Social Change and Stratification in Eastern Europe

Alexander Matejko

The Praeger Special Studies program—
utilizing the most modern and efficient book
production techniques and a selective
worldwide distribution network—makes
available to the academic, government, and
business communities significant, timely
research in U.S. and international economic, social, and political development.

Social Change and Stratification in Eastern Europe

An Interpretive Analysis of Poland and Her Neighbors

PRAEGER SPECIAL STUDIES IN INTERNATIONAL ECONOMICS AND DEVELOPMENT

Praeger Publishers   New York   Washington   London

Library of Congress Cataloging in Publication Data

Matejko, Aleksander.
    Social change and stratification in Eastern Europe.

    (Praeger special studies in international economics
and development)
    Bibliography: p.
    1. Social classes—Poland.   2. Social classes—
Europe, Eastern.   3. Europe, Eastern—Economic
conditions.   4. Europe, Eastern—Social conditions.
I. Title.
HN539.5.S6M38   301.44'0943   74-9424
ISBN 0-275-09570-3

PRAEGER PUBLISHERS
111 Fourth Avenue, New York, N.Y. 10003, U.S.A.
5, Cromwell Place, London SW7 2JL, England

Published in the United States of America in 1974
by Praeger Publishers, Inc.

Printed in the United States of America

Dedicated to Jan Wolski, the eminent Polish
advocate of industrial democracy based on
cooperative principles. His teaching has
always inspired my understanding of
social reality.

PREFACE AND
ACKNOWLEDGMENTS

After leaving Poland in 1968, I became committed to problems and subjects mostly far distant from Eastern Europe. However, during these years (first in Zambia and afterward here in Canada) I kept a close watch on my native country and its neighbors. My participation in the Polish-Canadian ethnic community, and especially my constant writing in the ethnic press, helped me considerably to keep in touch with East European affairs.

After publishing several articles on Eastern Europe in the professional journals, I decided to summarize my understanding of that part of the world in a book. It is based not only on sociological investigations done by me, my students, and professional colleagues, but also on my personal experience. I worked until 1968 not only in Poland but also in Czechoslovakia (study of public opinion polls and study of the cooperative movement in 1946-47; lectures in 1965), Yugoslavia (lectures in 1965), and the Soviet Union (study of the social impact of technological progress and lectures in 1962 and 1963). I visited Rumania, Bulgaria, and East Germany. All these experiences have contributed to the contents of this book.

I would like to thank Jan Krotki, Eva Luczynska, and Janet Howell for editorial suggestions and corrections. In addition, Jan Krotki has translated some parts of the manuscript from Polish, particularly in the last chapter. I also thank my wife Joanna for preparing the bibliography. I should like to give full credit to publishers of journals and magazines in which some parts of the text have already appeared. In particular, I am referring to the following articles, most of which have been greatly revised for inclusion in the present volume: "Planning and Tradition in Polish Higher Education," Minerva 7: 4, Summer 1969 (in Chapter 8); "The Executive in Present Day Poland," Polish Review 16: 3, Summer 1971 (in Chapter 6); "Poland's New Social Structure," East Europe 22: 1-2, January-February 1973 (in Chapter 1); "From Peasant to Worker in Poland," International Review of Sociology 7: 3, December 1971 (in Chapters 4 and 5); "Swiadomosc inteligencka" (Consciousness of the Intelligentsia), Kultura (Paris) 7-8, 1971; "Status Incongruence in the Polish Intelligentsia," Social Research 33: 4, November 1966 (in Chapters 7, 8, and 9); "Steel-workers' Attitude to Their Occupation," Polish Sociological Bulletin 1965, 1 (in Chapter 5); "A Newspaper Staff as a Social System," Polish Sociological Bulletin 1967, 1, also in J. Tunstall, ed., Media Sociology (London: Constable 1970; in Chapter 8); "Some Sociological Problems of Socialist

Factories," Social Research 36: 3, 1969 (in Chapters 5 and 6); "The Industrial Workers," Canadian Slavonic Papers 15: 1-2, 1973 (in Chapter 5); various articles in Polish in Zwiazkowiec (Alliancer) 1971-73 (in Chapters 3 and 9).

CONTENTS

LIST OF TABLES

In Eastern Europe under communism there is an unavoidable and permanent conflict between the democratic and the authoritarian interpretations of the system. As Zbigniew Brzezinski says (1970, p. 192), it is a struggle between sectarianism and universalism. With the general progress toward industrialization and universal education, which is an indisputable achievement of Communist ruling elites, the authoritarian style of ruling becomes more and more out of date. It seems to be particularly valid for East Central Europe (about this term, see Seton-Watson 1972; Halecki, 1950)—Poland, East Germany, Czechoslovakia, Hungary, and Rumania. There is a growing awareness, not only among intellectuals but also among the masses, in at least some of these countries that some kind of participatory democracy is the only solution. One of the main difficulties in progressing toward this solution in the Soviet bloc countries is of a doctrinaire nature. Officially, there is participatory democracy in all areas of social life, but primarily in the field of work. Why, therefore, look for something new? If under socialism alienation no longer exists, then why join Western Social scientists (Likert 1967; Blauner 1964; Pateman 1970; Blumberg 1968; Hunnius et al. 1973) in studying various ways of overcoming it? In many East European studies done from the orthodox Marxist viewpoint, it is taken for granted that nationalization of production automatically leads to the overcoming of alienation (Osipov 1966).

However, it is against the liberal orientation of many East European intellectuals to accept the doctrinaire interpretation without reservations, and under the bureaucratized system the intelligentsia suffers status incongruence (Matejko 1966b) to such an extent that some deep inclination toward alienation becomes unavoidable. Among members of the intelligentsia there is a feeling of responsibility for the fate of the nation that leads to a search for solutions to the problem of alienation.

Of the countries in Eastern Europe, Poland has the most influential intelligentsia, which took over from the gentry not only several elements of its social culture but also high sociopolitical aspirations. The influence exerted by the intelligentsia explains to a large extent why in Poland, on any possible occasion, there appears an evidently widespread criticism of the highly bureaucratized Soviet-style model. This was so in 1956 as well as in 1970, when, in both cases workers' uprisings shook the entire system (Cieplak 1972).

Changes in Eastern Europe must be appraised not only on the basis of statistical facts that show more or less economic improvement (such as progress toward egalitarianism) but also on the basis of an interpretative approach. What is the real meaning of empirical facts? It seems necessary to agree with George Lukacs (1971, pp. 7, 13) that

> . . . in order to progress from the "facts" to facts in the true meaning of the word it is necessary to perceive their historical conditioning as such and to abandon the point of view that would see them as immediately given: they must themselves be subjected to a historical and dialectical examination. . . . The intelligibility of objects develops in proportion as we grasp their function in the totality to which they belong. This is why only the dialectical conception of totality can enable us to understand reality as a social process.

Paradoxically, some social scientists who actively cooperate with the current East European establishments play with facts without bothering to establish their real meaning in terms of social transition, They tend to forget that the blinkered empiricist "will of course deny that facts can only become facts within the framework of a system—which will vary with the knowledge desired. . . . He forgets that however simple an enumeration of 'facts' may be, however lacking in commentary, it already implies an 'interpretation'" (Lukacs 1971, p. 5). These social scientists abandon the dialectic approach even while paying lip service to it. A kind of neofunctionalist thinking seems to prevail in present-day Eastern Europe for the sake of providing an optimistic image of a society in which everything basically goes in the proper direction toward utopian social harmony (Matejko 1972a).

For those studying social changes under the Soviet type of communism, Poland represents a particularly suitable and interesting case. According to Jan Szczepanski, Polish sociologists have a unique opportunity to study the transformation of a capitalist socioeconomic system into a Communist one (Szczepanski 1970, p. 5). Statistical and sociological data are much more easily available in Poland than in any other Soviet bloc country. Internal contradictions are relatively open for a scientific analysis. The tradition of Polish sociology is close enough to that of the West to make possible a meaningful exchange of data and insights.

However, there are some differences in approach that have to be taken into consideration. According to several establishment-oriented sociologists, the multidimensional stratification of the new Polish society does not allow opportunity for social class based on political authority. But they seem to exaggerate the degree of egalitarianism and tend to forget about the broader historical perspective. According to Jan Szczepanski, in Poland "the emerging order is indeed more egalitarian and closer to the ideal Marxian image of a classless society" (1970, p. 146). Wlodzimierz Wesolowski (1969a, pp. 470-77) admits the presence in the society of contradictions resulting from uneven distribution of goods but relates these contradictions to the failure of economists to develop precise measures of labor quality, the sensitivity of people to the fact that some of them earn more than others, the relativism of human judgment with respect to one's own economic position, and disequilibrium between the supply of certain goods and the demand for them.

The actual configuration of power relations is entirely missing from all these considerations. Criteria of social stratification allegedly appear independently of one another, and therefore "both the objective contradictions of interests and the subjective awareness of conflicts of interests tend to decrease in socialistic society when compared with capitalistic society" (Wesolowski 1969a, p. 476). Also, Szczepanski maintains the view that the multidimensional stratification of the new society makes it "hard to forsee the formation of a social class based on political authority" (1970, p. 142).

Shortly after these views had been published, Polish blue-collar workers revolted against the elitism and authoritarianism of the Gomulka regime. In this way they offered evidence that, according to their judgment, the predominantly egalitarian character of the Polish society exists only in the minds of establishment-oriented sociologists.

It is obvious that by remaining quiet and accepting the status quo, social scientists in Eastern Europe may gain security and official support. They are therefore strongly tempted not to expose the distance existing between the official myth and reality. Wesolowski alerts his readers to contradictions between the principle of paying "each according to his work" and the principle of egalitarianism (1969b, p. 145). However, he entirely misses the point that when basic democratic freedoms of self-expression, initiative, and social action cease to exist, the gap unavoidably grows between the vested interests of the establishment and the common interests of the masses.

Inequality in ownership of private property, political power, importance of the job, and home background—the obvious criteria of stratification—continue to exist under state socialism (Lane 1971, p. 129). However, the crux of the problem is not whether there is inequality, but how well-accepted the elite is and to what degree it contributes to the general welfare of the society. It is almost impossible to ascertain this when basic democratic freedoms and mechanisms are not available. Any social research that neglects this aspect of the issue misses the main point. For example, it does not make sense to talk about the function of trade unions in Eastern Europe without recognizing that they are neither "unions" nor do they deal with "trade."

The speed and magnitude of the socioeconomic progress in general, and the increase of productivity in particular, have a decisive importance for the power and ability of elites to manipulate the rest of their societies. "When national income is rising rapidly and promises to continue to rise as long as political and economic stability are maintained, the dominant classes find it in their interest to make some concessions to the lower classes to prevent costly strikes, riots, and revolutions" (Lenski and Lenski 1974, p. 388). In Eastern Europe the national income does not rise fast enough to stop the revolution of growing expectations that are constantly stimulated by the unquestionably rapid sociocultural progress. The bureaucratic version of socialism leads in the long run to the dominance of status orientation over task orientation (Matejko 1970), and ultimately it becomes self-defeating in the sense of its historical utility. However, for the time being the structure of power in Eastern Europe appears to be strong enough to prevent any basic overhaul from inside the East European societies.

The East European social scientists who have committed themselves to the political status quo find it impossible to reject their "background assumption" (Gouldner 1970, p. 34) that everything is basically sound, that social differences gradually disappear and egalitarianism prevails, and that people who earn more deserve it because they simply work more. However, without rejection of this optimistic assumption, it is not possible to understand anything about what is really happening in Eastern Europe.

The data on the East European societies show several disproportions and contradictions in economic, social, and cultural growth. Basic among them is the contradiction between the growing economic and cultural sophistication of the population and the authoritarian structure of power relations. Even the private farmers in Poland are largely dependent on the state, not to speak of the rest of the population, which is employed in state-owned or state-controlled enterprises, offices, and institutions.

All the unquestionable achievements in the advancement of lower-class people in Eastern Europe have to be measured, among other things, in terms of new desires and expectations. Equality of basic-need satisfaction has not enough social appeal so long as all the better opportunities and privileges are under the full control of the establishment. Heilbroner (1970, pp. 85-86) makes the following point:

The real resistance to development comes not from the old regimes which can be quickly overcome, but from the masses of the population who must be wrenched from their established ways, pushed, prodded, cajoled, or threatened into heroic efforts, and then systematically denied an increase in well-being so the capital can be amassed for future growth. This painful reorientation of a whole culture, judging by past experience, will be difficult or impossible to attain without measures of severity; and when we add the need to maintain a fervor of participation long beyond the first flush of spontaneous enthusiasm, the necessity for stringent limitations on political opposition and for forcible means of assuring economic co-operation seems virtually unavoidable.

It is the aim of this book to estimate, on the basis of available data, just how much real social and economic progress there has been in Eastern Europe, and to what extent it is followed by egalitarianism. East Central Europe, and particularly Poland, is the main field of observation. The Soviet Union is considered only in relation to East Central Europe, as is Bulgaria. So far, the most fully reliable sociological data and insights regarding the Soviet bloc countries come from East Central Europe, and have limited the scope of my analysis to the area I know best. The Soviet Union as a society was recently very well analyzed by Paul Hollander (1973) and the interested reader should consult his book.

Polish society is treated here as an object of experimentation in state socialism of the Soviet type. Foremost has been the issue of reallocation of resources among various social strata.

The Polish strata are discussed from the standpoint of their social mobility and relative well-being. It seems quite obvious that the upwardly mobile people have many problems related to the upper limit of their life achievements. In Eastern Europe the ceiling is relatively low, and it leads to growing dissatisfaction that in the long run may create much trouble for the present and future rulers, no matter what political orientation they present.

At the present time there is some built-in instability within the East European societies; and the question is who will try to stabilize these societies, and when and how. It is an issue not only of a material nature but also of a spiritual nature. Probably the presently dominant doctrines are to a large extent obsolete, and they no longer provide the basis for social and economic improvement. Sooner or later new doctrines must appear in order to contribute to further social change. So far, the authoritarian role of the orthodox Marxist establishment has effectively prevented the official doctrine from being defeated. However, the situation will not last forever.

The first chapter of this book deals with the main problem considered here—the contradiction between egalitarian and elitist tendencies in Eastern Europe, particularly in Poland. Depending on the changing balance of various socioeconomic and political forces, one or the other of these tendencies becomes more influential. The relationship between egalitarianism and elitism provides, according to my judgment, the key to understanding social change in Eastern Europe.

It would be wrong to make any extreme simplifications in this respect, such as assuming that the political establishment represents only elitism and that the socially advanced masses have purely egalitarian aspirations. On both social levels, the upper as well as the lower, one may find elitism and egalitarianism interpenetrating one another, thereby confusing the picture. The spokesmen of the establishment claim, of course, that the entire system is becoming more and more egalitarian. This is true only in part. On the other hand, it does not make sense to claim the contrary, that the entire system is purely elitist. The truth is somewhere between, and the purpose of the first chapter is to expose it.

Chapter 2 concentrates on the contradictions that appear in the socioeconomic development of Eastern Europe: the fast progress in industrial investments versus the underdevelopment of agriculture; the growing expectations of consumers and the inability of the rigidly centralized economy to achieve a much higher level of efficiency; the growing scope of the economic sphere and its total subservience to the political sphere; the growing industrial employment and the underdevelopment of services; the great dependence of families on the state and the inability of the system to satisfactorily solve the major problems of their welfare; the growing education and sophistication of the working masses and the very modest extent to which their needs are satisfied; and the ideal of international brotherhood among Comecon countries and the obvious differences among them in standards of living. Particular attention is paid to the income level of people employed in the nationalized East European economies. The buying power of incomes is compared on the basis of data available in the East European statistical yearbooks. The major conclusion is that the progressing discrepancy between the aspirations of the masses and their modest satisfaction (heavy industrial and military investments cost a lot) leads to an imbalance that will probably influence to a large extent the political future of Eastern Europe.

Chapter 3 describes the historical background of the present-day Polish social structure, The position of Poland changed considerably with the growth in that part of Europe of three absolutistic monarchies that ultimately partitioned Poland among themselves at the end of th eighteenth century. However, national identity and ideology were cultivated successfully—first by the gentry, which was particularly large and influential, and later by the intelligentsia. The Polish national myth, which is to some extent the continuation of the myth cultivated by the gentry, managed to survive all historical handicaps. The social structure during 1918-39 was dominated by the intelligentsia, even though it accounted for only a small percent of the total population. The take-over by Communists in 1945 led to a substantial change in the socioeconomic basis of the society: abolition of the traditionally privileged classes, nationalization of the means of production, and the massive social upgrading of the lower strata. Poland, as the close ally of the USSR, shares with her and with other countries of the bloc all the dramatic oscillations of the Soviet style of communism between its traditional totalitarian version and its more humanitarian perspective. It is a historical paradox that the Soviet Union, in deciding to move Poland geographically more to the west in order to take over her eastern part, contributed to a Westernization of Poland; this phenomenon is also treated in Chapter 3.

In Chapter 4 the social transformations experienced by Polish peasants from the nineteenth century to the present day are discussed. The national consciousness of the peasants grew considerably between World War I and World War II; but at the same time their economic situation did not improve, and ever deteriorated because of the low prices of agricultural goods and the progressive division of agricultural holdings into smaller ones. The vicious circle of poverty ended only when Poland progressed well toward industralization after World War 11 and when the attempts of the Communist authorities to force peasants into collective farms were abandoned. However, the situation of Polish farmers is still critical: young people do not want to stay on farms, there is not enough investment in agriculture, the country does not produce enough to feed itself, and many inhabitants of villages are in the precarious position of peasant-workers. It is an open question when and how Polish agriculture will be substantially overhauled in order to meet modern needs and standards.

Chapter 5 is devoted to Polish blue-collar workers. Their numerical strength has grown enormously under the conditions of state-sponsored industrialization, but they remained a silent class until 1956. The Party rules in the name of the blue-collar class, but its real influence is quite meager. Young people, especially, have several reasons to be dissatisfied with their living and working conditions, and even with the dominance of intellectual tastes in the mass media. The Polish blue-collar workers' stratum never managed to establish its full social identity. Not long ago these workers left the peasantry, and now their children join the ranks of white-collar workers in large numbers. Therefore, it is a stratum in constant historical transition, lacking in its own well-established institutions.

Chapter 6 deals with the managerial establishment in Poland, which is at the same time a substantial part of the political establishment (almost all upper managers are active Party members). The people about whom we are talking here came to a large extent from the lower strata, and they made a real career in the Polish People's Republic. However, this does not mean that they have every reason to be fully satisfied. The bureaucratic machine turns them into obedient cogs, and there is no escape from the frustrations typical for civil servants all over the world. In addition, Polish executives have good reason to feel inferior to their professional colleagues as well as to the cream of the intelligentsia. They know that bureaucracy has never been popular in Poland and that they epitomize its shortcomings, even if it is very often against their wish.

Chapter 7 is devoted to the intelligentsia as the traditional social elite in Eastern Europe, and particularly in Poland. Its members are much more than just white-collar workers. They have an informal claim to the governance of Polish souls, even if they are sometimes not willing, able or worthy to govern. It is the intelligentsia that originates and maintains national myths of various kinds and quality. In Poland it is largely liberal, and in this respect it is far removed from the Marxist-Leninist political establishment. However, members, of the intelligentsia, as well as members of the ruling Marxist elite, justify their existence by offering the masses and bureaucratic machine (more the latter than the former) goals and projects. In this respect they share a common interest. In addition, both are afraid of the masses and of their pressing questions regarding what has really been done to make daily life more comfortable, work easier and more pleasant, and the whole system more bearable. Therefore, in critical situations in which the lower strata appear on the political scene, the intelligentsia is rather inclined to keep quiet in order not to embarrass the ruling establishment too much. It then appears suddenly that the preservation of the status quo is in the vital interest of many people who in the less critical periods had preached the necessity of democratizing the system.

Chapter 8 shows the variety of problems characteristic for the whole spectrum of white-collar groups, from clerks at the bottom, through teachers and engineers, to the elite of the so-called creative intelligentsia. It is not a systematic coverage of all these groups but a review of problems familiar to me on the basis of my own studies (academic staff, journalists, researchers, engineers), investigations done by my professional colleagues, and personal experience.

Chapter 9 presents my personal impressions of the social and cultural infrastructure of contemporary Polish society. It is also a summary. Most of the discussion here is difficult to prove by specific data, and therefore must be taken by the reader as opinion.

Insight into the Polish problems allows one to understand better what happens in Eastern Europe in general, and particularly how Soviet state socialism works in a basically pro-Western society. Of course, it would be impossible to generalize on the basis of Polish experience alone. The East European societies differ so much that what is valid for Poland may not be valid for her neighbors. In this respect it is enough to look into the past and the present of various East European societies (Staar 1971). However, Poland, as the second power in Eastern Europe after the USSR), seems to be of crucial importance to the experiment of a Soviet-style state socialism. For several reasons, discussed in detail in this book, the conditions for this experiment were more difficult in Poland than in the rest of Eastern Europe. Full success would make it easier to apply the experiment to the countries that are more Western in their character and tradition than Poland. On the other hand, failure would be a warning light. It is up to the reader to decide what Poland is really like under state socialism. It has been my aim to provide sufficient data and insights to help make a judgment possible.

Among other reasons, Poland is sociologically interesting because the very rigid bureaucratic structure of the Soviet style of state socialism was imposed upon a society with certain strong individualistic traditions. In addition, this society has a long historical experience of following its own plans even under highly unfavorable circumstances. The Soviet style of communism had to adapt to the peculiarities of Polish society, which resulted in a unique mixture of individualism and collectivism, private entrepreneurship within the framework of state enterprises, full-scale commitment of people to their own goals under the cover of a public interest, and continuation of religious practices simultaneously with membership in the atheistic ruling Party. After considering various alternatives in approaching this complicated topic, I simply decided to put on paper what I think about it without bothering too much about being "objective." I do not claim that my understanding of the Polish reality is the best one. My modest intention is to confront the reader with one of the possible interpretations.

Of course, my subjective interpretation of Poland has been influenced by my own experiences, and therefore it is worth summarizing them briefly

During my life in Poland until 1968, I held a wide variety of jobs that allowed me to learn something about Polish society, probably more than I learned afterward on the basis of systematic sociological research. I started my professional career as an organizer of participatory democracy in the cooperative productive enterprises (in 1972 13 percent of all persons employed in the nationalized economy outside of agriculture worked for cooperatives). When Stalinism went so far that I could no longer practice democratic cooperation (see Matejko 1973b, 1973c), I took a position as assistant editor of a professional journal in labor policy and social welfare. A few years later I was accepted to the staff of an institute of public housing, and in that capacity I visited many households of manual workers and intelligentsia. After a stay (1957-59) at the University of Michigan as one of the first visiting scholars from Poland (at that time) on a U.S. grant, I worked at an institute of work safety, visiting factories all over Poland. Later I was accepted on the faculty of the University of Warsaw. But even in that position, in addition to the regular teaching of students, I spent much of my time training managers, teaching extension courses, and counseling people in industry. My major interest in sociotechnics (Podgorecki and Schulze 1969) brought me even closer to the Polish working people than to academia. I therefore feel positively biased to the blue-collar workers, farmers, and those white-collar workers who by their labor have to supplement what has been lost because of blunders committed by power-hungry politicians, pretentious intellectuals, corrupt managers, and malicious lower-rank bureaucrats. It is the former who build a better future for Poland, despite all the hardships created by the highly depersonalized system of command.

Social Change and Stratification in Eastern Europe

1

EGALITARIANISM VERSUS ELITISM

The social structure as "a system of human relationships, distances and hierarchies [conceived] in both an organized and unorganized
form" (Ossowski 1963, p. 11) will be treated here as influenced by
two opposing tendencies: one oriented toward social equality and the
other toward social inequality. Those who approve of the existing
order usually accept the inequality. On the other hand, those who
question the existing order very often tend to see the inequality as
unjust (Ossowski 1963, p. 179). Contemporary Eastern Europe does
not differ in this respect from the rest of the world, even though the
state socialist order established there since the end of World War II
is in many respects more egalitarian than feudal or capitalist orders.
"If socialist societies lag in terms of political equality, they appear
to be ahead in terms of economic equality" (Lenski and Lenski 1974,
p. 387.

Abolition of economic inequality, or at least a considerable
diminution of it, is treated by the adherents of East European socialism as socialism's moral and social justification. However, there is
now enough empirical evidence to demonstrate that the uneven distribution of goods and services persists even under a far-reaching
nationalization. "The really significant difference in the system of
social stratification compared to Western industrial societies is the
absence of a private propertied class possessing great concentrations
of wealth. Otherwise, the USSR is not dramatically unlike Western
industrial societies" (Lane 1971, p. 69). According to the data on
social stratification in Czechoslovakia, substantial differences in life
styles persist even though differences in skill and income have diminished substantially (Machonin 1970). Polish data show a correlation
between the prestige hierarchies of various occupational groups in
Poland and in the West (Sarapata 1966b). In general, "although income
inequality in state-socialist countries of the Soviet type has a narrower

1

span than in capitalist countries, there is, nevertheless a considerable variation in the actual consumption patterns of different social strata which indicates a marked differentiation of life styles. . . . State-socialist societies do have a definite system of prestige and . . . individuals regard themselves as members of distinctive status groups" (Lane 1971, p. 106).

The official ideology of Eastern Europe states that all men are equal; but in reality there are several built-in inequalities related to the relative shortage of goods, the monopolistic position of the Party and state elite, local elitist traditions, and internal contradictions of the socioeconomic and political structures of communism, pressure groups, and private ambitions of individuals. Common people socially upgraded thanks to the new system are committed to equality; but with the passage of time they acquire some elitist aspirations, at least for their children if not directly for themselves. The strict formal rules are supposed to make factors other than class origin, political loyalty, and work merit equal for everybody. However, as long as people actually differ in power, income, and prestige, the issue of inequality and of social injustice does exist. There are some limits, obvious to people in their everyday experience, on the extent to which inequalities under state socialism can be altered.

The claim that "men should all be treated in the same way save where there is sufficient reason for treating them differently" (Rees 1971, p. 92) is interpreted differently by people in Eastern Europe depending upon their incomes, wealth, power, and prestige. These contradictory interpretations lie behind the major sociopolitical tensions in Eastern Europe.

However, the perspectives of social change are probably influenced in that part of the world not so much by the "structured social inequality" (Heller 1969, p. 4) as by the limited ability of the state socialist system to satisfy the rising aspirations of people. In the Western countries, "production has eliminated the more acute tensions associated with inequality. . . . increasing aggregate output is an alternative to redistribution or even to reduction of inequality" (Galbraith 1962, p. 76). The major problem for East European state socialism is how to achieve this condition under its own rule.

Soviet-style communism gained much of its original strength from the massive upgrading of lower classes. "The rapid economic development of Russia under Communist control has created large numbers of upwardly mobile groups whose positions depend on the unity and stability of the Communist government" (Davies 1970, p. 94). The same phenomenon was later repeated in the East European countries after the Communist take-over. However, several historical and political circumstances have permitted these countries to preserve local ethnic, religious, and class traditions that still shape their social structures.

2

Totalitarian bureaucratization (Friedrich and Brzezinski 1965, pp. 205-18) remains the decisive factor determining the social structure. It is the ruling political establishment that distributes rewards and privileges among various groups and strata (Parkin 1971, p. 182). The operation of the market is highly restricted by the central planning authorities. However, the growing strength of various occupational groups that results from the increasing division of labor in the higher stages of development puts the political establishment in a difficult position. The scarcity of resources available for distribution allows it to generously reward only those groups that are of primary importance for the survival of the system. Recruitment to the elite is influenced much more by the relative pressure of a given group than by the principles of justice and equality. "One of the main cleavages in state socialist society is between those groups whose authority lies in the Communist Party (for example, party secretaries) and others whose position is technocratic and professional. . . . With the maturity of the state-socialist system, the social structure becomes less flexible and more rigidly stratified with benefits and advantages accruing to the professional, executive, and technical groups" (Lane 1971, p. 128).

When striving for higher levels of common welfare, it becomes almost impossible for the ruling elite to rigidly follow the principle of egalitarianism. The vested interests of various strategically located groups have to be taken into consideration. Consumers suffer constantly because they do not constitute an effective pressure group except in a political crisis, when the planners and decision-makers become apprehensive of the masses (Zielinski 1971b, p. 101). Any reforms that would be in the interest of consumers are effectively resisted by pressure groups that are much stronger and closer to the centers of ultimate decision. All these pressure groups promote their own vested interests. Take, for example, the technocrats as characterized by Zielinski: "Managers are essentially bonus maximizers and their behavior can be explained, to the degree comparable to a profit-maximizing assumption of market economy, in terms of this goal" (1971b, p. 416).

People who have learned how to manipulate the system for their own benefit are, of course, not really interested in reforms that would undermine their vested interests. The economic reform proposed in Poland in 1970 was "bound up with the resolve of the leadership to minimize the changes in decision-making and maintain a large part of current economic decisions in their own hands in order to avoid a loss of economic and hence of political power" (Flakierski 1973, p. 14; see also Brzeski 1971b). It would be naive to expect the beneficiaries of the system to resign their privileges voluntarily. "The centralization-decentralization struggle is a struggle for power" (Bauman 1971a, p. 28).

It does not matter what the intentions of the political establishment are; it loses in the long run in dealing with powerful pressure groups, not so much because of their strength but because of the necessity to offer higher rewards to those who are more essential. "The most effective way of holding such groups in check is by denying them the right to organize politically, or in other ways, to undermine social equality. This presumably is the reasoning underlying the Marxist-Leninist case for a political order based on the 'dictatorship of the proletariat'" (Parkin 1971, p. 183). In practice this leads to bargaining in which the strong gain and the weak lose. Managers must be bribed in order not to squander materials; but blue-collar workers' families may wait almost forever for a reasonable improvement of their industrial accident compensation, which is below the subsistence level (Gorecki 1971).

The success of state socialism in Eastern Europe should in the long run be evaluated probably not so much in terms of an achieved social equality but primarily in terms of the general welfare of the total population. This welfare does not necessarily need to be based on an egalitarian social arrangement. It depends very much on the model of social energy mobilization, its goals, its motivating forces, and its ability to gain the acceptance of the masses. It does not seem possible to reconcile for long the authoritarian political and economic model with the rising expectations of various increasingly sophisticated groups.

NEW STRATIFICATION: THE CASE OF POLAND

Since the Communist take-over in Eastern Europe, that area's human resources have been mobilized to a very high degree for a modernization that is equated with industrial progress and heavy investments. Agriculture no longer represents a substantial part of the gross national income. However, a disproportionately high percentage of the total labor force is still in agriculture, and the general agricultural productivity is low. The progress of urbanization, education, and the sociocultural aspirations of the masses expose more and more the inequalities among the almost 100 million people who live in Poland, Czechoslovakia, East Germany, Hungary, and Rumania.

The progressing industrialization of Eastern Europe has led to a substantial reallocation of human resources and to growing sophistication. The current formal structure is too bureaucratized and conservative to accord with changing human needs and rapidly growing aspirations. From the Marxist standpoint it would be possible to say that the clash between the infrastructure and the superstructure is unavoidable in the long run. However, it can also be asked to what

4

extent Marxist reasoning is applicable to the Soviet socioeconomic model of modern society. Blue-collar workers are now the majority, and their standard of living is becoming similar to that of white-collar workers. The traditional differences between the town people and the peasants have substantially diminished. However, the reality is still very far from the ideal of social equality (Lipset and Dobson 1973). Even if in Eastern Europe there are far fewer relatively rich people than in the Western countries, some new criteria of social stratification have become dominant. Political or administrative power offers some people the guarantee of substantial privileges that are tax-free. Various occupations differ in their relative income and in the opportunity to profit from fringe benefits. The distance between lowest-paid and highest-paid employees is more or less evident in various economic branches (see "The Ideal of Social Equality," below).

The elimination of the private sector under communism has completely changed the social structure of East European societies. Only in Poland is there a considerable number of private earners. Of 16 million economically active people in 1972, 31 percent were in the private sector, mostly as individual farmers (Concise 1973, p. 40). In the nationalized Polish economy (except for agriculture and forestry) 65 percent were employed as blue-collar workers. (Rocznik 1972, p. 112).

Contemporary Poland is full of contrasts. Religion practiced openly can be found side by side with the orthodoxy of the Party. Workers and peasants advance socially en masse, but a goodly portion of the climbers end up in traditional, conservative positions. The intelligentsia has been forced into a subordinate role, but Poland is today even more intellectualistic than during the interwar period. Poles go through the motions of religious ritual, but they do not take religion quite seriously. The tradition of the nobility still has a strong effect on Polish behavior, but it is easier to reconcile socialism with this tradition than with the peasant's or worker's ambition of becoming better off. The ideals of socialism still constitute the official ideology, but the social reality quite often is very far from them (Fiszman 1970, pp. 30-88). Szczepanski (1964b, pp. 10-11) describes the situation thus:

> With the exception of religious institutions, all others in Polish society are under the direct influence of the political institutions through the party organizations functioning in them. In this manner the whole state system of administrative institutions of economic management and of services, information, science, dissemination of culture, etc., are guided by a centrally fixed system of directives. . . . In a society based on planned economy

5

an individual's career is formed within the framework of
a centrally directed system of institutions. And the fulfillment of personal aims and ambitions, the acquisition of
prestige, etc., depend on the operation of the system.
Apart from this, the possibilities are very slight of realiz-
ing one's personal aims. Thus does the institutional system affect the creation of the personality type characteristic of a socialist society.

According to the 1970 census, the total Polish population is
half blue-collar workers, one-quarter private farmers, almost one-
quarter white-collar workers, and almost 3 percent other small groups
(See Table 1.1). Of people on pension three-quarters are blue-collar
workers. In the big cities blue-collar workers range from 40 percent
(Warsaw) to 61 percent (Lodz) of the labor force (Kozlowski and Turos
1973, p. 10).
   The present social structure in Poland favors a certain type
of egalitarianism. Rapid industrialization brought about many basic
changes, abolishing the distinctness of strata and groups marked by
skill (skilled workers, semiskilled workers, unskilled workers),
branch (heavy industry, small industry), ownership (state workers,

TABLE 1.1

Social Categories in Poland, 1970

	Thousands	Blue Collar Workers	White Collar Workers	Private Farmers	Others
		(percentage)			
Total	32,642	49.8	22.4	25.1	2.7
Employed	16,429	41.5	22.9	32.9	2.7
Not working	2,452	74.1	23.5	2.1	0.3
(students, pen-					
sioned, etc.)					
Maintained	13,761	55.8	21.7	19.6	2.9
(family members)					
Total					
in thousands		16,098	7,248	8,127	847

Source: Kozlowski and Turos 1973, p. 10.

private business workers), nationality (dominant nationality, minorities), and religion. Many of those distinctions still exist, but to a much lesser extent than was the case before World War II.

The high inter- and intragenerational vertical social mobility, as well as advanced egalitarianism of earnings and living conditions, favor to some extent the strengthening of the workers' positions. According to research done in Poland (Sarapata and Wesolowski 1961), the hierarchy of socio-occupational status is as follows:

1. Intelligentsia
2. Skilled workers
3. Private farmers
4. Private enterprise
5. White-collar workers
6. Unskilled workers

The social structure of the Polish society has changed considerably in comparison with the prewar period. Among the Polish population in the early 1970s, in comparison with the early 1930s, there were fewer independent farmers (25 percent instead of 46 percent), fewer handicraftsmen and small merchants (1 percent instead of 6 percent), more manual workers (50 percent instead of 35 percent), and many more white-collar workers (22 percent instead of 6 percent) (Zarnowski 1973, p. 377). Polish society now consists to a much larger extent of wage earners or salary earners. The traditionally lower classes now have much better access to schools, attractive jobs, and fringe benefits. However, the trends that developed fully only in the 1960s and 1970s started much earlier than 1945, when Communists came into power in Poland (Lane 1973a, pp. 2, 5; Taylor 1952; Zweig 1944). It seems that even under capitalist industrialization the new social structure would be quite similar except for handicraftsmen and small merchants.

The growing numerical strength of blue-collar workers is also evident in other East European countries. For example, in Czechoslovakia in 1970, 58 percent (in 1950, 56 percent) of the total population consisted of blue-collar workers, 8 percent of farmers in cooperative communes, and 1 percent of people maintaining themselves from work in other cooperative establishments. The percentage of the private sector in the total population has diminished from 27 in 1950 to 4 in 1970 (in Slovakia alone, from 39 to 5) (Statisticka 1972, p. 103).

In East Germany, among all persons economically active, in 1972 92.5 percent (53 percent in 1952) were employed in the nationalized economy, most of them probably as blue-collar workers. Members of the agricultural communes constituted 10 percent of the total labor force, and the private earners represented less than 3 percent.

7

(Statistisches Jahrbuch 1973, pp. 19, 52). Skilled blue-collar workers
in the industrial sector constituted 52.5 percent in 1970 (45 percent
in 1964)—ranging from over 60 percent in the power industry and the
machine-building industry to 36 percent in the food industry. Unskilled
workers constituted 20 percent in the food industry and in construction
(Statistisches Jahrbuch 1972, p. 141).

In Hungary in 1971, only 4.5 percent of the working people were
employed in the private sector, as compared with 36 percent in 1950.
The state sector employed 68 percent of gainfully employed people
(in 1950, 35 percent), and 28 percent worked in the cooperative communes (only 2 percent in 1950) (Statistical 1971, pp. 6, 7).

In Rumania in 1971, out of over 5 million employed people 75
percent were blue-collar workers, most of them concentrated in industry (48 percent of all blue-collar workers) and in construction
(15 percent of all blue-collar workers). Taking the employment of
blue-collar workers in 1950 as 100, the rate in industry in 1971 was
303 and in construction 452, which means that in these branches the
growth of employment was particularly fast. Among the remaining
25 percent of employed people in Rumania in 1971, 5.5 percent were
engineers and technicians, 7 percent occupied positions requiring
secondary education, 5 percent occupied positions requiring higher
education, and the rest were lower functionaries (Anuarul 1972,
pp. 100-02, 108).

THE RELATIVE STRENGTH OF VARIOUS STRATA

The relative social equilibrium in the East European countries
depends not only on the authoritarian rule of the Communist Party
but also, at least to some extent, on the mutual relationships between
all the major socioeconomic strata. It is a very important analytic
question as to how these strata make claims on the whole system
and how their demands are aggregated into the system. For example,
in Poland private farmers resist authority as a veto group, but they
are not organized into a coherent pressure force. The intelligentsia
is much too internally differentiated to be able to act in a coherent
manner. As for blue-collar workers: "Paradoxically, their weak
capacity for articulation as a political interest group through institutional channels may lead to wider class action. This is because,
having common objective life chances and faced by a threat to their
own security, groups of workers may spontaneously rebel against the
authorities to assert their own rights. Thus in October 1956 and in
December 1970 the workers briefly turned from being a fragmented
set of groups to become a class 'for itself'—though this was limited
in scope and did not include all workers" (Lane 1973b, p. 319).

In comparison with the prewar situation, blue-collar workers have increased their numerical participation in the society; they have acquired considerable opportunities for social advancement; and they have ameliorated their position with respect to the traditionally higher classes. And yet, the bureaucratic regime did not give them an authentic chance by socially dignifying physical labor. The establishment's principles of action derive their source not from the nature of labor, its needs, and its requirements, but from the historical necessity of consolidating power at the civil-service level. It is true that to an important extent this level has its genealogical origins in the workers' classes, but genealogy per se is not yet evidence of unity or disparity of concrete interests.

By subordinating the interests of the working world to its utter dictatorship, the bureaucracy has created a system of human relations in which upward flight to the intelligentsia has taken on a particular attraction. And the intelligentsia is highly differentiated. The bureaucratic system dominates, for even the majority of creative professions have become bureaucratized. To be sure, the intelligentsia is continually growing numerically, but it remains somehow suspended in a social vacuum. The East European establishments want to have a large number of specialists, but at the same time they remain suspicious.

Before World War II peasants were numerically stronger in Poland but had little say for a number of reasons. At present they are gradually being transformed into professionally qualified farmers, though the process is being hindered by a feeling of material uncertainty, by the disinclination of the younger generation to remain in the villages, by the insufficiency of agriculture investment, and by bureaucracy that is averse to peasants and that reaches into their pockets at every opportunity.

On the borderlines of the three basic socioprofessional strata in Poland there is a range of groups that are secondary from a numerical point of view but that often have considerable historical, cultural, or political importance. The question "Who controls whom?" is relevant to the mutual relationships between the basic and the secondary groups. For if the latter serve the interests of the basic strata, and are at the same time under their effective control, we can then say that the national interests, and thus the society's interests, are being placed above particular interests. In all other cases, the secondary groups become centers of exploitation, oppression, and lawlessness.

The interrelations between the three basic strata is a separate matter. State socialism has to a very considerable extent brought about a rapprochement of these strata, for all their members have found themselves, if not in identical circumstances of state employees, then at least in similar ones. Even the farmers in Poland, as owners

9

of individual farms, are so dependent on the state, both economically and administratively, that their possessing something has become considerably less important. The contemporary Polish farmer is closer to the circumstances of a semiprivate agent, whom the state deputizes to manage a café, a beer stand, or a gas pump, than to the circumstances of an owner who tries to acquire more land, more property, or more livestock.

BARGAINING WITH THE ESTABLISHMENT

In Poland, as in several other countries that experienced rapid modernization, "the authoritarian structure remains tied to the party elites in which legitimacy is enshrined, whereas 'participant orientation' to politics has spread to social groups. In Poland this might be groups of writers, factory directors and workers who without a well-based democratic societal infrastructure lack confidence in pushing their group interests. Changes in State socialist societies since 1956 may be explained by the fluctuating influence of those groups" (Lane 1973b, p. 321). The growing number and strength of various pressure groups in modernized Poland creates new demands on the political system. The ruling party is a "fulcrum in a consultative but authoritarian political system." (Lane 1973b, p. 322). The system depends on the ability of the Party to deal with various groups that have their own sanctions against the establishment. "In extreme circumstances, they may refuse to produce, as peasants; they may work inefficiently, as members of the technical intelligentsia; or they may riot, or absent themselves from work, as the manual working class has done" (Lane 1973b, p. 324).

Lane makes clear that "the cement which holds together the social system is political: the institution of the party provides for State socialist society what private property supplies for capitalism, namely a value system which is codified into laws and which promotes social and political solidarity" (Lane 1973b, p. 326). The question is how it would be possible in Poland to promote a participatory political system that would best suit the higher level of industrialization, urbanization, and the general sophistication of masses. Is there any peaceful way to move from state socialism to participatory democracy? Lane is probably wrong in stating that "the absence of a body of competent and educated citizens contributed to the setting up of a centralized bureaucratic system and was a major obstacle to the development of participant democracy within the framework of Polish socialism" (1973b, p. 310). The system was already rigid and highly centralized when brought from Russia. In Czechoslovakia the general educational level of the population was much higher than in Poland or in Russia, but exactly the same model was imposed there.

THE IDEAL OF SOCIAL EQUALITY

Income has become more equally distributed in the last few decades in the West as well as in Eastern Europe, but this trend is more evident in the Soviet bloc countries, especially in the USSR, than in the United States or even in Great Britain (Wiles and Markowski 1971). More than 1.5 times median income was received in 1970 by over 20 percent of all U.S. families, but the share of the top 5 percent of families scarcely changed during the twenty years 1950-70. The highest 20 percent of all families preserved their control of two-fifths of the total aggregate income, whereas the lowest 20 percent did not improve to any considerable degree its modest share of only 5 percent of the total aggregate income (which means only 25 percent of what they would have in case of equal distribution) (Statistical Abstract of the United States 1972, p. 323). A comparison of the United States and Great Britain in the late 1960s shows that people receiving more than twice the national average income numbered about 10 percent in the United States and 6 percent in Great Britain. On the other hand, the people receiving less than 25 percent of the national average numbered 8 percent in the United States and only about 3 percent in Great Britain (Wiles and Markowski 1971, p. 367).

How much of the population of Eastern Europe may be treated as an income elite? In Poland in September 1972, only 4 percent of people employed in the nationalized economy earned more than double the average income, 5,000 zloty and over per month* (among white-collar workers, 5 percent; among blue-collar workers, 3 percent), and 27 percent earned over 3,000 zloty (among white-collar workers, 31 percent; among blue-collar workers, 24 percent (Concise 1973, p. 264). However, the percentage of people earning over 5,000 zloty per month increased in the period 1960-70 from 0.7 to 4.2; among white-collar workers, from 1.2 to 5.6, and among blue-collar workers, from 0.4 to 3.3 (Rocznik 1972, p. 559).

According to the official Polish estimate, the cost-of-living index in 1971 for all people employed in the nationalized economy was 120.1 if 1960 is taken as 100; and the index of real income was 125.6 if 1960 is taken as 100. The cost of living for an average working family in 1971, with 1960 taken as 100, was 123 for food 129 for housing (furnishing and maintenance), 123 for transportation and communication, 98 for clothing and shoes, and 146 for liquor (Rocznik 1972,

---

*In 1973, Polish citizens paid 50 zl for one U.S. dollar when given official permission to buy dollars from the state owned banks. This exchange rate seems to be economically reasonable in terms of the buying power of both currencies.

p. 535). I do not believe that the Polish cost-of-living index takes adequate consideration of the changing preferences of the population. The government keeps the prices of basic foodstuffs on a relatively stable level, but people who are becoming better off are anxious to restructure their expenditure in favor of more luxury goods and services. For example, many Poles desire to own a car. Yet the government almost doubled the price of gasoline early in 1974, which led to much frustration among present and future car owners, many of whom, even before the increase in gasoline prices, spent quite a substantial part of their income on car maintenance.

In Czechoslovakia 44 percent were earning over 2,000 Koruna per month in 1970 (the average was 1,937 Koruna). In 1968, the figure was 45 percent. Only 2 percent earned over 4,000 Koruna per month (3 percent of the men and 0.2 percent of the women) (Statisticka 1971, p. 146). In Rumania the 6.3 percent of wage earners who received over 2,500 lei per month in 1971 may be treated as an elite (the average income was about 1,300 lei). Among Rumanian blue-collar workers in 1971, 43 percent earned from 900 to 1,300 lei per month, and 40 percent from 1,300 to 2,000 lei per month. Ten percent earned over 2,000 lei and 7 percent earned less than 900 lei. The percentages for all employed people were 40, 39, 15, and 6, respectively. This means that there is not much difference between the incomes of blue-collar workers and of other categories of employed people (Anuarul 1972, p. 110). In the Soviet Union probably only 2.5 percent of the population earns double the average income or more (Wiles and Markowski 1971, p. 506).

The ruling elites of Eastern Europe constantly create new social tensions, sometimes quite unintentionally. Measures oriented toward egalitarianism lead to certain elitist consequences. Strict planning gives rise to chaos. The doctrinaire propaganda depoliticizes people instead of making them more committed. All these paradoxes result not so much from the ineptitude or the doctrinaire approach of the elite, but basically are caused by applying a centralistic system to modern and relatively well developed societies. There is a growing cleavage between the authoritarian style of managing people and the pluralistic nature of emerging social structures. The majority of people maintain themselves through nonagricultural pursuits within the nationalized economy, and they are dependent on the state as the monopolistic employer; and even in Poland, with her private agriculture, farmers trade mostly with the state. The large numbers of employed married women strengthens the economic bond between the family and the state. At the same time, expectations regarding housing facilities, buying power of incomes, promotion, leisure, and opportunities for the young generation are growing faster than the ability and willingness of the states to gratify them. Even in popular culture, achieved progress is not keeping pace with growing demands.

In education, much has been achieved and the system is now much more accessible to masses of people than during the interwar period. The general intellectual level, teaching, learning, and research are in many cases now as advanced as in some Western countries. However, the totalitarian character of the system obviously has its impact. The conflict between old (traditional values) and new (the Communist Party, industrialization, urbanization, secularization) does not explain much, since "conservatives" and "progressives" are to be found on both sides of the fence. People who enjoy almost absolute power tend to attempt to retain it as long as possible, and with the passage of time their orientation becomes more and more "conservative." They seek support from the established social powers: bureaucrats, secret police, military, and highly paid specialists. The rest of the people are able to participate only as more or less obedient servants. Their situation may improve only if and when public opinion starts to carry any weight and the rulers are forced to pay more attention to urgent social needs as articulated by the majority of the society.

MOBILITY OF THE POLISH POPULATION

Poland has one of the highest indexes of economically active population (49 percent in 1972). In contrast with the prewar period, marked by extensive unemployment in the cities (23-29 percent in the 1930s) and great overpopulation in the country, the period after World War II has been characterized by a very rapid growth of employment in the nonagricultural nationalized branches of the economy, particularly in industry.

In 1970, 70 percent of the population supported itself with non-agricultural jobs (mostly working for state-owned enterprises), compared with 40 percent before World War II and 53 percent in 1950. More than half (54 percent in 1973) of the population lives in towns, and 43 percent (in 1970) of the rural population is employed outside agriculture, with many people commuting every day to work in towns. Forty percent of the population of Poland resides in urbanized and industrialized areas, which constitute 9 percent of the nation's territory. In these areas only 8 percent are employed in agriculture. Of the net increase in the urban population during 1946-65, 43.5 percent consisted of peasants who left their villages. In the big cities 20-40 percent of the population are first-generation urban dwellers, and in smaller cities the figure is even higher. (Kosinski 1970a; Leszczycki and Kosinski 1967). During the period 1960-72 the net yearly increase of the urban population through the migration from rural areas more than doubled—from 75,000 to 165,000 (Concise 1973, p. 37).

The intense migration of the Polish population during the period between the late 1930s and 1960s has had a deep impact on the egalitarian ethos of the society. People have become uprooted, less conservative, much more flexible, and easier to socialize into the new environment. The high rate of territorial mobility in Poland was closely correlated to the massive social upgrading. It seems necessary, therefore, to appreciate the magnitude of these migrations.

During World War II and immediately after it, one-third of all Poles, about 7.5 million people, moved (Kosinski 1970b, p. 82). During World War II, 5 million Poles were either deported to Germany (2.5 million) or to the Soviet Union (1.25 million) or deported and resettled within German-occupied territory (1.25 million). During the first few years after the war 4.3 million Poles either returned from the West (2.3 million) or resettled from the East (2 million) (Kosinski 1971). Internal movements among provinces (voivodships) in postwar Poland involved 4 million people. In the 1950s almost 14 million people changed their addresses. The same happened to 6.7 million people during the period 1961-67. In the period between the late thirties and the late sixties the number of Poles inhabiting their own ethnic territory grew from approximately 24.5 million to 33 million. The territorial mobility was at a very high level during that whole period of time and a very considerable proportion of Poles left their previous home areas. Of course, this was most evident in the new areas that were incorporated into Poland from Germany in 1945. In 1950 the population of those areas was only 20 percent indigenous, and the rest came either from old territories of Poland or from abroad.

In the 1960s and the early 1970s the territorial mobility in Poland diminished considerably. The percentage of people who changed their permanent residence by moving from one town or village to another diminished from 4 percent in 1960 to 3 percent in 1972. In the same period the percentage of people who moved from the countryside to towns stayed at the level of 2 percent. However, the percentage of people moving from towns to the countryside decreased from 1.6 to 0.7 (Concise 1973, p. 37). In comparison with the Western countries there is very little territorial mobility in Poland, mainly because of the housing shortage.

PROGRESS TOWARD EGALITARIANISM IN POLAND

The degree of egalitarianism in Polish society may be measured, at least to some extent, by a comparison of the income levels of various socio-occupational categories. However, this is not a fully indicative source of information because it does not reveal various hidden sources of income and privilege. People in managerial positions have benefits in the form of special tax-free financial bonuses, official cars, and cheaper sources for buying certain goods.* On the other hand, the state offers people, on a differential basis, low-rent apartments, inexpensive vacations in state-owned holiday hostels, theater tickets at reductions, and free use of sports facilities. A comparison of incomes gives at least some idea of the distance between various groups of the population.

Table 1.2 shows how blue-collar workers and white-collar workers are related in terms of income. At the bottom there are agricultural workers together with librarians and nurses, and at the top of the hierarchy miners appear above medical doctors. Such a mixture is fairly common in developed societies, which means that the situation that arose in the West as a result of economic booms and the pressure of trade unions also developed in Poland as a result of entirely different factors.

However, depending on the economic branch, the situation of blue-collar workers may be better or worse than that of white-collar workers. Of the nine economic branches enumerated in Table 1.3, in only one are there proportionately more white-collar workers earning less than the average income in comparison with the blue-collar workers. In all other cases the opposite is true.

The distance between lowest-paid and highest-paid employees is more or less evident in various economic branches. In the construction industry, for example, at the end of 1970 the 20 percent of employees at the lowest level of the income hierarchy received 9.7 percent of the total income fund, while the 20 percent at the highest income level received 36.3 percent of the total income fund. Thus the ratio of the lowest-paid workers' share to the highest-paid workers' share in the total income fund was 1:3.7 among the white-collar workers in construction, while among manual construction workers it was 1:3.4 and among white-collar workers employed in construction, 1:4.0. The same ratio (of the income share of the lowest-paid 20 percent to the highest-paid 20 percent of employees) was 1:2.9 in transport and communication, and only 1:2.1 among blue-collar workers in public health. The ratio was the highest for

---

*This also occurs in the West. Gabriel Kolko points out that fringe benefits in the United States render the offical statistics regarding income distribution of doubtful value (Kolko 1962). However, in Eastern Europe the average income level is much closer to the survival minimum, and therefore the large hidden fringe benefits make more difference there than in countries with substantially higher general standards of living.

TABLE 1.2

Income Comparisons Among Occupations and
Professions in Poland,
1970 (100—the monthly income
of an average employee in
the nationalized non-agricultural sector,
2,500 zloty)

Forestry manual workers	64
Workers in state-owned agricultural enterprises	68
Librarians (public libraries)	68
Nurses	69
Salespersons (mostly women) in retail trade	80
Elementary school teachers	87
Industrial manual workers	101
Industrial administrative staff	102
Construction manual workers	110
Manual workers in private farming (25 days at 110 zloty per day)	110
Secondary school teachers	110
Editors	119
Foreign trade staff	130
Postsecondary school teachers	143
Industrial technical staff	154
Medical doctors	158
Miners	171
Design engineers and technicians	227
Mining engineers and technicians	255

Source: Rocznik 1971. Compiled by the author.

TABLE 1.3

Percentage of Polish Employees Earning Less Than
the Average Monthly Income, September 1970

Branch of Economy	Blue Collar Workers	White Collar Workers
Industry	55	36
Construction	45	33
Agriculture	81	58
Forestry	75	80
Transport and communication	60	57
Trade	87	73
Municipal enterprises	66	46
Education, culture, and science	92	67
Public health and welfare	94	78
Total	62	57

Source: Rocznik 1971, p. 591.

white-collar workers, not only in construction (1:4.0, as mentioned above) but also in public administration and the judiciary (1:3.6). In cultural, educational, and medical services the ratio was 1:3.0 (Dmoch 1971).

The income differences between blue-collar and white-collar workers, as shown by Table 1.4, document their high level of equalization with clerical staff, as well as some distance between blue-collar workers and technical specialists. This distance decreased in some branches of the economy during the 1960s; but the better-paid occupational groups, such as engineers and managers, enjoy financial bonuses and other privileges that are not revealed in their regular incomes. These additional sources of remuneration are very carefully controlled by state and Party authorities. To a large extent, the loyalty and usefulness of a particular person are the principal criteria for deciding how much he or she will obtain in bonuses and fringe benefits, and whether these benefits will be continued.

How much actual equality is there in terms of the standard of living? Studies of family budgets provide interesting data in this respect by documenting some significant employment category differences in the structure of expenditures (see Table 1.5). White-collar worker families spend less on food and more on culture and leisure. Their households are equipped with more appliances related

TABLE 1.4

Income Comparisons Between Blue-Collar Workers and Other
Occupational Groups in Poland, Various Years

Industrial Branch		A Blue-Collar Workers (zloty)	B Engineers and Technicians (col. A=1)	C Administrators and Clerks (col. A=1)
All industry	1960	1,781	1.6	1.0
	1970	2,515	1.5	1.0
	1972	2,815	1.5	1.0
Power plants	1960	2,034	1.5	0.9
	1970	2,852	1.5	0.9
Coal mines	1960	2,728	1.8	0.8
	1970	4,281	1.5	0.8
Ferrous metallurgy	1960	2,235	1.5	0.9
	1970	3,198	1.5	0.9
Electrotechnical industry	1960	1,679	1.5	1.1
	1970	2,245	1.6	1.2
Chemical industry	1960	1,663	1.7	1.2
	1970	2,538	1.5	1.1
Textile industry	1960	1,460	1.9	1.3
	1970	2,056	1.7	1.2
Foodstuffs industry	1960	1,482	1.4	1.2
	1970	2,116	1.4	1.1
State agricultural enterprises	1970	1,709	2.0	1.3
Forestry enterprises	1970	1,594	1.6	1.4
Foreign trade enterprises	1970	1,985	1.6	1.2
Municipal enterprises	1970	2,210	1.5	1.1

Source: Rocznik 1971, pp. 205, 206, 307; Concise 1973, p. 95.

TABLE 1.5

Family Budget and Household Equipment of Blue-Collar and White-Collar Workers and Farmers on Various Income Levels in Poland, 1971

	Total			Low Income			Middle Income			High Income		
	B	W	F	B	W	F	B	W	F	B	W	F
Work earning as percent of total income	87	88	—	74	72	—	84	81	—	88	89	—
Food as percent of expenditures	45	39	50	55	52	52	48	45	49	43	40	48
Lodging as percent of expenditures (includes light and heat)	13	14	11	12	13	12	13	13	10	13	14	9
Clothing and shoes as percent of expenditures	15	15	16	14	11	15	15	15	16	15	15	15
Culture and leisure as percent of expenditures	7	10	5	6	8	4	7	9	5	8	10	6
Annual consumption of meat and fish (kg. per person)	60	56	43	40	41	37	55	51	49	70	58	53
Radio sets per 100 households	85	99	76	63	90	64	85	119	84	94	105	93
TV sets per 100 households	75	79	41	66	62	35	80	79	49	82	82	77
Washing machines per 100 households	81	81	64	84	79	55	89	89	73	82	85	82
Refrigerators per 100 households	38	58	9	12	28	10	38	47	10	48	68	13
Vacuum cleaners per 100 households	43	65	11	17	38	12	47	58	12	51	71	15
Sewing machines per 100 households	40	35	44	46	48	48	45	44	45	38	35	47
Motorcycles and motorbikes per 100 households	9	8	39	5	—	25	8	10	40	11	8	80
Bicycles per 100 households	27	25	100	34	31	72	31	38	118	25	30	139

B = Blue-Collar.
W = White-Collar.
F = Farmers.

Notes: "Low Income": for B and W, 9,600 zloty or less per person per annum; for F, indicates owners of farms less than 3 hectares. "Middle Income": for B and W, 12,001–15,000 zloty per person per annum; for F, indicates owners of farms 7–10 hectares. "High Income": for B and W, 18,001–24,000 zloty per person per annum; for F, indicates owners of farms 15 hectares or more.

Source: Rocznik 1972, pp. 543–53; Concise 1973, pp. 277–78.

to convenience (refrigerators) and cleaning devices (vacuum cleaners). This is due, at least to some extent, to the higher employment of wives outside of the household. Among farmers there is a strong emphasis on transportation vehicles (motorcycles, motorbikes, bicycles) and such utilitarian items as sewing machines. On the other hand, the equipment of households is still behind that of the urban population (for instance, a very limited number of refrigerators); the same is true of expenditures for culture and leisure. It must be mentioned that the farming families included in the budget studies were recruited from among the more prosperous and modern, and therefore do not fully represent the rank-and-file of the Polish peasantry.

EGALITARIAN ASPIRATIONS AND THE SOCIAL REALITY

Egalitarian aspirations are quite strong in the traditionally lower strata and certainly are stronger there than among the intelligentsia (Nowak 1969). Unskilled workers and people with less education feel they are being deprived of status. Although 40 percent of the urban population is upwardly mobile, the feeling of real improvement seems to be much stronger at higher social levels than at the bottom. According to data collected by Stefan Nowak, the feeling that their present social status is higher than that of their fathers at the same age was shared by 46 percent of the creative intelligentsia but by only 23 percent of unskilled workers. Among the latter only 20 percent were convinced that social distinctions between people of various groups in Poland are generally much smaller than before World War II; among the creative intelligentsia and top professionals such a conviction was shared by almost 33 percent. Differences in income, educational level, political power, formal status, and even religiousness (ruling Marxist atheists versus the Catholic majority) were commonly perceived by unskilled workers as important factors of social conflict (Nowak 1969, pp. 240-46).

It seems reasonable to accept Nowak's conclusion that the higher the social position of people, "the more rarely are they convinced that certain social differences create divisions among the people in Poland. This pertains to earnings, education, to the distinction between manual and non-manual labor, importance of positions or posts held, etc. The higher the social position, the greater the chance that the respondent will regard the structure as a non-conflicting one in both directions. . . . The higher the respondent's position the greater the tendency to see the animosity as coming from the bottom. The lower the position—the greater is the tendency to see it as coming from the top" (1969, p. 246).

Egalitarian postulates are positively stronger among manual workers than among the relatively privileged strata of Party and state officials, managers, specialists, and intellectuals.

How realistic is it to believe that free education leads to equalization of life opportunities in Poland? White-collar workers, who constitute 23 percent of the total population, occupy a much stronger position in the educational system than blue-collar workers and farmers. The latter are particularly underrepresented in almost all types of schools, except for vocational schools and nonresident postsecondary education. Blue-collar workers are also relatively numerous in vocational education and in evening or nonresident postsecondary education courses. Members of the intelligentsia are enrolled in secondary schools, art-vocational schools, and day courses in postsecondary education to a much greater extent than would be expected from their numerical strength.

CONFRONTATION OF THE IDEAL WITH THE REALITY

It seems quite obvious that in Eastern Europe there are still many social distinctions, and that egalitarianism is far from being a reality. Among the lower strata there is an evident awareness of social injustices and distances. Unfortunately, the available statistical and sociological data do not provide sufficient insight into the formation of the elite. It is common knowledge that fringe benefits for people located at the centers of power are often much more important than their official salaries. Many attractive goods at discount prices are distributed among the elite on a semiformal or informal basis. For example, given the opportunity to buy an imported Western car officially priced, low, an individual may make a tremendous profit by reselling this car at the high official market price.

In the nationalized East European economies there is a small percentage of people who earn well over the average. There are, in addition, some private businessmen, craftsmen, and individual farmers in Poland who are well-to-do. But taken together, people with high incomes constitute only a small percentage of the total population. However, the main issue is not how many are economically privileged, but to what extent the society's distribution of benefits based on work is justified. Table 1.6 shows some obvious distinctions in Poland that are dependent upon the sector of the economy and the level of education. Technicians in industry on a secondary education level earn as much as scientists on a post-secondary education level. Teachers' and nurses' earnings are well below average.

In 1972 people with graduate education earned 3,140 zloty per month, people with vocational education earned 2,545 zloty per month,

TABLE 1.6

Income Comparisons Among Various White-Collar
Groups in Poland, 1968 (as percent of average monthly
income, 2,334 zloty)

Field of Employment	Postsecondary Education Graduates	Secondary Education Graduates
Technology	198	134
Agriculture	145	92
Science	134	—
Public health	145	76
Humanities	141	—
Economics	165	101
Education	—	83
Total	164	106

Source: Rocznik 1971, p. 592.

people with general secondary education earned 2,475 zloty per month,
and people with only primary education earned 2,031 zloty per month.
The highest average earnings—3,654 zloty per month—were those of
specialists with a graduate education. The differences are not dramatic, but there is some social significance in the fact that the ratio
of the income of specialists to the income of people with only primary
education is of 1.7 to 1.0 (Concise 1973, p. 234).

To what extent do the people accept the priorities laid down by
the ruling Party? So far the East European establishments have not
been successful in gaining wide social acceptance for their specific
version of distributive justice. For example, data on the social prestige of occupations in Poland show that people substantially disagree
with the official income hierarchy insofar as status distribution is
concerned. According to public opinion, teachers and medical doctors
are at the top of the status hierarchy, but in actuality they are much
lower in the income hierarchy (Sarapata and Wesolowski 1961).

It is obvious that any political establishment is vitally interested
in rewarding people according to their contribution to what the establishment considers useful and therefore valuable. Cynical establishments tend to offer priority to any service that contributes to the
status quo. The East European establishments, apart from their
vested interests, must reward people, such as technologists and

scientists, who further the socioeconomic modernization of the society according to Communist principles. There is also an official tendency to progressively upgrade the incomes of blue-collar workers, especially those in lower income brackets, and to diminish the differences between the lowest-paid blue-collar and white-collar workers (see Table 1.7).

In Poland, the official ideology has so far had little appeal. People pay lip service to Party slogans and utilize them as a suitable cover for pursuing their personal interests. Consequently, a gap has arisen between what is expected by superiors and what is actually done by subordinates. The masses find that administrative procedures are sluggish, and that civil servants are at least indifferent if not unfriendly. This probably results from the fact that all agencies are oriented primarily to the commands of higher Party authorities. The Party saturates "all other organizations whether internally through the affiliation of their members to the party or externally through the influence exerted by party groups, sections or committees running parallel to these organizations" (Taras 1973, p. 265). Most people who belong to local political elites are members of the Party. "The party committee and party councillors are the most influential ways of shaping a town's politics". (Taras 1973, p. 270). Common interests are articulated through direct informal contacts and pressures. The Party leaders do not take direct responsibility for many things that happen at the local level, but their preferences have to be recognized and followed by the rest of the local elite.

The fact that an overwhelming majority of local civil servants on an executive level is recruited from the ranks of blue-collar workers

TABLE 1.7

Percentage Comparison of Monthly Gross Income Structures of Polish Blue-Collar and White-Collar Workers, 1960-72

Gross Monthly Income	Blue-Collar			White-Collar		
	1960	1970	1972	1960	1970	1972
1,200 zloty or less	29	12	7	23	4	1
1,201-2,000 zloty	44	30	29	47	33	27
2,001-3,000 zloty	21	35	40	22	34	41
3,000 zloty or more	6	23	24	8	29	31
Total	100	100	100	100	100	100

Source: Rocznik 1972, p. 559; Concise 1973, p. 264.

and peasants does not imply that these people represent the interest of their strata. Of the 168,000 representatives in the Seym and in the People's Councils in 1969, almost a half were members of the ruling Polish United Workers' Party; 20 percent were members of the United Peasant Party, which is totally subservient to the ruling party; and 30 percent were not politically affiliated (Zakrzewski 1973, p. 13). In the presidia of People's Councils the percentage of non-Party-affiliated members was only around 16. Membership in the Party among local councillors was 50 percent at the provincial level (wojewodztwo), and the same at the level of the villages (gromada) in 1969. It is quite obvious that at all administrative levels, in a general way "Party control is powerful, the administrative apparatus is extremely influential, the economic directorship cadres are well represented and the doctrine of unity of power vested fully in representative organs is equivocal" (Taras 1973, p. 301).

However, the absolute control exerted by the Party upon the unified state and community system of public administration has its obvious side effects. People know little about the councillors who are supposed to be representing them in "democratic" bodies. The electorate would like their representatives to be modeled on professional social workers (Dzieciolowska 1973, pp. 195-96), but in reality these representatives are primarily oriented toward the higher authorities. Therefore, it is not surprising that the general evaluation of the local people's councils in public opinion polls in the 1960s was far from enthusiastic. Only 12 percent of the respondents said that their problems were settled effectively by civil servants. "The procedure for dealing with human problems and the inefficiency of the apparatus, are criticized much more sharply than [even] the personal attitudes of the officials" (Dzieciolowska 1973, p. 205).

With respect to social justice, the major issue in Eastern Europe is not how equal people are but to what extent they are able to fulfill their expectations. Blue-collar workers complain primarily about the organizational ineffectiveness of their bureaucratized work places, which prevents them from doing more, and from earning more. Members of the intelligentsia feel restrictions on their acting and thinking freely. A large proportion of the status- and wealth-seekers who took advantage of opportunities opened by new regimes find themselves limited to little more than a modest standard of living. The rigidity of the bureaucratic setup makes it virtually impossible to develop any substantial initiative that would remain within the given legal framework, and extralegal activities have therefore become common. One of the best examples of this is the private trading of goods on any suitable occasion (excursions, visits, official travels) by people from neighboring countries.

The people of Eastern Europe are probably unanimous on at least one specific issue: that the system does not deliver a high enough standard of living. Most of the indicators show constant improvement, but that does not mean that people are satisfied. There is too great a gap between promises and reality. There is also too much obvious waste and rigidity. Differences in the standard of living between various social strata and even various countries probably count for less in the final analysis than the built-in inability of the whole system to enter higher stages of common welfare.

The fact that the inhabitants of Eastern Europe do not "live by bread alone" may be true to an even larger extent than in many other parts of the world. Mass media, culture, leisure, and education are formally controlled by state and Party officials; but in reality they are run by members of the intelligentsia who impose their own tastes, aspirations, and practical choices upon the masses. The young generation of blue-collar workers and peasants is being socialized primarily to intelligentsia values. Paradoxically, the ideal of being culturally sophisticated and following the examples of the "well-mannered" people who know how to enjoy life has become the latent function of the Communist take-over. It is in reality neither the blue-collar workers' class, nor even the tiny minority of Party and state bureaucrats, but the intelligentsia that has gained the most in terms of prestige, influence, attractiveness, and even numerical power. By generously subsidizing mass culture, education, mass media, sports, and leisure, the East European regimes contributed, against their own manifest intentions, to the establishment of a social force that now represents a major challenge to the concept of egalitarian totalitarianism. This seems more true for Poland and Hungary than for the rest of Eastern Europe, a situation that may be explained by the prestige inherited by the intelligentsia from the gentry in those countries. This also seems more true for East Central Europe, except East Germany, than for Eastern Europe in general, and for the Soviet Union in particular. The authority of the state and of the ruling elite has traditionally been much more strongly established in the territories directly dominated by Russia and Prussia than in the territories that formerly belonged to the Austro-Hungarian Monarchy.

The standard of living has become a bone of contention for the political establishment versus the intelligentsia. With a growing sophistication of mass needs and mass tastes, the man on the street becomes dissatisfied and looks for more—which, of course, undermines the concept, characteristic of the static Soviet type of state socialism, of a "perfect" sociopolitical system. On the other hand, growth of the intelligentsia leads to further upgrading of common expectations without making any direct commitment to fulfilling them. Under the authoritarian rule of the Party and state bureaucrats, the intelligentsia enjoys the freedom of asking for more without taking responsibility for the delivery. It is probably the most significant paradox of the East European social systems that the authoritarian rule contradicts itself by trying to satisfy people without asking for their participation. In Poland and in Hungary during the past few years, the regimes have started to cooperate with the intelligentsia; but to a large extent this is still merely a token cooperation, undermined by lack of mutual trust.

2

SOCIOECONOMIC PROGRESS

TENSIONS OF GROWTH

The economic, social, and educational modernization of East European societies is an unquestionable achievement of communism. However, the question is whether the regimes established by the communists in the 1940s are able and willing to restructure themselves with regard to new advances in technology, education, and the growing sophistication of the masses. In this respect Soviet-style communism shares the fate of all major political powers in history. It is not enough to create an empire; in the long run the maintenance of peace and prosperity becomes more important than the seizure of power. "The mechanism of decline is the struggle of the rulers for inputs of resources to meet demands beyond the capacity of the system to supply" (Rostow 1971, p. 51). It is still an open question whether and how rulers of Eastern Europe will be able and willing to alter this trend toward decline. In the long run, the well-being of the masses is of unequivocal importance for the survival of the system.

A sense of community in Eastern Europe does not extend far enough beyond the ruling elite because there is not enough widespread participation based on differentiation that would progress according to the developing division of labor. The single acceptable official doctrine does not allow enough flexibility and innovation. Therefore the social organization, as in traditional empires (Eisenstadt 1963, p. 69), is rigid and even to some extent ascriptive, especially in the allotment of rewards to individuals and in the personal dependence of administrative officers on the rulers (Hollander 1973).

The inability to make a clear distinction between the economic sphere and the political sphere prevents East European systems from achieving higher stages of differentiation "through which the main social functions or the major institutional spheres of society become dissociated from one another, attached to specialized collectivities and roles, and organized into relatively specific and autonomous symbolic and organization frameworks within the confines of the same constitutional system" (International Encyclopedia 1968, vol. 5, p. 229).

The East European establishments constantly have to deal with tensions that result from their doctrinaire approach to socioeconomic problems. The future of the establishments and programs promoted by them depends on the gap between doctrinaire plan and human reality. Unfortunately, there are no effective internal mechanisms in Soviet-style communism that would prevent the gap from growing constantly.

Let us consider, for example, the gap between investments and consumption. In Bulgaria, Czechoslovakia, East Germany, Hungary, Poland and Rumania (treated together here as East Central Europe) during the period 1950-68 the economically active population grew by 16 percent, but its participation in agriculture declined by 20 percent (in East Germany and Czechoslovakia, by as much as 40 percent). In the same period participation in nonagricultural pursuits grew by 56 percent. Almost half of this growth took place in industry (Ellias 1970, p. 150). These shifts in the allocation of human resources have considerably stimulated the growth of the masses' expectations regarding the standard of living. The question is how the East European systems will be able to deliver more, especially if "beyond doubt, technological change has been slower in Eastern than in Western Europe since World War II, and efficiency has risen more slowly" (Snell 1970, p. 240).

The gross national income (in its Marxist sense, which excludes services) had grown in 1971, according to official data (taking 1960 as 100), to 252 in Rumania, 182 in Hungary, 194 in Poland, 160 in East Germany, and 161 in Czechoslovakia. However, a large part of it is spent on accumulation (23-31 percent in each of these countries in 1971) and not on consumption. Investments in 1971 doubled in comparison with 1960 in Poland, East Germany, and Czechoslovakia; tripled in Rumania, and almost tripled in Hungary (Statistisches Jahrbuch 1973, p. 5). In 1971 Polish industry provided 60 percent of the gross national income (services excluded), in comparison with 50 percent in 1960 and only 33 percent after World War II. The relative position of Poland is good in coal, sugar, sulfuric acid, and even cement; but it is still fairly far behind other countries in iron, steel, electric power, artificial fabrics, and paper. This means that in order to become a developed country, Poland has to put much additional capital and human effort into overcoming current developmental disproportions. The same is to a large extent true of other countries in East Central Europe, except East Germany (see Table 2.1).

TABLE 2.1

The Comparative Position of Poland in Industrial Production, 1971

(kg. per inhabitant)

Industrial Product	Poland 1960	Poland 1971	Czecho-slovakia	East Germany	West Germany	Sweden	Canada	Yugo-slavia
Electric power (kh.)	987	2,134	3,257	3,870	4,393	8,200	10,050	1,431
Electric raw materials	3,653	5,000	5,615	4,466	3,710	797	10,260	1,122
Bituminous coal	3,516	4,443	1,987	50	1,824	3	668	34
Crude steel	225	389	832	209	681	648	507	119
Sulfuric acid	23	69	80	60	71	88	121	39
Artificial fabrics	1.4	8	17	22	77	32	15	5
Cement	222	399	549	472	661	472	390	289
Cellulose	10	14	32	24	14	833	484	19
Paper	22	29	59	62	92	542	528	29
Sugar (raw)	46	47	67	35	34	27	5	19

Source: Rocznik 1972, p. 651.

Several vital conflicts exist in regard to the structural nature of those countries. First, there is the question of a relative dispro- portion between underinvested agriculture and overinvested (at least in certain aspects) branches of industry. The relatively slow growth of agriculture has an obviously unfavorable influence on the living standard of the population. In the period 1951-67 the average growth of the gross national income in agriculture, in comparison with in- dustry, was 3 times lower in the USSR and Rumania, 5 times lower in Poland, 42 times lower in Hungary, and in the GDR almost the same; construction was in a situation similar to industry (Rozwoj 1969, p. 44). In Poland in 1972 the national income from industry grew to 266 if 1960 is taken as 100, but only to 119 in agriculture (Concise 1973, p. 50).

However, the main dilemma seems to be the conflict between the need for greater economic efficiency and the rigidity of the bureau- cratic model of management. Within the system there is insufficient incentive to utilize existing resources to their fullest extent. Many consumer goods are in very limited supply or are very expensive (Lipinski 1972).

Eastern Europe still suffers to a large extent from poor housing, shortage of communication media and private transportation, and underinvestment in several important social services. On the other hand, the exposure of the population to higher social and cultural needs leads to the constant growth of aspirations. Among Polish urban in- habitants reading is a common recreation for 25-33 percent of blue- collar workers and 50 percent or more of white-collar workers. Theaters and operas are regularly attended by 6-12 percent of blue- collar workers and 20-30 percent of white-collar workers (Czerwinski 1967, p. 51). People who watch television programs (more sophisti- cated than commercial television in the West) help their children acquire a higher education, read many good books, and communicate with their numerous relatives who have settled abroad are not so easily satisfied. They seek a better life, decide rationally about having either a car or a child, compare their own situation with what is available in other countries, and grumble about the ineptitude of the ruling elite.

With the growing sophistication of the administrative and eco- nomic machinery of the modernized societies, the Communist Parties ruling in Eastern Europe find it more and more difficult to face the new reality. How can they reconcile the doctrine with the current pressing social demands? How can they satisfy the local needs with the priorities coming from Moscow?

Around 1970 white-collar workers represented 38 percent of the Communist Party in Hungary, 28 percent in East Germany, 58 percent in Czechoslovakia, 24 percent in Rumania, and 44 percent in Poland (Starr 1971; Rocznik 1972). The real power of the white-collar stratum in these parties was much higher. Instead of being an avant garde of the industrial workers' stratum, the typical East European Communist Party is an avant garde of bureaucracy. However, even in this role the Party does not meet expectations. Among other factors, the educational level of its membership is not high enough. For example, among members of the Polish United Workers' Party in 1971, 37 percent (in 1960, 25 percent) had completed at least secondary education; but in the general population 26 percent are at this level of education, and 33 percent of the women. The general educational level of the Polish Party membership is far from being impressive (Rocznik 1972, pp. 62, 116). In the state administrative and judiciary branches taken together, 64 percent of the workers have at least secondary education.

The central rule and planning (on planning in Poland, see Montias 1962; Karpinski 1963; Feiwel 1971b) promoted by the ruling parties suffer from time to time because of tensions within the Party ranks. In the name of ideology or politics, various groups and strata struggle for power. Some of them are more rigid and doctrinaire than others. The issue of liberalization divides party ranks into hostile camps. For example, the anti-Jewish incidents in Poland in the late 1960s were correlated with liberalization. According to Celia Stopnicka Heller, they "were essentially not manifestations of an ethnic problem but rather of the struggle of factions within the Polish political elite, generating in the context of Poland's position in the Soviet orbit. . . . The Jews were the pawns in this factional struggle" (1969, p. 134).

The ruling Communist Parties do not have any opposing institutionalized groups within their home countries; Poland is the exception, for in 1972 the Roman Catholic Church had 18,000 priests and 6,700 parishes (Problemy 1973, p. xii). However, the major challenge comes not from politics but from the problems originated by the progress of industrialization.

THE IMPACT OF INDUSTRIALIZATION

The emphasis on industrial development has been the key issue of economic development in Eastern Europe. It is necessary to remember that most of this territory had been extensively agricultural. As recently as the 1950s one worker in agriculture produced enough food to feed only 2.6 persons in Poland (3.7 in 1966), 5 persons in Hungary (5.6 in 1965), and 4.2 persons in Rumania. Only in East Germany (15.2 in the 1950s and 10.5 in 1965) and in Czechoslovakia (4.6 in the 1950s and 12.8 in 1965) was the situation better (Rocznik

1972, p. 622). The fast progress of urbanization created some additional problems in feeding the population. In 1950 less than 40 percent of the total population lived in towns in Rumania (25 percent), Poland (37 percent), and Hungary (38 percent). Only Czechoslovakia and East Germany were urbanized to a considerable extent, 51.5 percent and 71 percent, respectively (Rozwoj 1969, p. 53). In the early 1970s the urban population in all these countries accounted for over 40 percent, and in Czechoslovakia and East Germany, over 60 percent.

Human resources are mobilized to a very high degree in Communist Eastern Europe, particularly for industrial progress based on a high rate of investments. However, the low productivity of agriculture provides an important obstacle in the progress toward modernization. A very considerable part of the labor force has to stay in agriculture (see Table 2.2).

The agricultural crisis in the USSR, which became more acute in the early 1970s, may in the long run have some very important implications for relations between East European Communist regimes and the Soviet Union, because agricultural efficiency does not improve fast enough. During the 1960s, the percentage of the labor force in agriculture and forestry diminished in Poland from 48 to 36.5; in Hungary, from 39 to 26; in Rumania, from 66 to 49; in Czechoslovakia from 26 to 18; and in East Germany, from 17 to 13. In the Soviet Union the change was from 39 percent to 27.5 percent (Rocznik 1972, p. 623). However, it is still a far cry from the low percentage of people in agriculture typical of the more highly industrialized countries.

The share of industry in gross national income (services excluded) increased in the period 1950-71 from 37 percent to 58.5 percent in Poland, from 43 percent to 57 percent in Rumania, from 36 percent (1960) to 42 percent in Hungary, and from 47 percent to 61 percent in East Germany; in Czechoslovakia it remained at 62 percent. It is now in general higher than in the USSR (52 percent in 1971). The output per person is also higher in several fields than in the USSR. At the same time the role of agriculture in the gross national income fell from 40 percent to 13 percent in Poland, from 27 percent to 22 percent in Rumania, from 25 percent to 18 percent in Hungary, from 28 percent to 11 percent in East Germany (in this case including forestry), and from 16 percent to 11 percent in Czechoslovakia; in the Soviet Union it decreased from 22 percent to 20 percent (Statistisches Jahrbuch 1973, p. 4). Nonagricultural workers in the total work force increased in 1950-70 in Poland from 43 percent to 63.5 percent; in Hungary, from 50 percent to 74 percent; in Rumania, from 26 percent to 51 percent; in Czechoslovakia, from 61 percent to 82 percent; and in East Germany, from 71 percent (1946) to 87 percent (Rocznik 1972, p. 623; Rocznik 1971, p. 657). These rapid

TABLE 2.2

Industrialization and Urbanization of Eastern Europe, West Germany, and Canada, 1970

	Rumania	Hungary	Poland	Czecho-slovakia	East Germany	West Germany	Canada
Population aged 20-64 (percent)	57	59	55	56	53	57	52
Urban population (percent)	40	45	52	62	73	79	74
Nonagricultural population (percent)	40	71	67	84	81	92	91
Industrial Employment (percent total employment)	23	37	42	38	42	41	23
Total Employment (percent population)	—	48	50	49	48	44	40
Agricultural and Forestry Employment (percent total population)	49	26	36	18	13	9	7
Number of People per Agricultural worker	2	6	4	13	10	18	24
Industry (percent gross national income)	60	44	57	62	61	49	35
Industry and construction (percent all investments)	54	36	43	42	54	32	32
Rate of investment (1960-100)	290	206	205	157	204	173	162

Sources: Rocznik 1972, pp. 610-29; Concise 1973, p. 41.

structural changes in employment were not accompanied by an adequate modernization in agriculture, trade, food service, and housing.

As may be seen in Table 2.3, the structure of industrial employment in Eastern Europe is already quite close to that of industrially developed countries; services, however, are still underdeveloped. In Czechoslovakia and in East Germany, close to 33 percent of all economically active people are in the tertiary sector (outside of industry, construction, transport, agriculture, and forestry), in comparison with almost 40 percent in West Germany and 60 percent in the United States. In Hungary it is little over 20 percent and in Rumania only 15 percent; no data are available for Poland (Rocznik 1972, p. 623).

The total population of Eastern Europe in mid-1973 was close to 100 million—Poland, 34 million; Rumania, 21 million; East Germany; 17.4 million; Czechoslovakia, 15 million; Hungary, 10.4 million—and the annual rate of population growth was 0.7 percent. The density was a little over 100 per square kilometer in Poland, Hungary, and Czechoslovakia; 158 per square kilometer in East Germany; and 85 per square kilometer in Rumania. One-fourth of the area's population consists of people under 15 years old (in Poland 28 percent), and the demand of the young generation for new jobs and better opportunities is increasing. These young people face the reality of a social structure that changed greatly over the course of 30 years but at the same time shows some tendencies toward stagnation.

CHANGES IN FAMILY STRUCTURE

Families tend to become smaller with the progress of economic modernization. In Poland in 1970, the structure and size of urban families and households differed greatly from those of rural families. In the towns there was a much larger percentage of smaller families (33 percent of all families) and one-person households. The rural families, in their size and structure, resembled the urban families before the Second World War (Concise, 1973, p. 33).

In 1970 the Polish family structure consisted of 67 percent families with children, 20.5 percent families without children, 11 percent single mothers with children, and 1 percent single fathers with children. Seventy-five percent of families lived alone, and the rest lived together with another household, either relatives (60 percent) or strangers (40 percent). In 75 percent of the marriages both spouses were gainfully employed. In 1970 in urban areas, 49 percent of the household members were economically active; in the rural areas the figure was 56 percent.

TABLE 2.3

Structure of Industrial Employment in Eastern Europe and
Selected Other Nations, 1970
(percentages of total industrial employment)

	Rumania	Hungary	Poland	Czecho-slovakia	East Germany	West Germany	Great Britain	United States	USSR
Power	2	2	2	1	3	2	4	3	2
Iron and steel	7	7	6	9	6	7	6	6	4
Machinery and metal fabrication	26	31	31	37	44	40	41	36	38
Chemical and rubber products	7	5	7	5	9	9	5	9	5
Wood and paper	16	5	6	6	5	4	3	8	9
Textiles, knit goods, clothing, leather	21	16	18	18	11	12	13	13	16
Food and beverages	8	10	11	8	7	6	9	9	9

Source: Rocznik 1972, p. 653.

35

Family size diminished in other East European countries. For example, in Hungary two-member families grew in the period 1949-70 from 19 percent to 27 percent of the population and three-member families from 26 percent to 31 percent, while the percentage of families with five or more members diminished from 31 percent to 14.7 percent. The percentage of people who remarried rose from 21.5 to 25.5 (Statistical 1970, p. 40).

Of all families in Czechoslovakia in 1970, 17 percent consisted of one person, 24 percent of two persons, 21 percent of three persons, 21 percent of four persons, and 17 percent of five or more persons (Statisticka 1971, p. 90).

The disruption of family structures is one of the common consequences of industrialization everywhere, including Eastern Europe. The number of divorces rose during the 1960s from 0.5 to 1.05 per 1,000 population in Poland, from 1.7 to 2.2 in Hungary, from 1.12 to 1.2 in Czechoslovakia, and from 1.4 to 1.6 in East Germany. Only in Rumania did it diminish, from 2.01 to 0.39. There is an obvious need for new family patterns that fit better into the entirely changed family situation and are based on lower fertility and limitation of family bonds to the nuclear family.

The fast-growing employment of women has had a strong impact on family life in Eastern Europe. Large numbers of women have entered professions that traditionally were masculine, although some occupations—executives, administrators, engineers (in some specialties)—have only a few women in their ranks. Professions such as medicine and pharmacy, which have come to be dominated by women, have had their salary scales lowered. There was a general governmental policy to upgrade the industrial professions at the expense of the service professions, but it was easier for women to enter the latter than the former. In practice women earn less than men, not because of discriminatory income rates (these were legally abolished) but because the female labor force is concentrated in low-income occupations. In addition, the growth of female employment has not been followed by an adequate improvement in social services that would ease the daily life of working mothers and wives.

In Poland in 1972, women constituted 41 percent of all wage earners: In trade, 70 percent; in industry, 38 percent; in transport and communications, 23 percent; in construction, 17 percent; and in public health and social welfare, 78 percent (Concise 1973, p. 45). According to survey data from 1972, 83 percent of working mothers with children up to three years old put them into day-care centers and 42 percent of mothers with children three to seven years old put them into kindergartens. The most important complaints of surveyed women were the inadequate supply of goods in the stores, the inconvenient location of stores, and the shortage of part-time jobs (Kulczycka 1973, pp. 44, 45).

The employment of women in other East European countries is also relatively high. In East Germany the highest percentages of women among all employed are in services (71.5 percent) and in agriculture (45 percent). In industry women's participation in the labor force increased from 36.5 percent in 1952 to 43 percent in 1972. The percentage of women in the total labor force grew in 1950-72 from 40 percent to 49 percent (Statistisches Jahrbuch 1973, p. 59).

In Czechoslovakia female participation in the labor force rose from 43 percent in 1960 to 47 percent in 1971 (in the services from 51 percent to 57 percent). Women constituted 80 percent of the workers in public health, 75 percent in trade and food service, 44 percent in industry, 51 percent in law enforcement, and 51 percent of all members of agricultural communes (Statisticka 1972, pp. 131-132).

In Hungary women constituted 42 percent of all wage earners in 1970: in trade, 62 percent; in industry, 43 percent; in transport and communications, 23 percent; in construction, 14 percent; in agriculture and forestry, 38 percent; and in other areas, 43 percent. Women constituted 32 percent of physicians under 31 years old, 25 percent of physicians 31 to 45 years, but only a small percentage of physicians over 45 years old (Statistical 1970, pp. 108, 423).

In Rumania women constituted 31 percent of wage earners in 1971: 32 percent in industry, 47 percent in trade, 40 percent in science, 32 percent in administration, and 71 percent in public health and social welfare (Anuarul 1972, p. 108).

The low-income policy that allows East European governments to save money for industrial investments is the major reason why married women seek gainful employment. However, with the rapidly increasing educational level of the female population, professional ambitions play a growing role. Discrimination against women is acute in Eastern Europe, not so much in employment as in home maintenance. Shopping takes too much time and becomes a nuisance when the stores are not well supplied; the public transportation is not adequate; private transportation is too expensive; household equipment is far from adequate; husbands are not eager enough to help in the household. All these factors create problems for gainfully employed women. They pay the mostly for the Party policy of promoting investment at the expense of consumption.

EDUCATIONAL ADVANCEMENT

Progress in education has been rapid in Eastern Europe. For example, in Poland during the 1960s the percentage of the population with more than primary education increased considerably and the

percentage of the population with less than primary education decreased
(see Table 2.4). In the labor force the indexes are even better (see
Table 2.5). Men and women do not differ much in educational level
except for higher education (see Table 2.6). Technical education dominates over any other types of education (see Table 2.7). The median
number of years of school completed by the Polish population seven
years old and over had grown from six in 1950 to over seven at the end
of the 1960s. The percentage of the population with less than primary
education diminished during the same period from 60 to below 50,
and the percentage of the population with secondary or higher education doubled (Searing 1970, p. 2).

The largest gains were achieved in vocational secondary education. The proportion of people with that education more than tripled
in the period 1950-69. The ratio of persons with vocational secondary
education to persons with general secondary education changed from
in 1950 1.1:1 to 3.6:1 in 1969. The percentage of primary school
graduates admitted to secondary schools grew from 68 to 83.5 in
1968, but many of them entered only basic vocational schools (29
percent in 1958 and 48 percent in 1968). In general the percentage
of persons aged 14-17 enrolled in schools increased from 14 in 1937
to 40 in 1948, 65 in 1960, and 81 in 1968 (Searing 1970, pp. 3, 11, 14).
In 1971/72, 16 percent of those aged 19-24 attended schools, and half
of all young people aged 18 were in schools (Rocznik 1972, p. 460).
In 1972/73, 87 percent of those 14-17 years old and 75 percent of
those 15-18 years old were in schools (Concise 1973, p. 222).

In other East European countries the growth of the education
level is no lower than in Poland, and in some cases even higher. For
example, in East Germany the number of employees with college education per 1,000 persons employed in the nationalized economy had
grown from 22 in 1961 to 49 in 1972 (in trade from 2 to 9.5 and in
industry from 6 to 22), and the number of employees with vocational
education per 1,000 persons employed in the nationalized economy
had grown from 39 in 1961 to 80 in 1972 (in trade from 4 to 29 and
in industry from 28 to 69) (Statistisches Jahrbuch 1973, p. 66).

In 1970 in Hungary, among people 15 years and older, 52 percent had at least eight years of school, in comparison with only 21
percent in 1949. In the same period, among people 18 years and older,
the percentage who completed secondary education had grown from
5 percent to 16 percent (among women from 3 percent to 14 percent).
Of the entire population over seven years old in 1970, 4 percent had
at least some higher education and 8 percent had completed secondary
education (Statistical 1970, pp. 36-37).

In the Czechoslovak employed labor force in 1970, the following
percentages of those in white-collar jobs had an adequate (or better)
education for the positions they filled: in jobs for people with higher

TABLE 2.4

Education Level of the Polish Population Aged 15
and Over, 1960 and 1970

| | 1960 | 1970 | | |
	Percent	Percent	1960=100	Thousands
Higher education	2.1	2.7	158	655
Secondary education	10.2	13.4	156	3,198
Vocational or some				
secondary education	4.6	14.5	379	3,458
Primary education	37.9	44.9	142	10,693
Less than primary				
education	45.2	24.5	65	5,828
Total	100.0	100.0	120	24,015

Source: Kozlowski and Turos 1973, p. 11.

TABLE 2.5

Education Level of the Polish Labor
Force, 1970

| | Thou- sands | Higher Education | Secondary Education | Vocational or Some Secondary | Primary Education | Less Than Primary Education |
				(percent)		
Nonagriculture	10,525	5.5	22.2	22.5	40.7	9.1
Nationalized						
Agriculture	667	3.7	15.5	13.3	46.9	20.6
Private						
Agriculture	5,754	0.1	1.3	3.9	42.2	52.5
Total	16,944	3.6	14.9	15.8	41.4	24.3

Source: Kozlowski and Turos 1973, p. 11.

TABLE 2.6

Education Level of the Polish Population Aged 15
and Over, by Sex, 1960 and 1970

	1960		1970	
	Men	Women	Men	Women
	(percent)		(percent)	
Higher education	3.1	1.2	3.8	1.8
Secondary education	10.7	9.9	12.7	14.1
Vocational or some secondary education	6.5	3.0	18.3	11.0
Primary education	37.1	38.5	44.0	45.7
Less than primary education	42.6	47.4	21.2	27.4

Source: Kozlowski and Turos 1973, p. 11.

TABLE 2.7

Polish Population Aged 15 or Over with More Than
Primary Education, 1970
(percent)

Type of Education	Total	Graduate Higher Education	Undergraduate Higher Education	Secondary Education	Vocational Education
General	17.7	—	—	35.5	—
Technical	42.7	31.0	14.3	28.1	73.7
Agricultural	5.4	8.0	1.9	4.5	6.6
Economic	10.2	12.4	9.0	17.7	0.6
Medical	3.7	13.2	14.3	3.1	0.9
Humanities	2.3	15.7	—	—	—
Natural sciences	1.0	7.7	—	—	—
Law and administration	0.8	7.4	—	—	—
Education	4.4	—	50.8	6.3	0.0
Art	0.8	2.9	1.4	0.8	—
Food Service	4.9	—	0.7	0.9	12.7
Other	6.1	1.7	7.6	3.1	5.5
Total numbers (1,000)	7,311	655	263	2,665	2,532

Source: Kozlowski and Turos 1973, p. 12.

education, 57 percent; in jobs for people with completed vocational secondary education, 62 percent; in jobs for people with completed general secondary education, 31 percent (among women the percentages were better). This means that in Czechoslovakia there were still many white-collar jobs occupied by unqualified people. This situation occurs to an even larger extent in the other countries discussed here, except probably East Germany (Statisticka 1971, p. 142).

Higher education has developed to a large extent in Eastern Europe (Table 2.8). However, there is the question of how many new graduates can be absorbed by the economies. The rate of economic growth is not high enough to create a real demand for a very large number of people with higher education. The present underqualified occupants of better positions are defensive when their present privileges become jeopardized by newcomers with better education.

In Eastern Europe there is still the myth that higher education opens all doors to social upgrading. White-collar workers, practically speaking, have much better opportunities to enter educational institutions in several fields than the traditionally lower social strata, which are still handicapped by their sociocultural backwardness. Yet young people feel disillusioned when, after completing higher education, they have to accept lower positions, meager salaries, poor living conditions, and very limited prospects. Even in culture the progress does not keep pace with the growing number of people with high aspirations. For example, the progress in publishing or in theater attendance is much slower in Eastern Europe than the progress in higher education.

Educational progress in Eastern Europe is one of the main sources of the local "revolution of rising aspirations." More educated people change their general outlook, are more demanding, push for a better standard of living, and look to the West for cultural inspiration. The high assimilating power of the local intelligentsia, particularly in Poland and in Hungary, is of great importance.

STANDARDS OF LIVING

The events in Poland at the turn of 1970 and 1971 had wide repercussions for the whole Soviet bloc, or at least its East European part, in that for the fifth time (East Germany, 1953; Poland, 1956; Hungary, 1956; Czechoslovakia, 1968) a wide and very evident pressure was exerted upon the establishment to improve the general living standards of the masses. This last pressure was much more successful than the previous ones because the Polish establishment had to accept the most urgent demands of the blue-collar workers.

The fight for better living standards has become one of the main sociopolitical factors in Eastern Europe. The countries differ

TABLE 2.8

Changes in Cultural and Educational Levels in
Eastern Europe, 1950-72

	Students in Higher Education per 10,000 Population		New Books and Pamphlets per Inhabitant		Theater Attendance per 10,000 Population	
	1950	1972	1950	1972	1950	1972
Poland	50	106	5	4	41	40
Hungary	35	83	6	6	32	53
Czechoslovakia	37	89	7	5	76	67
Rumania	33	72	3	4	28	37
East Germany	16	89	4	7	73	72
USSR	69	187	5	7	38	47
Bulgaria	46	112	2	6	27	67
Albania	3	112*	1	1*	11	65*

*1961-70.

Source: Statistisches Jahrbuch 1973, pp. 26-27.

in their levels of development and socioeconomic backgrounds, but their political and economic systems are more or less the same, and they depend on the Soviet Union to a similar extent. A labor and consumer crisis in any of these countries, and especially in the USSR, affects the whole Soviet Bloc. The rise of living standards in one of the participating countries becomes a pattern for the other countries.

The growth of personal consumption, as opposed to centrally provided services, leads unavoidably to individualization and diversification of demand that in the long run may change the nature of the system. There is a constant progress in food consumption (Table 2.9), as well as in health services and communications (Table 2.10). However, there is also an obvious gap not only in comparison with Western Europe but also among the East European countries themselves. Consumers are much better off in East Germany and Czechoslovakia than in the other countries. The Soviet diet is still qualitatively inferior to the East European diet, and the same is even truer in housing (Byrne 1970, pp. 273-315). There are severe discrepancies in progress in education, culture, aspirations, and the standard of living among the countries of Eastern Europe.

TABLE 2.9

Changes in the Consumption of Foodstuffs per
Inhabitant in Eastern Europe, Austria, and
Sweden, 1960 and 1970
(kg.)

	Meat		Fat		Milk		Sugar		Fruit	
	1960	1970	1960	1970	1960	1970	1960	1970	1960	1970
Czecho-slovakia	57	71	19	20	173	196	36	38	70	42
East Germany	55	66	27	28	—	108	29	35	80	55
Poland	43	53	14	18	234	267	38	39	—	—
Hungary	48	59	24	24	114	112	27	34	55	71
Rumania	—	38*	—	9.5*	—	116*	—	18*	—	35*
Austria	60	69	17	25	211	199	35	34	—	105
Sweden	49	52	21	20	262	263	41	41	72	94

*1964-66.

Source: Rocznik 1972, p. 687.

The monthly incomes of employed people are highest (in real
value) in East Germany. Differences in the average monthly earnings
between various branches of the economy are not great. For example,
the blue-collar workers employed directly in industrial production
in 1972 earned monthly wages of 911 marks in metallurgy and 863
marks in the power industry, but only 706 marks in light industry
and 663 marks in the textile industry. The average monthly income
of blue-collar workers in all production industries was 807 marks,
and in construction 856 marks. Blue-collar workers in state-owned
agricultural enterprises earned 745 marks; those in post offices,
661 marks, and those on the railway, 890 marks (Statistisches Jahrbuch
1973, pp. 136, 161, 199, 256).

In East Germany the ownership of durable consumer goods improved considerably in the period 1960-72. The percentage of households with cars grew from 3 to 19. Indexes for television sets are 17
percent and 75 percent; for refrigerators, 6 percent and 70 percent;
for washing machines, 6 percent and 63 percent. Even in relatively
poor households, with incomes below 600 marks per month in 1970,
55 percent had television sets, 28 percent had refrigerators, and 23

TABLE 2.10

Indexes of Relative Well-being in Eastern Europe, 1950/60-70

	East Germany	Czechoslovakia	Poland	Hungary	Rumania	USSR
Radios per 1,000 population						
1950	180	194	59	66	19	73
1970	351	325	174	245	152	388
Television sets per 1,000 population						
1960	60	58	14	10	3	22
1970	264	213	129	171	73	143
Private cars per 1,000 population						
1960	17	18	4	3	–	3
1970	68	58	15	23	21	–
Telephones per 1,000 population						
1960	75	74	30	–	19	13
1970	123	138	57	80	33	56
Doctors per 10,000 population						
1950	11	11	5	10	9	15
1970	20	23	19	22	15	27
Dentists per 10,000 population						
1950	4	1	1	–	1	2
1970	4	7	4	2	2	4
Hospital beds per 10,000 population						
1950	102	62	51	53	42	56
1970	111	80	74	77	81	109

Sources: Rozwoj 1969, pp. 111, 137, 138; Rocznik 1972, pp. 677, 682, 699, 700; Statistisches Jahrbuch 1972, p. 26.

percent had electric washing machines (Statistisches Jahrbuch 1973, pp. 336-37).

In 50 percent of all households in East Germany the wife was employed full-time, and in an additional 33 percent she had a part-time job. Even in families with three or more children, 76 percent of the wives were employed: 43 percent full-time, 12 percent part-time up to 24 hours per week, and 21 percent part-time more than 24 hours per week. The income of the husband did not make much difference to whether the wife was employed or not. Even if he earned over 1,000 marks per month, his wife was employed in 76 percent of the cases (in 1960 only 36 percent of the wives worked in such a case) (Statistisches Jahrbuch 1972, pp. 362-63).

In the typical three-person East German household in the earning category 800-1,000 marks per month in 1970, 34 percent of expenditure went for food, 9.5 percent for beverages, 9.5 percent for clothing, 2 percent for shoes, 4 percent for rent, 2 percent for culture and leisure, 2 percent for transportation, and 13.5 percent for various durable consumer goods (Statistisches Jahrbuch 1972, p. 357).

The pattern of expenditure differed very little with the size of the household. However, if one considers only the three-person household, the expenditure on food varied from 41 percent in poorest households (below 600 marks per month) to 18 percent in the wealthiest (over 2,000 marks per month). Expenditure on household appliances varied from 13 percent in the poorest households to 25 percent in wealthiest, but the expenditure on clothing did not vary at all (Statistisches Jahrbuch 1972, pp. 356-57). It is also very characteristic of the progressive equalization of life style in East Germany that there are no differences in the patterns of expenditure pattern between cooperative farmers and employees of the state enterprises (see Table 2.11).

The average monthly income in the state sector of Czechoslovakia in 1971 was 2,009 koruny (in industry, 2,026 koruny; in construction, 2,040 koruny), and in general the differences between branches were small: from 2,300-2,400 koruny in transport and in science and research to 1,300 in housing administration, 1600 in communal services, and 1700 in trade. In 1971 industrial blue-collar workers averaged 1,974 koruny, in comparison with 2,628 koruny earned by technical personnel (engineers and technicians) and 1,692 by other white-collar workers (mostly clerical staff). The average monthly incomes of all employees differed between industrial branches from 2,827 koruny in the fuel industry to 1,518 in the clothing industry (Statisticka 1972, pp. 132, 138, 247-48).

The availability of household appliances also has improved in Czechoslovakia. In 1964-71 the number of people per appliance

TABLE 2.11

Comparison of Expenditures in East German Four-
Person Households, Cooperative Farmers and State
Employees, 1972 (percent of total budget)

	Farmers	Employees
Food	28	27
Beverages	9.5	8.5
Shoes	2	2
Clothing	11	10
Industrial wares	18	16.5
Transport	1	1
Rent	1	3
Utilities	2	1
Culture	2	3

Source: Statistisches Jahrbuch 1973, pp. 337-39.

decreasea from 5 to 3 for washing machines, from 13 to 5 for refrigerators, from 7 to 4 for television sets, and from 3 to 2 for radios.
The number of people per private car fell from 35 to 15. In 1971
there was a washing machine and a television set in each household
and a refrigerator in each second household (Statisticka 1972, p. 465).

It is common among Czechoslovak families to have more than
one member employed. Among the households studied in 1970 (the
average size was about 3.5 people) two or almost two members were
employed; 1.89 among farmers, 1.79 among white-collar workers,
and 1.78 among blue-collar workers. The earnings of the wife constituted 20 percent of all incomes in both white-collar and blue-collar
households, and 12.5 percent in the farmer households (Statisticka
1972, p. 467).

When comparing expenditures by various classes and levels of
income in Czechoslovakia (see Table 2.12), the differences seem to
be significant only for farmers and not for the distinction between
blue-collar and white-collar workers. Farmers spend less on food,
installment payments, industrial goods, and savings. This indicates
that farmers are in general more oriented toward investment than
toward direct consumption.

A comparison of Czechoslovak households of various sizes in
1969 shows that, depending on the number of children in the family,
the role of food in the total expenditure grows, but not much: in blue-

TABLE 2.12

Comparison of Expenditures of Households of Blue-
Collar Workers, White-Collar Workers, and
Cooperative Farmers in Czechoslovakia, 1970
(percentage)

	Income in Koruny per Year for One Household Member											
	Below 7,200			7,201-12,000			12,001 and More			Average		
	B	W	F	B	W	F	B	W	F	B	W	F
Food and drinks	46	44	39	36	34	30	29	26	23	33	29	26
Industrial goods	25	24	36	27	27	36	27	28	35	27	27	35
Services	9	11	9	11	14	10	12	14	10	11	14	10
Installment payments	14	16	4	17	16	8	19	20	9	18	18	8
Savings	6	4	10	8	8	14	11	11	20	10	10	17
Other	1	—	2	1	1	2	2	1	3	1	1	3

B = Blue-collar workers.
W = White-collar workers.
F = Cooperative farmers.

Source: Statisticka 1971, p. 476.

collar families where the wife was not employed, it increased from
38 percent with one child to 42 percent with four or more children,
and in white-collar families from 33 percent with one child to 41
percent with four or more children. When the wife is employed, the
percentages are different: 30 and 39, respectively, in blue-collar
families, and 26 and 33 in white-collar families. In both these categories, employment of the wife leads to more savings and to investment in household equipment. The same may be said about the impact
of general material improvement. A comparison of blue-collar households differentiated according to income level shows that the role of
savings in the total expenditure grows from 5 percent in the poorest
families to 11.5 percent in the wealthiest families. Most of the
increase in family wealth is spent on transportation (private car,
motorcycle) and sporting goods (Statisticka 1971, pp. 472, 473, 475).

In Poland the average monthly gross earnings in the nationalized
economy were 2,760 zloty in 1972 (2,500 zloty net income after

deduction of income tax and pension contribution), the highest being in construction (3,342 zloty) and in science (3,288 zloty) and the lowest in forestry (1,985 zloty) and public health and social welfare (2,007 zloty).

The study of household budgets done annually by the Central Statistical Office in Poland (see Table 1.5) shows that in 1971 food constituted a greater part of the expenditures of farm families (50 percent) and blue-collar workers (45 percent) than of white-collar workers (39 percent). Manual workers who have higher incomes eat more meat and buy more clothing and shoes, motorcycles and motorbikes, and sewing machines. Farmers are particularly fond of bicycles and motorcycles. They have fewer refrigerators and television sets than the other categories. For other items there are many similarities in patterns of consumption and the equipping of households. There are no significant differences in the typical household equipment of four-person blue-collar and white-collar families. In both categories almost all families have television sets, radios, and washing machines. Refrigerators are owned by 40 percent of blue-collar families and 60 percent of white-collar families. Sewing machines are owned by almost 40 percent of both groups. In farm families all these household appliances are less common, but even for small farms of seven acres or less, 33 percent have television sets, 66 percent have radios, and more than 50 percent have washing machines and sewing machines (see Table 1.5).

The Polish masses show dissatisfaction with the current standard of living. They have good reason for this. The buying power of the average income is relatively low (see Table 2.14). The Polish diet includes a large amount of potatoes and cereals, and the consumption of meat is below that of the Western countries (from time to time there is a shortage of meat in stores). However, the food supply in general is quite satisfactory.

In 1960-72 the major interest of the population switched from goods for direct consumption to more luxury goods and services. Taking the purchasing power in 1970 as 100, the index for 1971 was only 147 for food but 267 for goods and services in culture, education, tourism, and sport; 237 for transportation and communication; 234 for personal hygiene, health, and welfare; and 232 for household equipment. The consumption of potatoes decreased in Poland between 1950 and 1971 from 270 kilos to 180 kilos per inhabitant, and that of cereals from 166 kilos to 129 kilos; at the same time, purchases of shoes, sugar, and silk almost doubled. The consumption of tea has increased nine times, and of wine seven times (Rocznik 1972, p. 538). Taking sales in 1960 as 100, the figures for 1972 were 235 in goods and 200 in food (Concise 1973, p. 172).

In Hungary the average monthly income in 1970 was 1,413 forints among blue-collar workers, 1,467 forints among cooperative farmers, and 1,887 among white-collar workers. Including social benefits, the respective sums were 1,625, 1,622, and 2,184 forints, which means that white-collar workers earned one-third more than blue-collar workers and farmers.

In 1971 the average monthly earning in the Hungarian state sector was 2,229 forints; in construction, 2,439 forints; in transportation and communication, 2,348 forints; in agriculture and forestry, 2,199 forints; in industry, 2,173 forints; in trade, 2,084 forints. The highest income in industry was in mining (3,251 forints) and the lowest was in light industry (2,046 forints), food processing (2,171 forints), and in the crafts and service co-ops (2,188 forints. Almost 40 percent (37.1 percent) of all people employed in the nationalized industry in 1970 worked in light industry and food processing.

The comparison of Hungarian household budgets in various occupational categories shows that there is a basic difference in the role of the food expenditure between the white-collar worker families and the blue-collar worker or peasant worker families (see Table 2.13). It is probably explicable to a large extent by the fact that the general income of white-collar workers is better and they therefore live on a somewhat higher level.

There was a fast improvement in household equipment in Hungary during 1960-71. The number of refrigerators per 100 households rose from 1 to 39; washing machines, from 15 to 51; vacuum cleaners, from 3 to 34; private cars, from 1 to 9; motorcycles, from 8 to 20; radios, from 72 to 76; and television sets, from 3 to 58. The per capita consumption of meat rose. In the same period the per capita consumption of cereals decreased from 136 kilos to 128 kilos and that of potatoes from 98 kilos to 75 kilos (Statistical 1973, pp. 103, 333, 340; Statistical 1972, 111, 119, 375, 381, 382, 384-87).

CROSS-NATIONAL COMPARISONS OF LIVING STANDARDS

When comparing the consumption of foodstuffs in Eastern Europe (Table 2.9), it becomes clear that in meat consumption Czechoslovakia and East Germany are at the top and Rumania at the bottom. In fats East Germany and Rumania are above and below, respectively, the standard typical for the other countries. In sugar Rumania is much below the others. In fruit consumption Eastern Europe is much below the West European standard.

Comparison of buying power (Table 2.14) shows that in East Germany the consumer is in a much better position than in the other

TABLE 2.13

Comparison of Expenditures of Households of Blue-
Collar Workers, White-Collar Workers, and
Peasant-Workers,[a] Hungary, 1970
(percent)

	White Collar[b]	Blue Collar[c]	Peasant Worker[d]
Food, drinks, tobacco	38	44	48
Clothing	15	15	13
Housing and mainte- nance	13	13	14
Household furnishings	9	9	9
Health and personal hygiene	3	2	2
Transportation and communications	8	5	5
Culture and leisure	7	6	4
Other	7	6	5
Annual expenditure per person	20,189 forints	15,489 forints	15,619 forints

[a]Some of the family members are engaged in agricultural work
and the rest are employed outside agriculture.
[b]The average size is 3.15, with 1.7 persons gainfully employed.
[c]The average size is 3.25, with 1.7 persons gainfully employed.
[d]The average size is 3 persons.

Source: Statistical 1970, pp. 389, 391.

countries. The data on household appliances are less reliable because
it is difficult to compare their quality. Probably the East German
statistical yearbook enumerates prices of such household articles
that are of better quality (and therefore more expensive) than in other
countries.

The volume of sales per 1,000 population gives some idea of
the relative availability of some goods, as well as of the financial
ability of the population to buy them. In 1967 sales of television sets,
radios, refrigerators, and vacuum cleaners were twice as high in
East Germany as in Poland, Hungary, and the USSR, in each of which
the purchase of these goods was at approximately the same level.

TABLE 2.14

Comparison of the Buying Power of the Average Monthly
Income in East Germany, Czechoslovakia, Poland, and
Hungary, 1970

	Unit	East Germany	Czecho- slovakia	Poland	Hungary
Potatoes	kilo	4,659	2,767	1,519	734
White bread	kilo	792	745	650	591
Sugar	kilo	483	242	247	222
Pork	kilo	99	65	46	56
Men's shirt	item	16.5	22	7.5	16
Washing machine	item	0.5	1	1	1
Refrigerator	item	0.75	1	0.5	0.5
Television set	item	0.33	0.5	0.33	0.33

Source: Compiled by the author on the basis of data available in the statistical yearbooks of appropriate countries.

Czechoslovakia was in between, and Rumania was lower (Rozwoj 1969, p. 127).

In East Germany housing conditions are definitely better (one person per room, on the average) than in the other four countries (in each about 1.4 persons per room). In Poland, Czechoslovakia, and Hungary 33 percent of all dwellings do not have running water (in Hungary as high as 44 percent), and in 50 percent the toilet is outside. The building of new dwellings does not go fast enough (4-7 new dwellings in each country per 1,000 population in 1971, in comparison with 13 in Sweden) (Rocznik 1972, pp. 693-94).

In Hungary in 1970, only 28 percent of the dwellings were equipped with flush toilets, 16 percent were connected to the gas system, and 36 percent had running water. Ninety percent of all economically active agricultural workers and 67 percent of blue-collar workers were better off in this respect: only 28 percent of them lived under the conditions mentioned above, and 11 percent had at least some of these "comforts" (Statistical 1970, pp. 414, 416).

In health, child care, education, and culture there has been a rapid growth in Eastern Europe. For example, in East Germany, 28 percent of the children under three years old are in kindergartens or day-care centers (only 1 percent in 1950) (<u>Statistisches Jahrbuch</u> 1972, p. 35). In Hungary the number of pupils in kindergartens per 100 children 3 to 6 years old grew in the 1960s from 30 to 53, and the percentage of the population of secondary-school-age actually attending schools rose from 26 to 30. Among Hungarian students in postsecondary education, the proportion receiving regular state grants went from 76 percent to 85 percent (<u>Statistical 1970,</u> pp. 437, 439, 440).

People's tastes become more sophisticated, and their cultural activities change appropriately. Television has a great impact on life styles. One result is that attendance at motion pictures goes down. In East Germany in the 1950s there were 1,000-2,000 cinema visits per year per 100 people, but the number decreased to less than 500 in 1971. However, the number of stage theater visits remained at the same level, 73 in 1950 and 72 in 1971 per 100 people (<u>Statistisches Jahrbuch</u> 1972, p. 34).

The rise of the general cultural level has had an obvious impact on the standard of living and people's expectations regarding it. Only in East Germany is there some harmony in this respect. In other countries of Eastern Europe the progress in health, education, and culture seems to be much faster than that in living standards. Such a situation introduces internal imbalance that may in the long run have far-reaching consequences.

It is an open question how much the East European establishments will be willing and able to satisfy the rising mass expectations. The bureaucratic structure of a state socialist economy is highly disadvantageous in this respect, especially when it is entering the higher levels of economic and social development. So far there is little flexibility and structural innovation. Poland has private agriculture and some small private business. East Germany left a margin for private entrepreneurship. In Hungary there is economic experimentation with allowing state-owned business to have some local initiative. Rumania trades with the West to considerable extent.

However, all these measures do not seem adequate to stimulate the local economic systems to better satisfaction of rising mass demands. East Germans may be much better off than Poles or Hungarians, but what really counts for them is the comparison with West Germans. Poles are in close touch with their relatives who settled in the West. Hungarians have as their reference group not Russians or Rumanians but Austrians. Rumanians are unhappy with their low standard of living.

It is quite difficult for the Soviet Union and the other East European establishments to prevent the population from comparing themselves with the West. In the early 1970s the governments in Poland and Hungary were forced to relax restrictions on travel to the West for their citizens. The resulting extensive contacts contribute to the further growth of local expectations. People question the rationality of not following the pattern of Yugoslavia, which gains much from allowing her citizens to work in Western Europe (Baucic 1972).

The main trouble with state socialism in regard to living standards is that under this kind of system people are not able to harmoniously reconcile their own well-being with the interests of the state. The main gain of the state comes from the exploitation of citizens, and the gain of individuals comes from taking advantage of the state. All mention of eventual economic reforms in Eastern Europe is oriented toward creation of intermediary mechanisms that would allow citizens to show some initiative useful for the state and profitable for them. However, must it not lead in the long run to the abolishment of state socialism? Members of the establishment firmly say "yes" to this question and therefore oppose any real reform.

3

HISTORICAL BACKGROUND
OF POLAND'S SHIFTING
CLASSES

POLAND'S DRAMATIC CHOICES

Since 1945, Eastern Europe has been under a single rule for the first time in its history. The Council for Mutual Economic Aid (CMEA) and the Warsaw Treaty Organization (WTO) are the institutional vehicles of military, political, and economic integration under Soviet leadership (Staar 1971, pp. 215-79). However, one should not be misled by the apparent unity. Throughout history Eastern Europe has been the battleground of divergent military, political, social, and cultural forces from the west (Catholicism and Protestantism), the east (Eastern and Russian Orthodoxy), and the south (Islam).

The fate of Poland was of great importance in the history of Eastern Europe in the periods when the Polish-Hungarian cooperation worked well (common kings, extensive trade, cultural and religious bonds), the internal unity was not substantially endangered, and there were no major competitive powers on the horizon. The Turkish invasion from the south weakened Hungary and made it in the long run subservient to the Austrian Hapsburgs in the seventeenth century. Bohemia also lost its autonomy and became incorporated into the Hapsburgian monarchy. The present territory of Rumania was for centuries the battleground of Turkish, Hungarian, Russian, Polish, Austrian, and German interests. With Poland unable to play an active political role in Eastern Europe, her neighbors were exposed to constantly increasing pressures exerted by big powers. Russia, Prussia, and Austria had decided the fate of Eastern Europe since the eighteenth century.

History placed Poland on the border of very basic political, ideological, and cultural divisions. At the creation of the Polish state, around 1000, it was necessary to choose between traditional Slavic paganism and Christianity. During the Mongol onslaughts in the thirteenth century, Poland sided with Western Europe; she then had a freedom of political move unavailable to the eastern Slavs conquered by Mongols. Poland's attitude toward Islam was based on her Christian allegiance and, in contrast with the southern Slavs, was never conquered by Turks.

When European Christianity split into two hostile camps during the Reformation, Poland sided with Catholicism. However, she offered a refuge to many Protestants persecuted in the West. The fact that Poland declared for Catholicism contributed to some extent to her later involvement in the Swedish wars in the seventeenth and eighteenth centuries.

The contrast between the democracy of the Polish gentry state and the strict authoritarianism of neighboring monarchies was a major factor in Poland's loss of independence.

Later there came further choices of a dramatic nature: between the Central Powers and the Allies during World War I, between Western democracy and totalitarianism during World War II, and between the bureaucratic model of communism and humanitarian socialism at present. In all these cases, whether she wanted to or not, Poland had to side with one of the antagonists and bear all the consequences. These choices should not be simplified with the statement that Poland was always on a particular, clearly delineated side. In fact, various Polish orientations were almost always in mutual conflict—for instance, the split between the pro-Russian and the pro-Prussian orientations among the Polish nobility toward the end of the eighteenth century.

It often happened that a particular orientation was forced upon Poland by circumstances, or that Poland was too weak to make a conscious choice that would better serve her interests. In all these historical choices, Poland could either become an ally of a given side or, what as a rule had much more advantageous results for her, she could play the role of peaceful emissary: Poland as a bridge for Western Christianity to the East; union with Lithuania (but not with Ruthenia); religious tolerance during the Reformation; transmission of the French Revolution's democratic slogans to Eastern Europe; the controversial attempt to apply the Uniate solution in Ruthenia; the thought of uniting Poland and the Ukraine; Panslavism among some prominent Polish political emigrants in the nineteenth century; participation in the revolutionary freedom movements in the nineteenth and twentieth centuries; the demilitarization of Central Europe; the democratization of the Soviet bloc; and the revision of Marxist doctrine.

As a rule, a nationalistic orientation was considerably less advantageous to Poland than a universalistic orientation—for examples, the ill-fated campaigns against Moscow at the beginning of the seventeenth century, which were to subjugate her to Polish rule; the antagonizing of the Ukrainian Cossacks; the deterioration of relations with Sweden; the unfortunate policy with respect to ethnic minorities in Poland between the two world wars; the anti-Jewish campaign in 1968.

Polish nationalism must inevitably lose out when in conflict with the nationalism of her great neighboring powers. If it does not, then Polish nationalism becomes a conscious or unconscious tool of foreign control over Poland, as in the insurrections of the gentry against the last Polish king at the end of the eighteenth century, Piasecki's fascist group in People's Poland (Blit 1965), or Moczar's group toward the end of the 1960s.

Poles have for centuries been identified with Western Catholicism, although this has not always been entirely in accord with the historical truth; it so happened that the majority of wars waged by Poland were against nations with different religions (Orthodox Moscow, Protestant Sweden, Moslem Turkey). One can with some certainty surmise that this was the cause of the identification of defending "Polishness" with defending Catholicism. Poles were proud, to the point of absurdity, of their position as "outposts of Christianity" and defenders of Western civilization.

It seems historically justified to say that Poland came into being precisely because she joined the Christian world and thus was not eradicated like the Pieczyngs and the Jadzwings, or subdued like the Baltic nations and the Cossack ethnic minorities of the old Russian empire, who were conquered and later transformed into Soviet citizens. Catholicism has played the major role in shaping the moral image of Poles. Poland shares with Catholicism the latter's vacillations between an open model and a closed model, between a particularistic conception and a universalistic conception, between a passively ethnic understanding of religion and a moral world outlook.

If we accept that for Poles and for Poland, in her geographical situation, the correct choice is an actively universalistic attitude, we should then analyze whether and to what extent this attitude was the guiding principle for Poles in various historical circumstances and the consequences of accepting or rejecting it. It was definitely not a guiding principle during the Counter Reformation, when the treatment of Protestants, although much milder than in the West, still had little in common with Christian brotherly love (Fox 1971). The attitude of the nobility toward the bourgeoisie and the villeins was also by no means actively universalistic, with the exception of a group of enlightened reformers toward the end of the eighteenth century. However, the participation of Poles in various national liberation movements during the nineteenth century was undoubtedly based on universalism. Poland's approach to the Jewish question was far removed from universalism. The radically nationalistic orientation during the interwar period, which directed its barbs against all ethnic minorities as well as against almost all of Poland's neighbors, certainly did not leave any room for universalism; it was its very opposite.

THE GENTRY TRADITION

In the sixteenth century the Polish middle gentry gained its highest power by shifting its allegiance between the monarch and the magnates, gaining privileges from both, developing estates worked by serf labor, restricting the freedom of peasants and burgher, and promoting the unique pattern of the gentry democracy (Boswell 1967). At that time the gentry constituted 8-10 percent of the population of the Polish Crown (Lithuania not included). At the end of the eighteenth century it constituted 8 percent in the whole state, in comparison with 72 percent peasants, 7 percent burghers, 10 percent Jews, and 0.5 percent clergy. In the rural areas (approximately 85 percent of the total population) the gentry ruled together with the magnates, very often as members of their manorial staffs (only half of the gentry owned their own estates) (Gieysztor et al. 1968, pp. 174, 344-45).

The gentry of various ethnic origins became Polonized and united in promoting their common well-being. The myth that most of them were descended from ancient Sarmatians, who had founded the ruling class, provided the following ideological rationalization: "Upon the gentry lay the historic duty to defend Christianity. The gentry, and only they, were identified with the Polish nation excluding other social classes, allegedly of different origin, from the national community. This concept of a nation of gentry, based on the community of a privileged estate, merged into a single entity the Polish nobility with the Polonized Ruthenian and Lithuanian gentry" (Gieysztor et al. 1968, p. 264).

Sarmatism as a style of life was a specific blending of Western and Eastern cultures. The taste for ostentation, luxury, rich garments, and parade were developed in Poland under Oriental influences resulting from contacts by the Poles with Moscow and the Turks in the sixteenth and seventeenth centuries.

At the end of the seventeenth century Sarmatism became very popular among the Polish gentry. 'Its predominating feature was intolerance of other cultural, political and religious beliefs, and intolerance which clearly reflected the megalomania of the gentry who were convinced of their superiority not only over other social classes in Poland but even over other nations. The conviction grew among them that nothing could be learned from foreigners, because the system prevailing in Poland was perfection itself. This opinion implied that the foreigners for this reason sought to plot not only against the existence of the Commonwealth, but also against the freedom, the rights and the incomes of its inhabitants. Hence in the seventeenth century, a straight path led towards a growing xenophobia" (Gieysztor et al. 1968, p. 265).

On the other hand, Western influence kept the Polish gentry to some extent apart from the East. In the Middle Ages, Poland was very profoundly latinized. The Catholic Church took into its hands the moral and intellectual education of the country. Latin was supreme in the Church and in the king's chancellery. All diplomatic correspondence and all official documents were written in Latin. It was also the language of the very first Polish chronicles, scholarly treaties, and poems.

Latin gave the Polish language a distinctly West European aspect. In the sixteenth century it was elaborated by the Polish nobility, which at that time had close social and cultural relations with Western Europe. The Polish language, a product of an aristocratic and intellectual elite, is one of the most difficult and capricious of the Slavic languages.

A number of sources of Poland's indigenous bigotry, parochialism, chauvinism, and isolationism may be related to the gentry tradition. The Polish nobility was concerned primarily with local matters and returned to private squabbles as soon as public danger passed. Precisely because of this, Poland for centuries could not strengthen and consolidate her national economy; she gained little from even considerable military victories; and she could not take full advantage of international agreements and unions. This underdevelopment of the nation-state guarded against absolutism, but it also constantly contributed to the weakening of the Polish state.

Attaining goals of a collective nature was neglected in Poland effectively from the end of the Piast dynasty (1370). National loyalty did not have sufficient foundations in an appropriately developed government apparatus. The greed of the nobility and its tendency to discriminate against other classes precluded a suitable evolution of thought and economic activity based on rational principles. The nobility's monopolistic position formed the greatest barrier to economic development. The enormous power of the aristocratic oligarchy, and the division of Poland into power centers of the more influential potentates with a mass of lesser nobility in tow, did not provide fertile ground for authentic citizenship attitudes.

Despite patriotic rhetoric, the attachment of the masses of the nobility, and even more so of the indigenous aristocracy, to the Polish nation was comparatively flimsy, since central power was an object of incessant conflicts between various pressure groups that placed their local interests above the public good.

The partitions of Poland and the extinction of the Polish state at the end of the eighteenth century resulted from the growing disproportion of power between the Polish gentry democracy and the absolutistic monarchies of Prussia, Austria, and Russia. It is difficult to expect stronger neighbors not to decide to plunder a weak and divided state, especially when its geography facilitates nibbling at it bit by bit.

The gentry lost not only the state but also all the insurrections they sponsored during the nineteenth century. The occupants expropriated the estates of insurgents, who then had to look for other sources of income. The abolition of serfdom also undermined the position of the gentry. In 1927 the landowners and their dependents accounted for only 180,000 people—about 0.66 percent of the total population. However, "a fair number of prominent figures in the interwar period in Poland came from landed families" (Polonsky 1972, p. 25).

THE INTERWAR SOCIAL STRUCTURE

The feudal traditions collapsed after World War I, but the division of society into masters and serfs still remained to some extent in the Polish mentality:

> Poland, like a number of countries related to her economically and socially, passed through a period of transition when the former historical leading class was leaving the stage and new social elements, sufficiently strong, and of a distinct character and defined functions had not yet had time to form (Hertz 1942, p. 151).

Interwar Poland was a result of World War I, and the destruction during that war greatly influenced the fate of the Second Polish Commonwealth. The population in the territory of interwar Poland diminished from 29 million in 1910 to 26.5 million in 1920, but it grew to 35 million in 1939 (growth of 1.2 percent per year in the period 1932-39). The urban population rose from 24 percent in 1921 to approximately 30 percent in 1939, and the agricultural population decreased in the same period from 64 percent to 59 percent. Manual workers had grown from 27 percent to 30 percent of the total population, but more than a half of them had lived in the rural areas and less than one-third were concentrated in big cities. At the beginning of the 1930s Poland had only half the percentage (19) of people employed in industry that Germany had (41) but double the percentage in agriculture. Peasants constituted half of the population, and their numerical strength decreased only slightly during the interwar period. White-collar workers, the intelligentsia, and the petite bourgeoisie grew faster than other classes. The real bourgeoisie and landlords together represented only 1.2 percent of the total population, but their power and influence were quite substantial.

Jews constituted most of the petite bourgeoisie (70 percent) and 40 percent of craftsmen. Over 60 percent of the Jewish nonagricultural population was economically independent, while among the Gentile nonagricultural population over 80 percent worked as salaried or wage-earning workers. In the cities over 20,000 population, almost half of the population were Jews. There was much possibility for conflicts between Jews and Gentiles arising from diverging interests.

The development of a Western-style bourgeoisie was limited in interwar Poland by the great role of the state and the fact that foreign capital owned almost half of the stock. Almost half the bourgeoisie were Jews, a small percentage Germans, and the rest Poles. From 1921 to 1938 landlords, mostly Poles and some Germans, controlled 30 percent of the land at the beginning of the period and 24 percent at the end. However, as a result of the gentry tradition, still vivid in interwar Poland, their influence was even greater. The ruling political elite looked to them for support.

The role of the state was very substantial in interwar Poland. Its share in the gross national income was between 20 and 40 percent. Two-thirds of the total profit accumulation at the end of the 1920s was achieved by the public sector, and almost half of all investments belonged to it. The function of the state was highly positive in the integration of various parts of the country (which had remained under the rule of three different foreign powers for over 120 years), the promotion of mass education, the dissemination of culture, and the institutionalization of the total social structure. One of the main failures was in dealing with the non-Polish ethnic groups, which together constituted one-third of the population. The occupational structures of various groups differed in Poland. Among Poles the peasants constituted almost half, and over one-third were manual workers. Among Ukrainians and Byelorussians almost all were peasants. Among Jews two-thirds were petite bourgeoisie in industry and trade. Among Germans the majority were well-to-do farmers and the rest middle-class.

The social stratification was very evident in terms of wealth, power, culture, and status. At the end of the 1920s the well-to-do professionals spent five times more than manual workers, over ten times more than middle-class farmers and almost twenty times more than poor farmers. The expenditures of nonprofessional white-collar workers represented a half of those typical of well-to-do professionals, and the expenditures of the petite bourgeois only a quarter. The

Intelligentsia and the military circles close to the ruling elite had
much power because of the great importance of the state apparatus.
Status and prestige were still dominated by the gentry tradition, and
there was a clear distinction between the masters (gentlemen) and
the rest of the population (common people). Among the children of
upper classes 20 to 30 percent had the opportunity for higher education, whereas among the manual workers and peasants (excluding
rich peasants) it was less than 1 percent. In this respect the clerical
occupations had better chances (10 to 20 percent), especially those in
public service (Zarnowski 1973, p. 321).

Peasants and workers of peasant origin did not really start to
gain national consciousness on a wide scale until the twentieth century. Even during the interwar period, national consciousness was
not universal among the peasant masses, and in any case their economic destitution was no stimulus for developing one. The young
peasant generation met with hopelessness both in the villages (not
enough land to go around, low prices of agricultural products) and in
town (unemployment, housing shortages).

The peasants were primitive and parochial, the blue-collar
workers represented only a minority, the bourgeoisie did not have
much influence in comparison with more advanced countries, as
Czechoslovakia or Germany. Only the intelligentsia flourished and
gained power by taking over the bureaucratic apparatus of the independent state. "Tendencies towards increased state control issue as
a rule from the intelligentsia, which is vitally or perhaps selfishly
interested in the development of the state's functions and its administrative apparatus" (Hertz 1942, p. 153).

However, the Polish interwar intelligentsia did not have the
solid middle-class economic background. Its social content was as
fluid as the whole of society. New leaders were looked upon for years
with indifference by traditional upper classes. The lower classes
did not even know of their existence. From the obscure role of
"marginal people" the active young members of the intelligentsia
suddenly rose after the regaining of national independence in 1918
to the leadership of the country. Most of them were amateurs in
dealing with bureaucracy, the military, economic policy, and foreign
affairs. In order to maintain themselves in power, they had to create
internal coalitions, which soon started to compete with one another.
Hertz analyzed the situation as follows:

> The historical gentry, which in the twentieth century was
> in the last stages of its decline, found successors in the
> new aristocracy which robbed the old of its sense of
> superiority, the attitude of patronage, the manner of
> looking upon the country as its own private property.

The new aristocracy identified itself with Poland, and
defined the role of the mass of the people as a means
which was to safeguard its existence and prosperity .
. . . It formed a political group whose raison d'etre
and whose political activity was the maintenance of the
state power possessed by them? . . . It was a group of
officials who saw in their power the guarantee of their
personal careers and on whom years of bureaucratic
activity had already imprinted a specific psychological
mark (1942, pp. 156-57).

The history of interwar Poland was filled with the power struggle
between the elite in control of the state machinery and the opposition
groups made up of specific social strata: blue-collar workers, peasants, petite bourgeoise, landed aristocracy, minority ethnic groups.
The state was strong enough to prevent the opposition from endan-
gering the unconditioned rule of the establishment, but not to prevent
the collapse in case of serious danger (Polonsky 1972).

THE ESTABLISHMENT AFTER 1945

After World War II a new establishment came to power, this
time provided by the victorious Soviet Union. Several interwar problems—overpopulation in the rural areas, unemployment in towns, and
ethnic tensions—disappeared almost automatically because of the war
losses, the geographic restructuring of the state, and the massive
postwar reconstruction. However, the old problem of the gap between
the political establishment and the large mass of population remained,
in a new form. The rulers brought to Warsaw from Moscow did not
have any large-scale social support, and in order to gain local power,
they had to show initiative and relative independence of thought. The
rigid Soviet socioeconomic model, however, did not fit well into the
Polish reality. Both these circumstances contributed substantially
to the maneuvers of the political establishment that became public
in 1956, 1968, and 1970. "For Polish Communism to survive on its
own, without reliance in the threat of Soviet intervention, the Party
will probably have to explore new directions. Thus seems to be the
implication of its quarter century experiment during which the PZPR
(Polish United Workers' Party) has managed to capture genuine popular
following briefly and only once—when it seemed least orthodox, least
doctrinaire, least Russophile" (Groth 1972, p. 140).

As a member of the Soviet bloc, modern Poland is forced to
participate in Soviet-style communism. Soviet direct intervention,
even armed intervention, was by no means very remote in the period

around 1956; and its threat also had a very strong influence on the internal policies of Gomulka and his team. The aspirations to freedom of the intellectuals and of those Marxists who became disillusioned seemed to the governing elite to be unrealistic fantasies that endangered Poland by publicly manifesting the very considerable existing differences between the margin of freedom allowed in Poland and the much more stringent restrictions of liberties in the USSR.

To Gomulka freedom to maneuver was very limited, and it was additionally restricted by suspiciousness of colleagues and his personal authoritarianism, if not outright dogmatism (although Gomulka's knowledge of Marxist doctrine was limited).

We should not close our eyes to the considerable achievements of Poles under Communist rule—to a significant extent achieved in spite of the bureaucratization of the system. Poland has become a country with a relatively high level of education, with a considerable scientific potential, a country that is known and respected throughout the world. Polish culture has been relatively autonomous with respect to political doctrines since the 1950s, which is in contrast with the situation in the USSR, where there have been no important changes since the 1920s and even that in Czechoslovakia, which has developed since 1948, with a short break during 1967-68. Contemporary Poland's development potential is quite noticeable; and at the first opportunity to shed the rigid autocratic model, the Polish economy may forge ahead very readily. Of course, this would also depend on a favorable arrangement of international economic relations. Poland is at present very strongly integrated into the economy of the Soviet bloc; and it would by no means be easy for her to switch over to other economic requirements.

Above all, however, one must stress the importance of the fundamental changes in social structure that have taken place in Poland since World War II. The peasants and working masses, which were formerly discriminated against, have risen to the foreground; they have acquired access to education; they have even graduated from institutions of higher learning (especially by working at the same time and taking evening courses); they have ousted the so-called higher levels and have brought about a basic redistribution of the nation's social substance.

It is a great historical paradox that despite the intentions of the ruling establishment, social advance in Poland was, and still is, an advance of the intelligentsia, which has not only survived all tribulations but has grown considerably. It dictates trends in many areas, creates and supports the prevailing norms of behavior, propagates its liberal world outlook, and continuously makes life unpleasant for those in power while simultaneously collaborating with them, for an employee must fear for his employment when he is robbed of

63

independence. Veterans of the Communist movement look with dismay on the Polish intelligentsia, who demonstrate snobbery, feelings of nationality, and sympathies for the West and tend to social isolation. After all, the Communist movement traditionally was, and is to a considerable extent, anti-intellectual; power was to have been exerted over the intelligentsia and not in collaboration with it. Now traditional moral and cultural formulas are victorious and the entire effort of the Party in the realm of social advance has led to increasing the influence of a class that in "capitalistic" Poland was numerically much more modest, though at the time far more attention was paid to it.

POSTWAR POLAND'S SHIFT TO THE WEST

The considerable geographical shifting of Poland to the West that took place in 1945 is one of many examples of how the fate and the character of an entire society can change as a result of territorial transformations. It is a paradox that while prewar Poland, despite all its pretenses to be the frontier of Christianity, was to a considerable extent an Eastern country, very intensively involved in the socio-political problems of the Slavic East, contemporary Poland is, despite being an integral part of the Soviet bloc, a country and a society with very Western aspirations. It happened by the common will of the great powers, which agreed that the Western Territories fell to a very considerable extent to Poland. Both western and eastern frontiers were shifted westward by approximately 150 miles (Kruszewski 1972, p. 11). From a multinational state Poland was transformed into a national state with relatively stable and secure boundaries.

One-third of present Polish territory belonged to Germany before World War II. In 1936 it contributed something like 6 percent of Germany's industrial output. Now 30 percent of the total Polish population lives on this territory, and 33 percent of all school-age children. Half of the export capacity is located there.

Many studies have been done by Polish sociologists on adaptation, integration, and welfare in the Polish West. However, most of them were influenced to a large extent by a vested interest. Until recently, the Oder-Neisse boundary was endangered by the West German territorial claims (Lachs 1964), and the Western allies of World War II hesitated to give their formal approval of this boundary. It was not in the national interest of Poles to offer any data that would weaken their claims to the Western Territories.

How much did Poland's westward shift contribute to the modernization of the country? It was, first of all, a unique opportunity to reallocate the human resources. (Ford 1972 [?]) The Polish village was overcrowded before the war. After 1945 it was necessary to resettle millions of people, mostly farmers, from the territory incorporated into the Soviet Union (Poland lost 46 percent of its prewar territory to the USSR). In the period 1945-50, approximately 3 million Germans left Poland, and their places which were taken over by Poles from central Poland, the Soviet Union, France, West Germany, Yugoslavia, and Rumania.

Large parts of the Western Territories had been destroyed. The transportation system was in a state of total collapse. In addition, the Soviet army had removed much of the transportation equipment and industrial facilities left by the Germans. It was a formidable task to start a new life under such conditions. The Polish local authorities were totally dependent on the Soviet occupation forces and had to please them. People from various places did not trust one another. There was great animosity between those Poles who were natives of the Western Territories and newcomers from other places.

Thanks mainly to the stubbornness and determination of Polish peasants, the resettlement was successful. In many cases whole villages were resettled and neighbors helped one another. Some local security arrangements were established on the spot. The Catholic parishes played a very important role in providing spiritual encouragement. The total result was that over 4.5 million people settled in the Western Territories during a few years. According to the data from 1950, colonists from central Poland constituted half of the population, repatriates from the East and the West 30 percent, and natives to the area 20 percent.

Now the territory is more urbanized than the rest of Poland, and most of the population earn their living from nonagricultural pursuits. In the early 1950s, the government tried to collectivize all rural areas, but the plan was abandoned when Gomulka came to power in 1956 (he was against the plan). Small towns and handicrafts suffered extensively because of the governmental policy oriented against private trade and industry. Kruszewski says, "The strict application of economic dogmas to an area that had just undergone a total changeover of its population delayed social stability in the region for many years" (1972, p. 112). There was a general exodus of the rural and small-town population to large cities. Poland still spends much money on importing grain, which would not be needed if a more liberal policy had been followed from the start. "If properly developed to a level surpassing the present output, the area's agriculture could be an equally valuable asset in solving the difficult economic situation of contemporary Poland" (Kruszewski 1972, p. 133).

For the Polish peasantry, the territorial gain in the west offered a unique opportunity to improve their standard of living. Until World

War II, poverty and the lack of opportunity blocked the enormous potential of peasant aspirations, which did not have an outlet until the settling of the Western Territories. Contemporary Poland is above all a country of this resilient element that has been uprooted from the villages and has not the slightest intention of returning to villages, but is full of typical peasant characteristics (both positive and negative).

After the war there was a general shortage of food, and peasants with enough land to cultivate could gain a good deal. Their dream of a better life was near fulfillment. However, the Communist government did not have any long-term interest in supporting private farming. Even after abandoning the general plan to collectivize all farms, the Party did not pay enough attention to the vital interests of private farmers. The investment in agriculture was generally low. The development of agricultural services was slow. All resources were concentrated in heavy industry without any direct profit for agriculture. Farmers had to pay for the rapid progress of industrialization.

Polish peasants were liberated from serfdom in the nineteenth century, but only in the late 1950s were adequate socioeconomic conditions established for their massive transformation into farmers or workers. The traditional peasant is a rural cultivator, but "he runs a household, not a business concern" (Wolf 1966, p. 2). Even if no longer bound to the land and to his landlord, even being a master himself, for a very long time he could not enter a new stage of social and economic development. The occupation of the country by foreign powers, the relatively slow progress of urbanization and industrialization, and the low prices of agricultural goods limited the perspectives of peasants. The short period of forced collectivization in the early 1950s had long-term repercussions for relationships between peasants and the state (Korbonski 1965), substantially undermining the trust of peasants in the Communist state. However, it was the Communist industrialization that was a substantial factor in the massive social upgrading of peasants to the position of workers employed within the nationalized economy.

The first contacts of Polish peasants with industry go back to the eighteenth century, when the first manufacturers badly needed labor—which, until serfdom became abolished, was in short supply, thus hampering the devlopment of industrial production. The employment of peasants in industry under serfdom rules, difficult working conditions, very low wages, and the wide use of coercion did not give peasants a positive attitude toward industrial work. Also, the very low standard living common to peasant families could not allow them to develop higher aspirations that would encourage them to change their way of living.

The growth of urbanization was relatively very slow in Poland in the first half of the 19th century. In the Polish Kingdom (under Russian domination) the percentage of the urban population rose in the period 1816-48 from 19.4 percent to 23.2 percent, and a very large part of that population was still employed in agriculture. Serfdom was abolished in the Polish Kingdom in 1864, several years after its abolition in the territories occupied by Austria and Prussia. Afterward the growing rural population became more and more interested in finding some source of income outside of agriculture. At the turn of the 20th century one-third of the total rural population in the Polish Kingdom consisted of landless peasants. In the territory occupied by Prussia only 30 percent of the peasants were able to cultivate agriculture effectively (in economic terms). In 1902 Galicia, which was an economically very backward Polish territory occupied by Austria, contained approximately 28 percent of the population of the Austrian state, but only 16 percent of the industrial enterprises and 10 percent of the people economically active in industry. In the same period, 80 percent of all Galician agricultural holdings had an area less than 5 hectares and 43 percent had less than 2 hectares. In the countryside there was twice as much manpower as necessary in the summer and, during the winter, around three times as much.

Despite the difficult political and national conditions in the initial period of the growth of capitalism in Poland, some industries began to develop, particularly from the end of the 19th century to World War 1. Industrial growth was especially rapid in Upper Silesia (occupied by Germany), involving a considerable part of the total rural population in mining and foundries. By 1910 the urban population still comprised only 25 percent of all inhabitants, but more than 66 percent of all owners of small agricultural holdings 2 hectares or less) worked outside agriculture. Of the peasants who owned agricultural holdings in the Polish Kingdom in 1904, nearly half were also economically active outside of own holdings. In Galicia the peasants found additional income mostly by working for landowners and for farmers.

In all parts of Poland except Upper Silesia, industry consisted mostly of small factories with a primitive technology requiring much physical labor power. Therefore, in most of the Polish regions the territorial distribution of industry was more even than in many of the more industrialized countries (Leszczycki 1964). Such a distribution favored the employment of peasants in industrial plants.

In the period between the two world wars, agriculture still dominated the Polish economy. In 1931, 60 percent of the people were in agriculture (in rural areas 81 percent) and only 13 percent in mining and industry. Agricultural production accounted for 66 percent of the total national production. Large estates accounted for more than 44 percent of the total area in agricultural use (Lipski 1962, p. 8).

In interwar Poland the internal division (one-third of the population were national minorities) and the external insecurity led to a situation in which only a very strong economic push forward would produce social harmony. However, it did not happen. During 1918-39 the urban population grew to 30 percent, and the nonagricultural population from 33 percent to about 40 percent (in comparison with 70 percent in 1970). The nonagricultural sector of the village population grew from 15 percent to not more than 25 percent in the interwar period; in 1970 it was 43 percent (Rocznik 1972, p. 87). Peasants did not have the opportunity to move to towns, and they had to continue subdividing their holdings. In southern Poland, according to data of Wincenty Stys, in 1930-31 the average acreage per capita had declined to 57 percent of what it was in 1787 (Krzyzaniak 1971, p. 4).

In interwar Poland the structure of agricultural holdings was very unsatisfactory. The percentage of very small holdings (less than 2 hectares) grew from 29 percent to 33 percent, and the percentage of small holdings 2 to 5 hectares) from 30 percent to 34 percent. All these holdings, which constituted 67 percent of all Polish agricultural holdings, were not of sufficient size to give their owners and their families a reasonable living. In 1935 Poland was overpopulated by an estimated 33 percent in the agricultural sector while having a relatively low agricultural production per capita (700 zloty in 1938, compared with 1,110 in Hungary and 4550 in the United States). In all these respects the situation in Poland was quite similar to that in most of Eastern Europe except Czechoslovakia, which had a much stronger demand for agricultural products, a healthier agricultural structure, and a much more progressive agricultural technology. The Polish peasant did not have adequate financial and cultural incentives to develop a really efficient farming business (Slomka 1941; Thomas and Znaniecki 1918). Low prices for agricultural products, the scarcity of mechanical power, the fact that 46 percent of the farmers did not have horses of their own, the striking contrast between big landowners and small farmers, and cultural backwardness were common in Poland and most other East European countries. The conditions of the interwar period were well summarized by Brodzinski, who wrote:

> Polish agriculture was subject to the vicious circle of poverty. Low productivity led to low income, low income led to low savings, low savings meant low investment and this consequently led to low productivity. . . . The depression years 1930-1935 greatly deteriorated the position of the Polish peasant. The consequent lack of capital and drastic fall in agricultural prices did not only considerably slow down the progress of the land reform (which is often forgotten), but also greatly increased the burden of agricultural loans. . . . The depression of 1930-1935 brought Polish agriculture to the verge of ruin (1971, pp. 113, and 115).

A moderate high natural increase of the agricultural population further aggravated the situation. In the early 1930s natural increase in the countryside was 16.7 per 1,000 population, compared with 8.4 per 1,000 in the city. In the period 1921-38 the equivalent of 67 percent of the village population increase remained in the countryside, 22 percent migrated to the cities, and 11 percent left Poland.

The population of Poland had grown by 15 percent in the interwar period, but in 1938 industrial production was only 95 percent of the 1913 volume. Therefore, the prewar socioeconomic situation implicitly included the strong demographic pressure of the mass of people abandoned in agriculture and remaining in the country-side because of the lack of other opportunities. The young generation of peasants was socially and psychologically ready to leave their homes and to disassociate themselves from the traditional way of life. This is quite clear from the memoirs of young peasants that were collected, analyzed, and interpreted by Jozef Chalasinski (1964). In 1921-31 the total number of people who stayed in rural areas was equal to 58 percent, and in 1932-39 it was equal to 82 percent, of the natural increase among the rural population. Forty percent of the peasant farms had a labor surplus that had to remain on farms because there was no other place for them (Zarnowski 1973, pp. 115, 168).

THE MOVE TO TOWNS AFTER 1945

In Poland net emigration from rural to urban areas grew substantially after World War II. This trend may be illustrated by comparing the net emigration from rural to urban areas as a percentage of the natural increase in the rural areas for various periods; 27 percent in 1919-31; 21 percent in 1932-38; 95 percent in 1946-50; and 46 percent during the 1950s. After achieving its peak during the late 1940s and early 1950s, the movement from rural to urban areas slowed down (Iwanicka-Lyra 1972, pp. 71-80). With the passage of time migrants gained a better education, and thereby became qualified for the more attractive jobs in manufacturing, construction, and transport.

The rapid growth of industrialization in the postwar period, undertaken within the frame of the new social system based on nationalization of all basic means of production, created favorable conditions for the employment of workers in the nonagricultural sectors of the economy and for migration from the countryside into the cities. According to M. Pohoski, the average annual rate of migration from rural to urban areas in 1946-60 was 2.5 times the figure for 1921-38 period (Pohoski 1964b). By 1960 the average real income of the peasant was 250 percent of the interwar level and the income disparity between rural and urban population had been considerably

70

reduced. Nevertheless, even with the much improved agricultural structure (the average size of the individually owned farmstead was 5 hectares), substantially higher prices for agricultural products, and a shortage of manpower in farming, the majority of the young peasant generation did not want to stay in the village.

An extensive migration from the rural areas into the cities during the period of intensive industrialization led to a transformation of the peasants into workers. At the same time the proportion of the rural population earning a living from nonagricultural sources increased greatly. The movement to nonagricultural activities exceeded the growth of urbanization: the rural emigration was most intensive in the regions that were greatly underdeveloped and overpopulated. The percentage of migrants from small farms was higher than that from large farms (Borowski 1967, p. 550).

In Poland, unlike other East European countries except Yugoslavia, private farmers now prevail in agriculture. They utilize 82 percent of the arable land and own 77 percent of that land. The rest belongs to the state farms and to the agricultural cooperatives. The working population in agriculture in 1972 was 85 percent on individual farms, 1 percent on agricultural cooperatives, 9 percent on state farms, and 5 percent employed in the agricultural service units (Concise 1973, p. 144). Even during the intensive collectivization in the 1950s, the socialized sector never exceeded 25 percent of all agriculture.

The population on private farms has diminished in 1950-70 from over 10 million to only 8 million, whereas in the period the population of Poland grew from 25 million to 33 million. The drop was particularly dramatic on the small farms of 25 hectares, where the number of people dropped by 33 percent. Only on the larges farms of 10 hectares or over was the number of people maintained on approximately the same level (Concise 1973, p. 32).

The young generation of Poland does not want to stay in agricultural occupations as much as young people in Communist countries with collectivized agriculture. When young peasants stay on the farm, they have to work for an extended period of time under the supervision of their fathers, with no hope of quick occupational independence. They also have to do heavy physical work, and their leisure time is greatly restricted. Even in the early 1970s there was less access to cultural activities in the village than in the city, and the social status of the farmer was lower than that of a skilled worker. As Ewa Jagiello-Lysiowa states on the basis of her survey in the early 1960s:

> The long hard work required in agriculture, and the
> small profit it gives, are the main reason for the flight
> of the younger generation from the land and for their
> ambitions to find a job elswhere; there are also reasons

71

of a more structural character—the organization of the
farm and the family based on it, which causes burden-
some family ties, especially the ties between parents
and children. Children who work on their parents' farm
continue even in adulthood to be subordinate to their
parents' will. They have no money of their own, it is
not always possible for them to make a marriage of
their own choice, and they have little free time. Mean-
while, growing contacts with the outside world allow
new patterns of personal behavior to penetrate into
thr rural areas. Young people on the farms look
longingly at the division of time in non-farming occupations into working time and leisure time. The
growing independence of attitude among the young is
the cause of increasing conflict in the family. Children employed on the farm also want to have their own
money, they want some independence in their work,
and above all they desire free time for entertainment—
entertainment of a new type. Parents differ in their
reaction to these modern interests and trends among
the younger generation. Some of the older generation
are completely against the new trends, yet nevertheless,
have no say in the matter since they are "old-fashioned",
and incapable of any real, effective opposition. In these
circumstances, the flight of young people from the land
and from farming may not only be a flight from the long
hours of ill-paid work, but also a flight from functioning in their role of member of the present family. It
may represent an attempt on the part of the young
people to seek their own occupational models, and
individual aims and way of life independent of the
family model (Jagiello-Lysiowa 1963).

The sons of peasants leaving the country have access to education and occupations that give them not only a better economic and
cultural position but also a higher social standing. Among the young
generation of peasants studied by Pohoski in the early 1960s, 42 percent became nonmanual workers and 64 percent held income positions
higher than that of the middle farmer (Pohoski 1964a).
Improvement in the educational progress of the rural youth is
evident in the early 1970s. The percentage of young people of farmer
descent at some educational levels in the 1971/72 term was similar
to the proportion of the peasantry in the total population, 25 percent
in the first year of the lower vocation schools, 26.5 percent of the
students were of farmer descent and in secondary vocational schools,

23 percent. However, students of farmer descent accounted for only 14 percent of the first-year students in general high schools and 14 percent of the day students in higher education (Rocznik 1972, p. 461). The rural youth are ambitious regarding education but are handicapped by the long distances to schools, inadequate cultural stimulation at home, and the poverty of their parents (Kozakiewicz 1972). In 1970/71, 33 percent of the students in Poland commuted, and most of them were inhabitants of villages. Half of them commuted by bus and 40 percent by train. Twenty-seven percent spent more than one hour each way commuting (Klimczyk 1973, p. 20).

The higher standard of living enjoyed by workers was for several years a very important consequence of mass migration from villages to towns. Even in the late 1950s the families of blue-collar workers spent much more than the peasants on clothing (in 1958, 18 percent of the total expenditure, compared with 12 percent by the peasants), culture (in 1958, 4 percent versus 1 percent among peasants), and alcohol and tobacco 4 percent compared with 2 percent among peasants). The budget of the blue-collar worker's family in 1958 was 40 percent higher than that of the peasant's family (Czerniewska 1961). With the gradual improvement of the living standard of peasants who became professional farmers (not uncommon in many parts of Poland by the 1970s), differences in the house-hold budgets and equipment of blue-collar families and peasant families started to disappear. Data from 1971 show that white-collar workers were still spending less on food than blue-collar workers and farmers (Table 1.5), and that farmers had larger families. All other differences were of no substantial significance.

According to a survey conducted by the Polish Center of Public Opinion Polls in 1961, there was a positive correlation between size of the peasant family and the tendency toward migration, but only with respect to young people. Intentions to migrate were also influenced by the distance of the current place of living from the town. The rural population living relatively close to an urban area preferred to remain in the rural area and to commute to their working place.

The acculturation of peasants to the urban environment has been a more acute problem in Poland, as it has been in other rapidly industrialized East European countries. Workers from the peasant stratum were long handicapped by their relatively low level of education, lack of industrial experience, and unfamiliarity with city life. According to M. Pohoski, a higher percentage of male migrants to cities, compared with nonmigrant urban males, had not completed their elementary education (28 percent versus 17 percent); a lower percentage of the male migrants had completed their elementary education (28 percent versus 36 percent); and a lower percentage of the male migrants had a high school education (25 percent versus 30 percent). The same was true of women except for high school education (Pohoski 1964, p. 120).

However, the social structure of the population flowing from the countryside to the cities has undergone some changes since the early 1950s. Migrants to the cities consist to a growing degree of young persons who want to complete their schooling or learn trades or work in industry as skilled workers. Some of those who are drafted do not return to the villages after their military service is completed. According to the data gathered by S. Borowski, the percentage of people going to the city in order to attend school became much greater in the 1960s (65 percent) than it had been in the 1940s (21 percent or in the 1950s (40 percent). At the same time the percentage of people leaving the country in order to work declined considerably: 66 percent in the 1940s, 48 percent in the 1950s, and 27 percent in the 1960s (Borowski 1967).

PEASANT-WORKERS

There is an evident trend in the rural areas to look for something other than private farming. The percentage of nonagricultural population in the villages rose in the 1960s from 31 to 43 (20 in 1931 and 23 in 1950). A survey taken in 1967, based on the national sample of villages, showed that only 38 percent of families maintained themselves exclusively from agriculture (Wyderko 1972, p. 2).

On very small farms (up to 2 hectares) 80 percent of the people support themselves with outside employment (Dziewicka 1972). On small farms of less than 3 hectares, 18 percent of the income in 1970/71 came from outside employment, mostly in the nationalized economy. The total number of people who support themselves solely by working on their private farms diminished by 22 percent during the 1960s. For the same period the number of people from farms who worked exclusively in nonagricultural areas grew by 41 percent, and the number of people who had some additional employment grew by 62 percent.

More and more owners of agricultural holdings are earning their living predominantly outside agriculture. According to Maria Dziewicka (1963) the number of such "farmers" amounted in the early 1960s to 25 percent of the total number of individual farms with an area of one acre or more. One-quarter of all wage earners in Poland are people living in the countryside, and most of them own very small farms (Widerszpil 1965, p. 220).

The peasant workers constitute a new social stratum that is one of the significant features of contemporary Polish society. This stratum is especially evident in more developed areas with better roads and transportation facilities, higher housing standards, and more opportunities for jobs outside agriculture in the nearby communities. As a result of increasing nonagricultural employment and limited opportunities for territorial mobility, a growing number of people commute from their homes in the countryside to their work places. Daily commuters constitute 20 percent of all people working in the nationalized economy.

Peasant workers are not as well off in education, occupation level, and income compared with urban workers who live in urban areas. In the early 1960s more than 80 percent of the males aged 18-49 living on farms and working in town had only an elementary education (55 percent of the same age group in the cities); 31 percent of peasant workers 20-29 years old were unskilled; and their incomes were decidedly lower than those of urban workers' families (Galeski 1964). All these factors contribute to an inferiority complex quite common among peasant workers. It is more difficult for them than for workers of urban origin to obtain work demanding higher skills; relatively fewer advance up the hierarchical ladder. Advancement for many of them seems not only impossible but also not very appealing, because of their relatively low urban acculturation. Therefore, they show little interest in acquiring additional education. The peasant workers do not have enough time, strength, or inclination to develop their farms, which is disadvantageous from the socioeconomic point of view. At the same time, the adaptation to modern skilled work comes more slowly to a man who is engaged simultaneously in two different occupations.

Yet the appeal of a peasant worker's social role grew steadily among the Polish peasantry. The peasant worker was enjoying a higher income, had more capital to improve his house and his farm, and had a more attractive daily experience. According to research done by Dyzma Galaj in the early 1960s, the small farm owner tended to hold a more positive view of the effects on the farm operation of a farmer's working simultaneously in another occupation. The opinion that agriculture benefits most by the farmer's limiting himself to working on his farm was found to predominate among farmers who had an educational level higher than the average among peasants and were more professionally oriented. Among the rural populations studied by Galaj, only 51 percent of the farmer respondents maintained their willingness to work on the farm and did not plan to change their occupation; 23 percent were willing to work on farms but were also attracted by other occupations; 21 percent would like to change occupations but saw no possibility; and 5 percent planned to change occupation (Galaj 1965).

Migration of the population from farms to cities and nonagricultural activities had unfavorable repercussions on agriculture in the

1950s and 1960s. There was a constant rise in the average age of the agricultural population, a decline in the average number of household members economically active, and a decline in the ratio of men to women. The average family on individual farms declined from 3.9 persons in 1950 to 3.3 persons in 1960. Those who stay are often too old to move. Among private farmers in 1970, 67.5 percent (in 1960, 74 percent) were 45 years old or more. The percentage of farmers 60 years old or more grew during the 1960s from 24 to 32. Among those who consider farming as their basic employment, 33 percent are 60 years old or over (Kozlowski and Turos 1973, pp. 9-10). This process of aging is related to some extent to the longer lifespan (in villages the average increase was 20 years when comparing 1965/66 with 1931/32) (Wyderko 1972, p. 3). However, the main reason is probably that young people just do not want to stay on farms. In the summary, people who stay on farms are too old, not very educated, and not adequately motivated. There is a shortage of labor. Less than 1 percent of farms hire outside workers for 100 days a year or more (Dziewicka 1972, p. 5). Some 6 to 7 percent of all farmers do not have heirs willing to take over the farm when they die.

PRIVATE FARMERS AND THE STATE

The changing position of Polish peasants in the sociopolitical system may provide a good example of how collective bargaining has developed between various social groups and the establishment. During the interwar period, among peasants "the idea of the state ('panstwo') remained etymologically and politically associated with the dominance of the 'gentleman' ('Pan')" (Lewis 1973, p. 35). Living on small holdings and not having sufficient opportunities to find jobs outside agriculture, the peasants were in a disadvantageous position in relation to all other classes as well as in relation to the government. After World War II they gained much by populating the devastated Western Territories and farms expropriated from the landlords, as well as by receiving much better prices for their products than during the interwar period. However, their freedom became endangered by the forced collectivization campaign (stopped when Gomulka returned to power in 1956), by obligatory deliveries, taxes, shortage of bank credits, and bureaucratic restrictions. The process of farm division continued despite all measures imposed by the state to stop it.

According to Paul Lewis, "Gomulka's policy had provided a structure in which the more pressing frustrations of the peasants could be eased; poor peasants who were unable to support themselves from agriculture could generally find off-farm work in the nonagricultural sectors of the economy. Enterprising peasant farmers had certain lucrative outlets for their produce and could find ways to circumvent formal restrictions within the decentralized bureaucracy that the scattered nature of peasant agriculture had forced on the State" (1973, p. 86). It is possible to agree with Lewis that Gomulka's version of communism was more irksome than oppressive for Polish peasants, and that they learned how to deal with bureaucratic institutions. However, it was coexistence rather than cooperation based on mutual trust.

In the early 1970s the state agencies still control the key elements of successful farming, and the modernization of farms depends on the mutual understanding between their owners and local bureaucrats. Of course, this relationship is not based on equality of partners; and in order to secure some advantages for themselves, farmers have to bribe officials. The heavy dependence of farmers on bureaucracy does not contribute to the security and the eagerness of owners to invest in their farms. It results in the relatively low efficiency of Polish agriculture and the inability of the country to achieve self-sufficiency in gain production.

In Poland in the early 1970s individual farmers produce 86 percent of the total agricultural product, but it represents only 13 percent of the gross national income (Rocznik 1972, p. 274). Of a total of almost 3 million individual farms, 14 percent (11 percent in 1965) are very small (no more than 1 acre or less than 0.5 hectare), and small farms with areas of 1 to 5 acres (0.5 to 2 hectares) account for 24 percent. Of the total population on private farms, 30 percent is concentrated on these small or very small farms, which cannot develop any profitable agricultural activity. It is therefore understandable that 36 percent of all people economically active and living on small farms are employed somewhere else than on their farms. Even on farms with an area of over 5 acres (2 hectares), 11 percent of the economically active persons are employed elsewhere.

Twenty-seven percent of all individual farms have an area of 5-12 acres (2-5 hectares), and 24 percent have an area of 12-15 acres (5-10 hectares). Farms over 25 acres (10 hectares) constitute only 11 percent of the total. Eighty percent of all farming area belongs to farms of 5-37 acres (2-15 hectares), which contain 66 percent of the people on farms who have farming as the only source of their income.

Among Polish private peasants there is great dependence on the government because the state functions as their main client and supplier. In 1971, 78 percent of the value of the total agricultural production of private farmers was sold to the state, and only 8 percent was sold to private persons (Rocznik 1972, p. 255). From 1965 to 1970, of all farm products sold by private farmers, 80 percent went to the state and only 20 percent to the free market. Since 1971 it has not been compulsory for farmers to deliver their products to state agencies. The state, and the cooperative enterprises fully controlled by it, enjoyed a monopolistic role of the entire farming trade. Therefore the state will always remain the most important customer of Polish farmers. However, the importance of compulsory deliveries has diminished considerably since about 1960 and the state has changed its position in regard to the farmers: from a position of command to a position of a quasi monopoly. The abolition of compulsory deliveries was the logical outcome of the general trend of state policy developed after 1956 (see Table 4.1).

Witold Lipski has noted:

> In the late 1960s many negative features appeared in the implementation of the agrarian policy. The most important among them were the following: methods were adopted which disturbed the process of commodity exchange between agriculture and industry, such as the quota deliveries; the principle of profitability of agricultural production was neglected; and overly complicated means of influencing agricultural production were used. At the same time, a dogmatic approach to some economic problems, such as the restrictions on the import of grain, was revealed. Administration suffered from excessive red tape. As a result, during the Five Year Plan (1966-1970), the real incomes of the peasants remained unchanged. The un-favorable relation between the prices of fodder and meat resulted in decreasing pig chattel. In general, ignoring consumption inevitably led to a serious neglect of agriculture (1973, pp. 102-3).

The value of imported agricultural products almost doubled in 1960-71, and the value of agricultural exports in 1970-72 represented only 60 percent of the agricultural imports. Poland in the early 1970s was not self-sufficient in food (Concise 1973, p. 194; Trzeciakowski 1973).

MODERNIZATION OF FARMING

There is a growing awareness in Polish society, including the rural population, that some structural transformations are needed. Private farmers were asked in 1969 and 1970 what should be done with the farm when the farmer is no longer able to work it: 23 percent mentioned the possibility of renting the farm to the state; and 60 percent of the respondents accepted the idea of cooperating closely with an external agency in running the farm instead of depending only on their own ability and experience (Adamski 1972, pp. 6-9). Comparative sociological data show that during the 1960s the proportion of farmers committed to the continuation of private farming diminished from about 50 percent to less than 20 percent (Galeski 1973; Jagiello-Lysiowa 1963; Kryczka et al. 1971). Even in the mid-1960s, the personal incomes of families on collective farms was over 20 percent higher than those in private agriculture (Czyszkowska and Grochowski 1966, pp. 52-56). These collective farms contributed only 2 percent of the total agricultural market product in 1971 (private farms contributed 79 percent and state farms 19 percent); but the growth of that product for collective farms was 230 (taking 1960 as 100), whereas for private farms it was only 136 (Rocznik 1972, pp. 250-51). Some socialization of farming is un-avoidable in the long run. The question, however, is how to preserve the freedom and commitment of farmers under the restraints imposed by collective forms of coordinating their efforts (Wierzbicki 1972; Hunek 1965). In this respect the Soviet model of socialism has so far failed to offer any effective and attractive proposals.

TABLE 4.1

Compulsory Deliveries as a Percentage of the Total Trade of
Private Farmers in Poland, 1955-70

Compulsory Deliveries	1955	1960	1970
Cereals	84	65	39
Potatoes	84	54	48
Cattle	35	23	28
Calves	89	45	83
Pork	48	28	16
Bacon	44	27	11

Source: Rocznik 1971, p. 332.

The mass social movement from the countryside to the cities that occurred in the 1950s brought concrete benefits to many. An additional factor was the real hope among peasants and blue-collar workers of advancement to white-collar jobs for their children. But as the years passed, the inability of the government to provide for the needs and aspirations of peasants and blue-collar workers became more apparent. The highly centralized and bureaucratized Polish economy of the early 1970s has features that limit, to a large extent, real progress toward modernization. On the other hand, these features go well with the conservative tradition of the peasantry. The peasant families still preserve some of their traditional characteristics that have disappeared from urban family life. For example, husbands still decide on the management of common property, even though there is a full equality of husband and wife in this respect according to the law (Gorecki 1963, pp. 156-73).

It is evident in the 1970s that Poland's modernization badly needs a real social and economic reform. The possibility of such a reform depends to a large extent on the further advancement of people who, until recently, had been peasants. It is not possible to manage modern enterprises on the same principles that prevailed on small farms and in traditional villages. Poland's westward shift must be accompanied by a mental Westernization of work and organization. The social and political perspectives in Poland of the 1970s have been influenced to a very great extent by the large influx of peasants into the towns during the previous decades. Many newcomers improved their conditions to such an extent that they were grateful to the regime.

> The pre-war blue collar workers became dissolved in a vast mass of peasant migrants, to whom the living conditions they met meant a genuine improvement on the standards they had known. The urban environment, with all its deficiencies was incomparably better than anything they had experienced so far in the thick of the "idiocy of the rural life"; the high job security they enjoyed from the moment they stepped on urban soil; the fresh experience of urban shopping, scarce as the supply of commodities was, untasted on a subsistence-oriented peasant household; the avidly exploited opportunity to turn the traditional peasant "hunger for acquisition" into purchasing durable goods on the account of the not-yet-earned-incomes; all this transformed the new "working class" of the socialist countries not only into loyal supporters of the new order of things, but also into a group with important vested interests in its continuation and stability. (The most telling propaganda item against the students rioting in Poland in March 1968 was that they choked the urban traffic

and so impeded "honest workers" from getting to their homes to enjoy the well-deserved afternoon nap....)(Bauman 1971a, pp. 38-39).

CHAPTER

5

FROM UNSKILLED LABORER
TO BLUE-COLLAR WORKER

The development of a blue-collar class in Poland started to a noticeable extent in the latter half of the 19th century. From 1860 to 1910 the index of people employed in industry on the present Polish territory grew from 12 to 43 per 1,000 population (in the part of Poland occupied by Germany, from 23 to 64), which was much less than in Western Europe but indicated some substantial economic progress. The urban population grew in that period from 18 percent to 29 percent (35 percent on the territory occupied by Germany, 26 percent in the zone occupied by Russia, and only 17 percent in the zone occupied by Austria). The textile industry accounted for 20 percent of all industrial employment; power, machine building, minerals, and foodstuffs each employed from 12 to 16 percent (Misztal 1972, pp. 120, 123).

The destruction during World War I prevented Poland from regaining the prewar level of production until 1929. Then came the Depression, which, together with the fast population growth, kept the index of industrially employed people at only 50 per 1,000 population in 1939 (43 in 1907-10). Foreign capital constituted half of total industrial investment (Misztal 1972, p. 133).

The manual workers' class grew faster than the total population in the period 1918-39, but at the end of this period 30 percent of them (in 1921, 41 percent) were poor agricultural workers and only half were in industry. The rest were employed in public service, trade, transport, and domestic service. Thus blue-collar workers in some significant industry represented only 5 percent of the total population. Among them 40 percent were skilled workers and the rest were semiskilled or unskilled. During the Depression a very substantial part of them were unemployed and approximately 33 percent were employed only part-time. According to survey data from the mid-1930s, half of all blue-collar worker families had some or all members unemployed. The unemployed famiies spent 75 percent or more of their budget on food. Usually the working blue-collar families spent 50 to 60 percent of the budget on food, but the figure decreased to 40 percent before World War II. Housing conditions did not improve at all; 70 percent of manual workers' families had more than two persons per room (Zarnowski 1973, pp. 19-128).

At that time in Poland there was a close connection between the manual workers and the peasantry. Forty percent of all industrial blue-collar workers lived in the countryside. Poor peasant families constituted 66 percent of all peasants. Even on the relatively large farms (15-50 hectares), only 33 percent had some hired labor. During 1918-39 the total agricultural area owned by peasants grew by 15 percent, as a result of the agricultural reform promoted by the state, but the number of peasant farms grew by 30 percent. There were some differences in the standards of living among the peasantry in various parts of the country; but in general blue-collar workers earned more and had a better standard of living, and it was therefore a common dream among young peasants to move out of agriculture. Unfortunately, the opportunity to do so was very limited.

Both manual workers and peasants were politically active only to a limited extent. Twenty percent of blue-collar workers belonged to trade unions, and only a very small percentage were active in political life. For the peasant parties it was difficult to gain even half of the peasants' votes.

The sociopolitical involvement of Polish blue-collar workers before World War II was considerably limited by the unfavorable labor market, the relatively low level of education and skills, the unfavorable political situation for movements that represented the interests of lower classes (except the state-sponsored branch of trade unions, which never become really influential among the blue-collar class), the dominance of the intelligentsia in the socialist parties and even in the underground Communist Party, and the general lack of security and democratic experience (after 1926 Poland had a semi-dictatorial regime). Many blue-collar workers supported the Polish Socialist Party, but the economic situation quite often made it very disadvantageous for them to show an open commitment to the political opposition. Even the Christian-democratic political and trade union movement had only a limited appeal, it was also in political opposition to the regime.

The blue-collar class was then still relatively new, and the industrial development was not fast enough to open new employment opportunities for young peasants who had to stay in overpopulated villages. The general lack of any broader opportunities for social and political advancement prevented the blue-collar class from crystallizing its collective consciousness. The socialist and Christian-democratic leaders of blue-collar movements had the best intentions, but their opportunities were seriously limited by disadvantageous socioeconomic and political circumstances.

During World War II, in addition to millions of lives being lost, half of the power equipment, 33 percent of all industrial buildings, and 45 percent of all manufacturing equipment were destroyed. The industrial production in 1946 represented only 45 percent of the production in 1937 on the same territory. However, the high rate of industrial growth in the following years substantially changed the socioeconomic image of the Polish society, and especially of its blue-collar class, which had developed simultaneously with the progress of industrialization and the general level of employment of men and women (women represented 40 percent of economically active persons in the nationalized economy in 1971). The role of industry in the gross national income grew from 33 percent in the late 1940s to 60 percent in 1972. Among the village population, over 40 percent are in non-agricultural pursuits, most of them commuting to the closest industrial center. Even with housing conditions still quite difficult, moving to towns is very attractive, especially for young people. In industry 25 percent of all employees commute to work from another locality. In some southern regions it is close to half of all employees. In Warsaw 23 percent of all industrial employees commute from outside the city limits (Leszczycki and Lijewski 1972, pp. 111-12). In 1968, 20 percent of all employed people commuted to work from other counties: in transport and communication, 32 percent; in construction, 28 percent; and in industry, 22.5 percent (Rocznik statystyczny pracy 1948-68, pp. 248-49).

Until 1956 the blue-collar class grew. The large employment, education, and promotion opportunities were widely utilized by people from the lower social ranks. The institutional framework of Party and labor organizations was imposed on the blue-collar class without its consent. There was no room nor opportunity for people in Poland, and particularly blue-collar workers, to establish institutions that would be autonomous (except the Catholic Church, which preserved its independence to a very large extent); but there was still plenty of opportunity to maneuver on an individual basis. Friends and relatives supported one another in achieving specific goals. A very high level of social mobility has widely extended the scope of social contacts and influence available to blue-collar workers. They now have colleagues, friends, and relatives almost everywhere. Political indoctrination among blue-collar workers has been much less effective than among intellectuals who have their own self-interest in deceiving themselves. The socioeconomic modernization promoted by the Communist regime was welcomed by blue-collar workers because it meant a very substantial extension of their life opportunities. Especially welcome was the promise of a better future for their children, in the sense of their rising above manual worker status and entering the ranks of intelligentsia (Sarapata 1965).

The Communist regime had an obvious tendency to rely on blue-collar workers, especially when they were adequately indoctrinated. People of blue-collar background had priority in advancement to influencial positions in the Party, administration, and industry. Yet both cases of a successful change of the regime enforced by the rank and file (1956 and 1970), the demonstration of power by the blue-collar masses was of decisive importance. In Pirages' words, "There are limits to the power that the state can employ in attempting to make allies. Values inculcated by church, family, and peer groups are not easily thrown aside in favor of the party line. When the true believers in the Party represent a small minority of society, even the clear control of coercive forces and most of the secondary socialization agents cannot sway the masses" (1972, p. 99).

THE SILENT CLASS

In the 1970s the industrial blue-collar workers constitute the dominant social class in Poland. A considerable part of this class has come to nonagricultural occupations only since the 1950s. Only about 50 percent of industrial blue-collar workers and only about 44 percent of construction blue-collar workers are of manual worker origin; the rest have come for the most part from the villages.

Some 6.5 million blue-collar workers are employed in the nationalized economy, most of them in the state-owned nationalized industry (2.9 million in 1972, versus 2.55 million in 1960) and in co-operative industry (over 460,000 in 1972, versus 360,000 in 1960). In the private nonagricultural sector there are 164,000 employees, mostly manual workers. There are 300,000 manual workers in the state-owned agricultural enterprises and 100,000 in the forestry enterprises. The total number of industrial manual workers grew from 1.5 million in 1950 to 3.35 million in 1972 (a growth of 223 if 1950=100). Of these, 86 percent are in the state-owned industry and 14 percent in the industrial cooperatives controlled by the state. In 1972 most of the industrial manual workers were in the textile industry (373,000), the food industry (343,000), coal mining (295,000), engineering (286,000), the machinery and metal structures industry 216,000, and the transportation industry (284,000) (Concise 1973, p. 88).

According to the official ideology, blue-collar workers constitute a ruling class in Poland. They account for 40 percent of the membership of the ruling Polish United Workers' Party (peasants only 11 percent), 66 percent of the membership in the workers' councils, and 25 percent of all jury members in courts and in the disciplinary committees of local governments. Politically, manual workers were for years a "silent class" in Poland. Even if, according to Marxist theory adored by Communist regimes, they constitute the basic class within the social order, it was really the Polish United Workers' Party that exploited the image of the working class. For all the years between the incorporation of the Polish Socialist Party into the Communist Polish Workers' Party in 1948 and the widespread demonstrations and struggles initiated by workers in December 1970, there was no mention of any distinction between the Party and the working class. However, such a distinction always existed even if the Party did not recognize it.

The Polish economy, even while growing relatively fast, is still in a stage of development distant from that of well-developed countries. This situation is a mixed blessing for the blue-collar class. On the one hand, this class does not diminish so fast as in some Western countries. The participation of blue-collar workers in the nonagricultural nationalized economy decreased in 1960-71 only from 67 percent to 65 percent—in industry from 84.5 percent to 82 percent, in construction from 78 percent to 73 percent, and in transportation and communication it stayed at 70 percent (Rocznik 1972, p. 112).

On the other hand, this kind of economy, overburdened by heavy investments, does not provide enough room for Western-style consumerism. Agriculture is still underdeveloped and the social, cultural, and recreational facilities generously subsidized by the state do not provide a sufficient substitute for a higher standard of living that would be particularly attractive to blue-collar workers.

The growing aspirations of the blue-collar workers are reflected by their relatively high mobility rates. Among the respondents (sample of total male urban population over 18 years old) surveyed by Stefan Nowak in 1961, 42 percent held higher positions than their fathers had at the same age. Twenty percent of respondents among the college-educated people and 50 percent of respondents among the white-collar workers who had not completed college declared a peasant or working-class origin. Among the investigated skilled blue-collar workers, more than one half had improved their social status in comparison with that of their fathers (Nowak 1964). According to Adam Sarapata, more than half of the engineering-technical personnel and of the administrative-clerical employees had performed at least several years of manual labor. More than 20 percent of teachers, engineers, journalists, and doctors are of working-class origin (Sarapata 1965).

In comparison with the prewar situation, the income diversification of the labor force is now much smaller. The spread between earnings has been substantially reduced. Also, there is now much less difference in earnings between blue-collar and white collar-workers. According to Michal Kalecki (1964):

> During the period 1937-1960 there has been a considerable rise in the living conditions of the working population. It is the result of an over two-fold increase in the real incomes of manual workers and a certain drop in those of salary earners. This increase in the standard of living is to a considerable extent a result of the increase of employment; the average rise per employee is much lower. It remains high for manual workers, but in the case of salary earners there has been a fall of about 25 percent. However the index for manual workers amounts to only 145 when the prewar "pariah" group, that is domestic servants and artisans' labourers, is excluded. This rise is a result of a 55 percent increase for industrial workers and an approximately 30 percent increase for workers employed in other branches of the economy (excluding domestic servants and artisans' assistants.

In the nonagricultural sector the ratio of salaries to wages per employee for all Polish employed persons was 2.8:1.0 in 1937, but only 1.2:1.0 in 1960. If we exclude domestic servants and artisans' assistants, the ratio was 2.2:1.0 in 1937 but only 1.1:1.0 in 1960. Members of the intelligentsia, especially those performing tasks of special importance (such as factory engineers promoting technical progress), have much less reason than the blue-collar workers to be satisfied with the equalization of incomes.

The social prestige of the blue-collar worker has risen in comparison with the prewar period, especially among miners, construction workers, and plumbers. But aspirations are rising even faster. Blue-collar workers no longer desire to perpetuate the same occupation in their families. They are eager to help their children into the ranks of the intelligentsia. A study shows that "the models for desired occupational careers among the manual and nonmanual workers are the engineer and doctor for boys and the doctor and teacher for girls; the tailor is also a model among the manual workers" (Sarapata and Wesolowski 1961). In that respect the aspirations of blue-collar workers do not differ very much from those typical for the white-collar professional groups.

There is an obvious status incongruence among Polish blue-collar workers, especially among the younger generation. By pushing forward with industrialization and egalitarianism in at least some areas, and by generating great expectations regarding the general improvement of working-class conditions, the Communist establishment paved the way for dissatisfaction. There was too great a discrepancy between the growing aspirations of blue-collar workers and the reality of low wages, limited opportunities for promotion, poor working conditions, and ineffective management. The mass demonstrations and bloody struggles in December 1970 were the outcome of these growing contradictions.

The growth of social aspirations may lead either to social conflicts or to constructive reforms. It was up to the new technocratically oriented Polish elite, which could become outspoken only after abolishing the old elite led by Gomulka, to institute real reforms. It seemed necessary not only to considerably improve the ossified and inefficient managerial system but also to give workers more of a chance to practice real, not merely token, industrial democracy. However, is such an industrial democracy imaginable without allowing basic political freedoms? The blue-collar workers who demonstrated in December 1970 talked not only about prices and wages but also about freedom of speech. It seems quite improbable that it would be possible to substantially improve the economy of Poland without instituting basic political reforms. However, such reforms depend not only on what happens in Poland but also upon the internal policy within the Soviet bloc.

Common sense tells the blue-collar workers that the highly bureaucratized economic system of a Soviet-type communism does not function effectively enough. According to available sociological data, blue-collar workers are even more apathetic and pessimistic than white-collar workers, and they blame the current organizational and managerial setup for the existing low efficiency and inadequate wages. The fact that an average industrial blue-collar worker wastes 25 percent of his working time is not due to his laziness but to the paradoxically chaotic state of a "planned" and centrally steered Communist economy. Alongside the rising expectations of blue-collar masses, the conservative stabilization of the existing system becomes unacceptable. The young generation of blue-collar workers is aware that without basic economic reforms, further modernization is impossible. The question is which regime, how and when, will have the courage and power to introduce any far-reaching reforms. The Gierek regime so far has been very slow in this respect.

The introduction of a market economy based on relatively free entrepreneurship of autonomous enterprises would be impossible without a substantial curtailment of the Party and the central state authority. On the other hand, any rationalization would cost the blue-collar class by increasing the number unemployed (overemployment is common in Communist factories), abolishing informal practices that have been common, relating incomes much more closely to productivity, and increasing the expectation that workers would give more effort to their work and that they would commit themselves to educational self-improvement.

It is highly doubtful that the blue-collar would be willing to accept all those changes. The new social consciousness of this class will not crystallize as long as the current artificiality of the institutional setup continues. The Party bureaucracy, with the help of the police and the army, has been able to prevent the blue-collar masses from seizing power; but it seems virtually impossible to commit the Party bureaucrats wholeheartedly to the realization of economic goals. There has been too much waste, contradiction, parochialism, and ossification in the current managerial system. The semifeudal structure of management has been based on influential individuals who enjoy at least temporary support from the top, as members of informal cliques that penetrate the formal organization from top to bottom. All these individuals have been vitally interested in building their own subcliques. The exchange of favors between various cliques and their supporters to a very large extent has influenced the circulation of funds, goods, and services in the economy (Feiwel 1965).

The blue-collar workers have been involved in this informal business of exchanging favors, which tends to be very demoralizing and damaging to the economy. The Party leadership in the early 1970s (after the Gomulka regime) has been fully aware of how ineffectively the system works; but changing it would mean, among other things, allowing the blue-collar class to formulate its own social identity more or less independently of the Polish United Workers' Party's organizational and ideological formula. This seems to be an impossibility under the current political line that dominates the Soviet Bloc. It helps to explain why the Seventh Congress of Trade Unions (November 13-15, 1972) did not bring anything new, why there has been a constant postponement of reforms in economic management, and why the internal arrangement of power in the nationalized workplaces has remained almost unchanged.

However, the regime is under constant pressure from inside as well as from outside. Changes within the current arrangement are urgently needed, and the support of blue-collar masses will be absolutely necessary if substantial socioeconomic progress is to be achieved. The question for the ruling elite is how to gain this support without losing control. Some kind of compromise has to be found in the long run. The bargaining for such a compromise is impossible without allowing the blue-collar class to elect its own representatives, to establish autonomous institutions in the workshops and occupational groups, and to challenge (at least peacefully) the existing Party groups, including state officials, business executives, state bureaucrats, and even various groups of intelligentsia. New sociopolitical alliances have to develop under such circumstances. These alliances and the power play based on them may change the nature of the whole system.

EDUCATIONAL LEVEL

The participation of the wage-earning class in the educational system has changed substantially in comparison with the prewar situation (Nowakowska 1970); however, it is still not fully commensurate with the numerical strength of this class. In the early 1970s students of blue-collar worker origin accounted for 44 percent of primary school graduates, and 44 percent of vocational secondary school graduates, but only 30 percent of the graduates of general secondary schools and 30 percent of first-year higher education students (day division). The figures for students of peasant origin were 29, 23, 18, and 14 percent. At the same time the analogous figures for pupils of white-collar worker origin were 19, 27, 47, and 52 percent, which indicates that students of white-collar origin dominate the general secondary education and the day division of higher education disproportionately to their numerical strength in the total population.

In the first year of secondary education in 1971/72, students of blue-collar worker origin accounted for 53 percent of all students, in comparison with 22 percent of peasant origin and 19.5 percent of white-collar worker origin. However, the figure resulted mainly from the high participation of blue-collar students in lower vocational schools (60 percent of blue-collar worker children, in comparison with 9 percent of white-collar worker children) and in higher vocational schools (50 percent of blue-collar worker children, in comparison with 27 percent of white-collar worker children). In the first year of general secondary education, which provides the most suitable entrance to higher education, students of blue-collar worker origin accounted only for 37 percent, peasants for 14 percent, and white-collar workers for 44 percent (Rocznik 1972, p. 461).

Among college students the blue-collar worker offspring constituted 29 percent in 1969/70 (in comparison with 50.5 percent of white-collar worker offspring), but they showed a much higher participation in evening classes (57 percent) and extension courses (47 percent; only 20 percent of white-collar workers).

The educational level of blue-collar workers has greatly increased, as can be seen from a comparison of the educational level of the workers with that of their parents. Such a comparison for Polish industrial blue-collar workers showed that, on the average, 50 percent of the fathers and 60 percent of the mothers did not complete their elementary education, compared with only 27 percent of their children (Sarapata 1965).

The traditional educational level of the working class is rather low in almost all East European societies except the Czech and the East German. In Poland in 1958, among wage-earning workers in industry, 40 percent had not completed elementary school. The educational level of blue-collar workers in construction was still lower; almost half of them had not completed elementary school. Among textile workers, 66 percent of them women, 38 percent had not completed their elementary education. Over 40 percent of the total wage-earning workers had not finished elementary school. In the 1960s the educational level rose considerably. However, of all wage-earning workers in 1968, 25 percent still had not completed their elementary education. (See Table 5.1).

The drive for better education is growing among the young generation, particularly among the males. About 7 percent of the industrial blue-collar workers and about 8 percent of the blue-collar workers in construction participate in some form of additional education. The study by Stanislaw Widerszpil (1965) showed that the percentage of blue-collar workers feeling a necessity for better education increased with the growing technological level of industry and the general educational level of all employees.

When asked why they do not participate in any program of learning, the blue-collar workers usually cited advanced age, concern with family responsibilities, and additional work; a relatively smaller percentage said that they do not see any necessity for it. Women

TABLE 5.1

The Growth of Educational Level of Polish
Blue-Collar Workers, 1958-68
(percentage)

		Elementary			Secondary	
		Incom-plete	Com-plete	Craft	Incom-plete	Complete or Higher
All blue-collar	1958	43	46	8	2	1
workers	1968	24	56	17	1	2
In industry	1968	20	56	20	1	3
In construction	1968	24	58	17	1	0
All White-Collar	1958	4	30	8	12	46
workers	1968	1	20	12	8	59

Source: Rocznik statystyczny pracy 1968, pp. 260-62.

and older blue-collar workers were much more satisfied with their low educational level than were other categories of wage-earning workers. The young blue-collar workers continue their education because they expect advancement, a better job, and higher status. Some 40-60 percent of Polish blue-collar workers felt that their employers were inclined to encourage acquisition of additional learning. However, foremen and the department chiefs express quite negative opinions about the necessity of improving wage-earning workers' skills:

> In accordance with these opinions the worker is only an instrument deprived of all initiative, performing operations determined in advance. When a plant management adopts this conception it is no longer interested in the development of both qualifications and professional ambitions of its employees. . . . The intention of education is not practically taken into account in personnel management neither when engaging new workers, nor when recommending workers for promotion and dismissing them from their post (Bursche and Pomian 1965).

WORK AND WAGE CONDITIONS

Professional and social promotions are most common among qualified male blue-collar workers with some education and, to some extent, among the semiqualified. Lack of a minimum education prevents many blue-collar workers from receiving further professional and social promotions. Also, the possession of an agricultural holding, even a small one, prevents blue-collar workers from spending enough time and effort in school to complete their education and to achieve significant professional advancement.

The opportunities for professional advancement by blue-collar workers vary in terms of the regional differentiation in the average level of qualifications. Where there is a relative shortage of skilled blue-collar workers, the semiskilled workers carry out work that requires a higher skill than they possess. This is evident especially in newly established large enterprises, which accept blue-collar workers with low qualifications, intending to have them trained later.

Technological progress greatly changes the situation of the blue-collar worker, which in turn affects his satisfaction. Some branches of industry have become more important than others, and they attract more blue-collar workers. If 1950 is taken as 100, the total employment grew in 1971 to 600 in the electrotechnical industry,

384 in the precision instrument and equipment industry, 380 in the metal industry, and 360 in the rubber industry, but only 135 in the textile industry and 157 in the clothing industry (Rocznik 1972, p. 177).

The progress in improving work conditions and opportunities to make employment more attractive is not fast enough to make blue-collar workers really happy. Jan Szczepanski noted:

> The workers are still hired labor. The socialist revo-
> lution does not change the relation of the worker to the
> machine, nor does it change his position within the
> technological system of the factory. It changes his
> position in the social and economic system of the in-
> dustry or factory. But his relation to the machine
> and the organizational system of work requires his
> subordination to the foreman and the management of
> the factory. He receives wages according to the quan-
> tity and quality of work performed, and he must obey
> the principles and regulations of work discipline. Thus,
> the status of workers is to some degree inconsistent,
> being at the same time that of hired laborers and that
> of co-owners of the means of production (1970, p. 125).

The group that came to power in Poland at the end of 1970 promised blue-collar workers improvement of their living standard. However, the improvement was quite modest. In the nationalized industry the gross monthly income of blue-collar workers in 1971 was 2,663 zloty, only 6 percent higher than in 1970. The improvement was as follows in various branches of industry (taking 1970 as 100): coal, 5 percent; ferrous metallurgy, 6 percent; transport, 8.5 percent; electrotechnics, 5 percent; and textiles, 7 percent. The material expectations of blue-collar workers are not particularly high (Sarapata 1963); but especially after the power contest at the end of 1970 and beginning of 1971, they learned that it is possible to push the ruling elite for some improvements and relaxations.

The blue-collar workers earned a monthly average in 1971 of over 4,000 zloty in mining, over 3,000 zloty in steelmills, close to 3,000 zloty in construction and the power industry, but only a little more than 2,000 zloty in the textile, foodstuff, leather, and clothing industries. In the state-owned agricultural enterprises the blue-collar workers earn even less (1,800 zloty in 1970/71), but they have additional income from their small agricultural holdings. Blue-collar workers who earned above the average of 2,500 zloty per month in 1970 were concentrated in construction and industry. In construction 55 percent, and in industry 45 percent, of blue-collar earned more than 2,500 zloty; the percentages for white-collar workers in these two branches were 67 and 64. On the other hand, the percentages of blue-collar workers earning less than the average income were 75 in forestry, 87 in trade, and 94 in medical care and social welfare; the percentages for white-collar workers in those branches were 80, 73, and 78. In nationalized industry the growth of monthly gross income in 1960-71, calculated using 1960 as 100, was 150 percent for blue-collar workers, 141 percent for engineering and technical staff, and 145 percent for administrative and clerical staff (Rocznik 1972, p. 196).

Compared with blue-collar workers, several white-collar professions do not earn more—or may even earn less. Medical doctors employed full-time in hospitals averaged just over 4,000 zloty; editors in publishing houses and television and radio journalists earned 3,000 zloty; and nurses made less than 2,000 zloty. Teachers average a little over 2,000 zloty in elementary schools, close to 3,000 zloty in secondary schools, and close to 4,000 zloty in colleges and universities.

Both in Poland and in other East European countries, the social and political activity among blue-collar workers increases with their educational level, the importance of the work done, and seniority. (The average occupational seniority among blue-collar workers was 16 years in the early 1970s.) There is also a significant difference in this respect between the sexes. Men are much more active than women, which is related not only to tradition but also to their higher skill, better education, and less commitment to family care.

DISCONTINUITY IN THE CLASS TRADITION

Little attraction remained for blue-collar workers' sons to take on their father's occupations. The young generation very easily breaks with the tradition of occupational inheritance and often is strongly supported in that inclination by the parents. The educational level of the peasants' offspring who migrate into the towns and cities has been rising, as have their aspirations. A general decline of migration from the rural areas by those with modest aspirations and still more modest requirements (as to the conditions of work and nature of the job) is obvious. The young migrants from the country no longer passively accept being treated as inferiors by urban people. There are no more basic differences in educational level and culture between them and their colleagues of blue-collar descent. Universal education and the mass communication media (radio, television, cinema) popularize the same patterns of thinking and behaving in the countryside as in the urban areas.

As an example consider what happens in the traditional miners' environment. According to an extensive study of 500 miners' families in 1958-61 by Wanda Mrozek, the traditional inheritance of the miner's profession began to disappear. The same was happening to the attitude toward heavy work. The miner's family has become less and less the source of labor for the mines. One generation ago it was common for miners' sons to follow the same trade, but now it has become rare. The regional homogeneity of the miner's professional environment started to disappear several years ago. In the community studied by Mrozek one could observe the loosening and decline of family ties. Thus the demographic basis for the strong professional tradition is weakening.

The labor shortage in the mining industry has been solved by attracting migrants from the rural areas outside Upper Silesia, the traditional mining region in which about 70 percent of all Polish miners still live. There have been conflicts between newcomers and old-timers, but gradually integration has occurred. The percentage of marriages of partners with different regional background has been increasing steadily. In the miners' population studied by Mrozek, it was only 2 percent in the old generation, and 34 percent in the young generation. In the new settlements for miners built during the first 20 years after World War II, the newcomers are an especially high proportion of inhabitants (50 percent or more), and therefore the predispositions for social integration are especially favorable (Mrozek 1965).

The traditional communities of miners and foundrymen, characterized by a high degree of integration, great territorial stability, and almost complete homogeneity, had a very important role in the occupational motivation and stability of workers employed in the heavy and sometimes dangerous work. Mutual help and mutual under-standing were typical. The great influx of new people, increasing urbanization, growing popularity of new family patterns (for instance, the average miner's family now consists of 3 persons), more opportunity for the young generation to study and to find attractive jobs outside mining or the steel industry, increasing contact with the outside world, and rising cultural aspirations disrupt the traditional community of workers employed in several branches of heavy industry. There is clear evidence of the breakdown of the specific isolation of that community within the society. Furthermore, the development of heavy industry favors the creation of new population centers with a pre-dominant blue-collar worker population but without traditionalistic integration.

According to the research done by me in the big new steel town of Nowa Huta (New Foundry), most of the inhabitants, who are pre-dominantly employed by the steel mill called Lenin Foundry, came from the villages and for a long time adhered to their old cultural patterns. The urbanization process has been slowed by the fact that the growth of the population was much faster than the growth of family housing. For several years, 40 to 45 percent of the inhabitants of Nowa Huta had been living in workers' hostels, without the opportunity to obtain dwellings, all of which belonged to the government and had been distributed among the workers according to how much they were needed and accepted by governmental officials. Married workers were separated in many cases for several years, the husband living in the male hostel and the wife living in the female hostel. In the early 1960s most of the town's population lived in family dwellings, but their urbanization and social integration had been slowed down by the previous poor living conditions (Matejko 1956; 1959).

A better situation has been created for the crew of the new steel mill erected in Warsaw. There it was possible to hire people living in the city and its vicinity without having to put them in workers' hostels. Also, the new housing construction around the mill had progressed very well, so that after few years every fourth employee lived in an apartment given him by the mill. The study done among the blue-collar workers at Warsaw's steel mill makes it evident that adaptational problems of that particular group of steelworkers were seldom found elsewhere in the Polish steel industry. The labor turnover, which was especially high in the first years after the mill had been constructed, was due mostly to the wide opportunities to find another job in the city. The inhabitants of Warsaw were not accustomed to heavy work in the steel industry. Many of them took the job in the mill only temporarily, until they could find an easier occupation in trade, in an office, or in the crafts. However, after some years the occupation of steelworker became accepted and appreciated by the population of Warsaw (Matejko 1964a).

URBAN ACCULTURATION

The traditional family patterns of East European blue-collar workers have derived in large part from the peasant class, both because of the high percentage of workers originally from the peasantry and because many of the families of blue-collar workers live, or lived until recently, in the countryside. Since the intragenerational family bonds are still fairly strong, there are close neighborhood relations and much mutual help. There is a clear-cut division between man's work and woman's work; men believe that women should do the household chores. The old parents help their adult children do the household chores and the young generation feels obliged to take care of their elders; very often two or three generations live together in one household. Relatives are expected to help each other.

The basic problem of all people newly arrived in the Polish cities is finding a dwelling and furnishing it. There is still great congestion in existing urban dwelling buildings (in 1970, 1.31 persons per room and 117 households per 100 dwellings); and many of them still do not have central heating (available in only 13 percent of urban dwellings in 1960), toilets, bathrooms, gas supply (each available in 50 percent of the urban dwellings in 1970), and even water (not available in 25 percent of the urban dwellings in 1970). For young couples there are not enough dwellings constructed by the state or by cooperatives. The situation is better than it was several years ago, but it is still quite difficult. For each 1,000 newlywed couples each year in Poland during the 1960s, there were only about 700 new dwellings (in cities about 1,000, but in rural areas less than 400) (Rocznik 1972, p. 419).

Even if manual workers' families who move from the country achieve a living standard similar to the traditionally more privileged social strata, they retain some specific preferences. Data from surveys done in the new urban settlements show that in dwellings occupied by the families of blue-collar workers, the kitchen still tends to be the center of the daily family life, as it had been for centuries in the country (Matejko 1959). There is a need for a garden and a tiny farm (rabbits, chickens, pigeons, a pig). In the blue-collar worker dwellings, in comparison with white-collar worker households, there are more common beds and traditional kitchen sideboards, and fewer cupboards, sofas, bookshelves, and worktables. There is also less place and less special furniture for the children. The whole decoration of the dwelling is in a traditional style. The need for privacy of each family member is more developed in the families of the intelligentsia as can be documented by the higher percentage of respondents preferring to have more rooms in their dwellings, even when sacrificing their space. There is a strong inclination in the blue-collar worker families to sacrifice one's daily comfort in order to keep a certain part of the dwelling as something "for guests," which corresponds to the peasants tradition of dividing their homes into a "black" part (for daily use) and a "white" part (for special occasions). There is also a common tradition of furnishing the bedroom with two old-fashioned beds even if the space is small and it would be more convenient to use space-saving modern beds (Matejko 1959).

With the progressing urbanization of the blue-collar workers from the country, the differences in household habits become less acute. A study done by Wanda Czeczerda (1964) of housing preferences among employed people in Warsaw showed only small differences between blue-collar and white-collar workers. The proper equipment of dwellings was most important for both groups. The white-collar workers expected a higher standard of accommodation than the blue-collar workers, but this difference diminished considerably when comparing the younger generation of both groups.

The free time of the blue-collar families is spent mostly at home, reading newspapers, listening to the radio, watching television, and visiting with their neighbors. In comparison with the white-collar families, they are much less inclined to go to the theater, to attend concerts, or to go to the movies. But sports events are above all the entertainment of the blue-collar workers (Skorzynski 1962). In general the free-time activities of blue-collar employees are not so varied as those of white-collar employees, who are culturally much more active and know much better what to do with their free time (Sicinski 1966; I. Nowak 1966).

Alcoholism, widespread among certain categories of blue-collar workers, is related to the lack of emotionally satisfying ways of spending free time (the consumption of alcohol in Poland in 1971 was 170 if 1960 is taken as 100, and constituted 9 percent of the total sale). Very illuminating in this respect are several studies dealing with the free-time expenditure of blue-collar workers of peasant origin living in an urban area in workers' hostels. They really "kill" their leisure time, not being able and willing to make full use of the cultural services available in the city, and at the same time being cut off from the village life. It is quite obvious that Polish blue-collar workers do not have enough recreational facilities that are really attractive to them. The mass media are dominated by the intelligentsia. The same is true with cafés, which are common in cities (they are also in villages now) and provide a place for social contacts. The sport clubs are financially sponsored by the trade union movement, but they are primarily for semiprofessional sportsmen. There is a general shortage of recreational and restaurant facilities, as well as a shortage of means of transportation, especially during the periods of high demand (weekends, summer). Therefore blue-collar workers are quite often handicapped either by lack of leisure facilities or by the fact that the content of what is provided does not suit them.

It is a paradox that the government that claims to represent the working class promotes culture and entertainment of an elitist character. The Communist establishment for obvious political reasons does not accept Western-type mass culture, which would please average consumers among the blue-collar worker ranks; yet blue-collar workers are strongly dissatisfied when the only easily available daily entertainment consists exclusively of television, radio, reading, and crowded beer stands. There are not enough restaurants in Poland. The number of people per restaurant decreased in 1950-71 from 3,800 to 2,200; but it is still far from being enough, especially when the quality of the restaurants is often poor.

The rising educational level of blue-collar workers has an important impact on their leisure time. Using a representative sample of all urban inhabitants in Poland, Zygmunt Skorzynski found that the higher the level of education, the more frequent the attendance of theater performances, concerts, movies, or sporting events. Especially important in this respect is the completion of secondary education. For people of peasant origin, education is the real bridge to the urban culture. Skorzynski observed:

> Workers who migrated from the rural areas after World War II, and who constitute a very large percentage of the present urban population, are gradually breaking away from the numerous traditions and customs of the rural area, and are becoming accustomed to new conditions. This assimilation is not without its difficulties, but the passive attitude toward free time (for in the rural areas free time is often unknown) is more and more frequently changing into an attitude where an active choice is made, although the choice is still usually limited to the simplest forms of consumption and the most primitive forms of entertainment. It is probable that apart from the influence of various social and political institutions, the greatest influence producing slow change in this direction is the example provided by the skilled workers (1965, pp. 186-87).

In leisure the important integrative role is played by organized recreation. The total number of people who used state-subsidized holiday hostels grew from 700,000 in 1960 to more than 2.77 million in 1972, 2.34 million paying reduced rates. Spending their holidays in the resort hotels with people from other social strata, the blue-collar workers assimilate new cultural values. Holidays outside of their home were unknown to most blue-collar workers before World War II. Increasingly blue-collar workers began to follow the holiday style of the intelligentsia; this was especially true of the skilled blue-collar workers and much less so for unskilled blue-collar workers, who followed to a large extent the old traditions of spending their vacations at home or with relatives in the country (see Table 5.2).

ADAPTATION OF NEW WORKERS IN HEAVY INDUSTRY

The problem of workers' adaptation to their work environment is especially acute in heavy industry, particularly in branches in

TABLE 5.2

How Holidays Are Spent by Blue-Collar
Workers and Intelligentsia, 1960
(percent)

	Unskilled Blue-Collar Workers		Skilled Blue-Collar Workers		White-Collar Workers with College Education	
	A	B	A	B	A	B
City	61	8	50	6	19	5
Country with relatives	21	9	23	9	13	3
State-sponsored inn	8	39	15	30	32	27
Country privately	—	19	3	21	18	22
Tourist trip	2	9	3	17	11	20
Other	1	1	1	4	2	11
No data	7	15	5	13	5	12

A = place where the last vacation was spent.
B = place most desirable for spending a vacation.

Source: Skorsynski 1965, pp. 241-42.

which the improvement of working conditions is relatively slow. For example, employment in heavy industry is not very attractive because of hard work in heat and limited opportunity for advancement. The technological progress is not rapid enough to relieve the worker of a number of arduous tasks.

Polish pig iron production increased (in terms of martin oven output) from 880,000 tons in 1938 to 1,533,000 tons in 1950 and to 7,815,000 tons in 1972. This growth was accompanied by an increased demand for manpower, and therefore the total ferrous metallurgy employment in 1971 was 176 if employment in 1950 is taken as 100. Steelworkers enjoy higher wages than workers in several other branches of industry. The average gross monthly income of blue-collar workers in the ferrous industry rose from 2,227 zloty in 1960 to 3,595 zloty in 1972, when the same indexes were for workers in the textile industry were 1,461 zloty and 2,282 zloty, for workers in the food industry were 1,485 zloty and 2,458 zloty, and for workers in in the machinery and structural metal industry were 1,730 zloty and 2,607 zloty (Concise 1973, p. 96).

With the rising general cultural level of the population there has also been a rise in the expectations concerning labor conditions. For several years the basic reservoir of labor for heavy industry was the rural population, which accepted heavy work and achieved in exchange the status of industrial worker, which is traditionally relatively much higher than the status of a peasant. At the same time the educational level of newcomers was unsatisfactory. Among all iron-workers and steelworkers in the mid-1960s, only 2 percent possessed secondary vocational education, which had become almost indispensable in the modern metallurgical enterprises; only 5 percent had completed elementary vocational schools and the rest had only a general elementary education (and many not even that).

During 1950-70 several new industrial enterprises were established in heavy industry; they had to recruit their crews from those at hand. Especially in those enterprises the problem of the workers' adaptation to the work environment was very acute. How to prevent high rates of labor turnover and absenteeism? How to attract workers for stable employment in a particular factory, at a particular job? How to convince them that they should strive for a higher educational level?

The sociological study conducted by me and my research team in four Polish steel mills in 1962 was an attempt to answer some of the above questions (Matejko 1964a; 1965). Observations were made and interviews were conducted with 220 production employees, mainly blue-collar workers, as well as with foremen and department chiefs. The study was conducted at two pipe-rolling mills and at two hearth departments.

Using data from intensive interviews, an attempt was made to establish a typology of the workers' professional careers and their adaptation to the working environment. The following criteria of professional adaptation were used:

1. Professional advancement. How much does the worker gain at the present job in terms of rising on the occupational ladder?

2. Qualifications. Are the qualifications of the worker enough for him to work efficiently at the present job?

3. Adaptation. How much does the worker adapt himself to the particular work, to his colleagues, and to his supervisors? Is he a stranger or a fully adapted member of his work group?

4. Motivation. Is the worker satisfied with his present social role and position? Does he accept his job?

5. Perspectives. Are the perspectives of the worker realistically in line with his abilities?

6. Aspirations. Does the worker have any aspirations that would advance him in his professional career? If so, is he able to realize these aspirations?

Using the above criteria, it was possible to classify the investigated workers, giving them one of three ratings for each criterion: + (presence of the criterion), - (absence), 0 (insignificance). The following five basic groups of adaptation appeared among studied workers:

1. Advancing

advancement +	perspectives +	motivation +
adaptation +	qualifications + or 0	aspirations +

This type of adaptation is especially characteristic of young people with a good educational background who have entered an occupational career that seems to be successful. Their present job is a step to another job that will offer higher prestige, better wages, and greater power. Workers do not become discouraged by the disadvantages of their present work because they think of it as being temporary.

2. Stabilized

advancement 0 or +	perspectives 0 or +	motivation +
adaptation +	qualifications 0 or +	aspirations 0

These are mostly people who do not have enough abilities to get ahead, but also do not aspire to become upgraded. The stable, relatively well-paid job in an acceptable human and physical environment is all that they really expect to have.

3. Relatively adjusted

advancement - or 0	perspectives 0 or +	motivation 0
adaptation + or 0	qualifications 0 or +	aspirations 0

In this group are workers generally satisfied with their present employment as a way of earning money, but at the same time not really happy with the present situation. The work does not give them any deep satisfaction, either because they do not have strong occupational interests or because the present job is boring. Most are workers with low educational backgrounds who have had many other jobs. They change their working place often, whenever it is convenient for them, and move easily.

4. Passively maladjusted

advancement 0	perspectives 0	motivation 0
adaptation -	qualifications + or 0	aspirations 0

These are the workers who accept their present job only for material reasons (good wages, company-provided housing, seniority). They give up any ambitions and become frustrated with the present job or with the occupation of steelworker in general. Many are relatively older people with limited life expectations.

5. Actively maladjusted

advancement - or 0 or +	perspectives -	motivation -
adaptation -	qualifications + or -	aspirations +

These people are dissatisfied with their present job and strive to change it in the future. Their frustration does not prevent them from trying to change their occupational situation; rather, the frustration motivates them to search for other occupational possibilities.

Of the steelworkers studied, most could be characterized as belonging to categories 2 (workers of peasant origin), 3 (young workers of urban origin), and 4 (older workers of urban origin). The great majority of the respondents considered their jobs as the ceiling of their occupational career. At most they hoped to gain more experience and to become upgraded automatically, without any special educational contribution on their part. The incentive to work was reduced to a passive force of habit accompanied by the conviction that since there were no alternatives, there was nothing to be done.

If the heavy labor, difficult working conditions (the heat), and the rather strict discipline are taken into consideration, it seems quite obvious why the occupation of steelworker has lost its social attractiveness in Poland. The above-mentioned research, as well as the research done by Franciszek Adamski (1965; 1966) shows that the steelworkers do not want their children to be puddlers, smelters, gutterers, and rollers: "Let them at least have some schooling so they won't be wage earners anymore. . . . If they entered the ranks of white collar workers, they would not be obliged to sweat like we are at the present time. . . . We would never wish our children to earn money doing such arduous work. . . . It is always better to work in the office than at the shopfloor." Some of them would like to have their sons employed in the steelmill, but only as engineers or technicians, not as regular wage earners (see Table 5.3). The workers were conscious of existing real opportunities for their children to acquire higher education through the free education system sponsored by the Communist government. They were also inclined

TABLE 5.3

Interest of Parents in Their Sons' Becoming Steelworkers
(percent)

Steel Mill in Which Husband Is Employed	Definite Yes		Perhaps		No		Perhaps Not		Don't Know	
	h	w	h	w	h	w	h	w	h	w
A	39	35	4	4	30	22	4.	4	22	35
B	30	20	20	7	20	17	17	20	23	37
C	17	25	-	9	33	33	8	4	41	33
D	24	17	31	24	19	19	9	7	17	33
Totals	25	22	19	13	23	26	18	9	22	35

h = husband.
w = wife.

Source: Adamski 1965, p. 196.

to help their offspring materially, for they wanted them to occupy a
higher socio-occupational status than their own.

ADAPTATIONAL PROBLEMS OF YOUTH

A good insight into the problems of rural youth adapting to the
working environment in a big city is provided in a sociological study
by Maria Jarosinska (1964). She surveyed the crews of four Warsaw
metalworks, arranging them into three categories (men only): young
blue-collar workers of rural extraction (180 interviews), young blue-
collar workers of working-class origin (150 interviews), and older
blue-collar workers (179 interviews). By comparing these groups,
she was able to formulate the following conclusions:

Nowadays young people from the villages, like those from working-class families, generally make their own choice of occupation:

> It is significant that the advice of relatives plays little
> part. . . . This indicates a shift of authority from the
> family to outside it. . . . Young people of peasant origin
> attach great importance to the opinions of classmates
> and friends. . . . Apart from friends the decisions of
> this group were influenced by a primary school princi-
> pal, teachers, uncle, foreman, and a recruiting officer
> canvassing labour in the village.

The main route to industry is through the vocational school.
Most of the young people who come to industry have graduated from
such a school, but some also study while they work (about 20
percent of those polled). Young men who are already employed improve their skills by taking vocational courses (50 percent of those
polled). On-the-job-training is becoming less important, although it
still embraces quite a large number (33 percent of both the peasant
and the working-class youth). The young generation of workers, says
Jarosinska, regardless of their origin, has better formal preparation
for trades, because a majority have finished vocational schools. In
this respect the position of the young generation is better than that of
older people. It should be added that by the 1970s young persons, especially those coming from the village, take jobs in industry only
when they are mature enough in age and education.

The ambitions of the young are striking. Hardly 33 percent
of the subjects appeared to be satisfied with their present position,
while the rest indicated that they would like to become overseers,
foremen, technicians, or engineers. Jarosinska observed that relatively more young people of peasant stock had ambitious plans than

those of working-class origin. None of the young people of peasant stock planned to return to the village; all their plans for the future were based on living in the city and working in socialized industry. Only a few dreamed of owning a private workshop. Jarosinska found that young trained metalworkers of rural origin were, in their aspirations, more "working-class" than the corresponding group of young workers of working-class origin. Among the latter a greater percentage displayed petite bourgeois aspirations.

Attitudes toward work were in general positive. Young workers liked the job mainly because of the kind of work they were doing and to the mental effort required by it. The bulk of the subjects, 75 percent, wished to continue working at their present place of employment. The tolerably good earnings, promotions achieved, and familiarity with the conditions at the factory were responsible for this disposition. The majority availed themselves, if necessary, of the help of their fellow workers, spoke well of the attitude of older workers toward them, believed they were well treated by the overseers, and got on with the other members of their team. In consequence, we may say that the process of adaptation to trade and the place of employment is proceeding smoothly.

Adaptation to the job goes along with adjustment to the environment outside the factory. Two-thirds of the subjects were married; more than half the wives also came from the rural area. Furthermore, Jarosinska found that the cultural level of women who married to young workers of peasant stock was similar to that of their coevals of blue-collar stock. The wives of the two groups differed in social origin but not in education. Among the wives in both cases there was a preponderance of white-collar over manual occupations—evidence of mixing between skilled blue-collar workers and white-collar workers.

While common peasant descent may often be the foundation of matrimony, the same is not true for other spheres of private life. Young people of peasant stock make friends both with townsmen and villagers. Social ties develop through common work and common pastimes, and less frequently through common origin. The "significant others" recognized by young people of peasant extraction have moved away from the rural communities to urban groups. Contacts with relatives who have remained in the village become considerably weaker. On the other hand, those who moved from the villages to the towns before the new migrants are frequently an important reference group. The family ties of respondents connect them with all the important social environments in contemporary Poland. There are contacts not only with other blue-collar workers' groups but also with intelligentsia.

If in the cultural and social spheres the adjustment of youth of peasant origin to urban life has been significant, the same cannot be said about their housing. Satisfactory and stabilized housing had been achieved barely by 25 percent of the respondents. However, in this they are not worse off than the young workers of blue-collar background, who also have a good deal of difficulty with housing.

Young people of rural origin identify almost universally with the status of a semiqualified modern worker, and not the worker-craftsman with whom older workers tend to identify. Two-thirds of the subjects of peasant stock studied by Jarosinska voiced the opinion that blue-collar workers had a higher social prestige than farmers, although only 15 percent thought this was as it should be. All of the interviewed groups had strong egalitarian feelings.

THE EGALITARIANISM OF BLUE-COLLAR WORKERS

Egalitarian feelings are widespread in Poland, particularly among blue-collar workers. A very large part of them have achieved social and educational upgrading under the Communist system. They have moved from poor villages to towns, industrial establishments, and even leading positions. Many of the Party and state officials, executives, and a large proportion of the intelligentsia are of a blue-collar background. The appearance of egalitarian aspirations does not mean, of course, that people are satisfied with the status quo. Egalitarian aspirations are even stronger in the traditionally lower strata than among the intelligentsia. Unskilled workers and people with less education often feel they are deprived of status.

Quite a high percentage of wage-earning workers covered by the quota sample of the total male urban population studied by Stefan Nowak (1964) defined their social status as lower than average: 66 percent among unskilled workers and 45 percent among skilled workers. The lower the educational level and the income of a blue-collar respondent, the more unfavorable his evaluation of his social status. Wage-earning workers, especially unskilled ones, were less optimistic, in comparison with higher social strata, regarding the decrease of distinctions between members of different social groups in Poland. Income, education, and managerial or nonmanagerial positions were perceived by blue-collar workers as primary sources of division in society.

Egalitarian postulates among blue-collar workers are related, among other things, to the fact that they have to depend so much on decisions of somebody at the top who is out of touch with reality. People at the bottom take full responsibility for the final outcome of their work, but the "cream and sugar" will be consumed at higher levels of authority. According to research done by Stefan Nowak in 1961, 53 percent of skilled wage-earning workers and 44 percent of unskilled wage-earning workers wanted to see the social differences disappear entirely in the future, as compared with 38 percent of the creative intelligentsia (Nowak 1964). It does not mean, however, that the blue-collar workers were in favor of the full equalization of incomes. Research done in Poland in 1959 by Adam Sarapata showed that the Polish people universally regarded the differentiation of earnings as normal and that representatives of different occupational groups constructed different wage hierarchies. The steelworkers, miners' wives, and various manual workers surveyed by Sarapata ranked university professor, cabinet minister, mechanical engineer, and physician among the top four occupations (there was relatively little difference in that respect in the opinions of wage-earning workers and representatives of other occupational groups). Such professions as actor, priest, building laborer, nurse, spinner, and recreationist (a community social worker in the field of recreation) did not receive a consistent ranking (Sarapata 1963).

The same research showed that the level of earnings postulated by blue-collar workers as desirable for their own occupational groups did not greatly exceed the level of actual earnings. Respondents were realistic enough to postulate no more than 20-25 percent their actual incomes. At the same time they were interested in limiting the highest possible incomes to the wage typical for the highest-paid wage-earning workers. Quite different were the opinions of highly qualified professionals. Their level of a reasonable income was much higher. There were several reasons: the incomes of these professionals often were higher before the war, there was a tendency (much stronger than among blue-collar workers) to compare one's own income with salaries paid in other countries, and there was a conviction that one's real contribution was much greater than real income (Sarapata 1963).

The main issue for Polish blue-collar workers is no longer the difference between them and white-collar workers or the numerical proportion in various occupations. In 1971, for every 100 manual workers in nationalized industry there were 14 technical staff members and 7 members of the administrative staff. This proportion differed depending on the branch of industry. It was roughly 100:10:3 in the coal industry, 100:9:6 in the textile industry, 100:15:8 in the chemical industry, and 100:23:23 in power industry.

Relatively light work, good working conditions, opportunity for advancement, permissive discipline, and a standard of living much higher than that of the parents were the values for which the young generation of workers strove. For the previous generation of blue-collar workers, who had experienced the unemployment of the interwar period, the war, and the German occupation, it was satisfactory just to get steady work in the state-sponsored industry and a place to live in the town. Their social aspirations were thus gratified to a large extent, and their hopes were more easily transferred to their children. The old generation's hope was that the young generation would advance further up the social ladder and would obtain better conditions of work, finally ceasing hard physical labor.

Starting in the late 1950s, several values very attractive to the old generation were no longer exciting to their offspring. What would be considered a real achievement by people deprived in the past of social facilities was taken for granted. For example, the son of a blue-collar worker was not satisfied just to find a job. If he was still willing to become an industrial wage-earning worker, he wanted to work in relative comfort and to take full advantage of all opportunities for promotion.

The younger generation of blue-collar workers takes for granted improvements in economic and health conditions achieved by the older generation. Its sociocultural aspirations have been stimulated by the rapid development of the mass media, which are sponsored by the state and therefore relatively inexpensive. Fewer and fewer young people are inclined to follow the way of life characteristic of their parents: to accept heavy physical work, poor living conditions, restricted opportunities to spend their leisure time outside their home, and to exhibit a passive attitude toward shortcomings at the workplace. The expectations of younger blue-collar workers are growing even faster than the effective progress in technology, the improved organization of work, knowledge, the social culture of people occupying supervisory positions, the average income level, the supply of material goods, and the real decrease of differences between blue-collar workers and the intelligentsia.

The rapidly rising sociocultural aspirations of the new generation of blue-collar workers play an important role in Poland, creating several social problems of great importance for the regime. First, there is a substantial increase in the supply of young labor because the generation entering the labor market is larger than previous ones (the percentage of people in the age group 15-19 increased from 6.5 in 1960 to 10.6 in 1972). The educational level of young people is rising (in the early 1970s, 90 percent of those 14-17 years old attended schools, in comparison with 40 percent in the early 1950s), but the more attractive jobs are occupied by older and uneducated people. Advancement into the clerical ranks is no longer attractive to the young generation of blue-collar descent.

In principle, the full-employment policy of the government guarantees younger people a place to work and live; however, this place is quite often not up to their aspirations and expectations. The transition from a permissive school environment to the average work environment is not an easy one. The young people have to overcome the negativism and defensiveness of the older generation, who feel endangered by their less experienced but better educated younger colleagues.

With their growing educational and cultural level, new generations of blue-collar workers expect not only a higher degree of social egalitarianism, but also a considerable reduction of physical effort and better operation of the enterprises. There is a growing awareness of shortcomings in the organization of work, in the intradepartmental and extradepartmental economic cooperation, and in the management. The question is how much room there will be in the political setup to accept the blue-collar workers' criticism as a constructive social force that will help to improve the total economic system. This is the problem of the autonomy of the enterprise as an economic and social subject able to engage the forces that originate in the growing social consciousness of the blue-collar and white-collar workers. It is also a problem of internal democracy at the workplace.

The wage-earning workers expect better treatment, higher wages, and better opportunities for their children. The prospect of social advancement, opened within the Communist system, was at first very attractive; but with the passing of time the new rights have come to be viewed by blue-collar workers less as privileges and more as self-evident facts of their daily life.

The political and social advancement of the blue-collar workers is another factor that stimulated their aspirations. About 66 percent of all industrial executives are of worker or peasant origin. Most of the ruling Party elite were manual workers or are of blue-collar origin. Party membership is relatively much more common among male blue-collar workers than female blue-collar workers, among skilled workers than among unskilled workers, and among people with seniority than among people without seniority (Bauman 1962).

The participation of workers in Party organizations increases with occupational status, and in this respect the unskilled workers are handicapped in comparison with their more skilled colleagues. About 33 percent of the technical staff is politically active, 20 percent of the foremen, about 15 percent of the clerical staff, about 9 percent of skilled blue-collar workers, and 4 percent of unskilled blue-collar workers (Krall, 1970).

> Degree of militancy is relatively highest among engineers
> and technicians, and lowest among unskilled workers (ex-
> actly seven and a half times less than among the engi-
> neers). This personal skill which as a rule is corre-
> lated to the position of engineer predestines him, more

than others, to behave in such a way as is accepted as a measure of Party militancy. Exactly the opposite is the case with the unskilled manual workers. . . . The percentage of Party militants among the factory personnel with a secondary education is four times more than among those with a primary education (Bauman 1962, pp. 59-60).

The blue-collar class in Poland is becoming more and more aware of its own strength. Its social consciousness cannot fully crystallize without establishment of autonomous class institutions. There is still too much pressure from both Party officials and the intelligentsia. Blue-collar workers used to live for years under the shadow of both these social powers, the first political and the second cultural. (It is significant that even in the state-sponsored holiday hostels, established originally for blue-collar workers, their participation had diminished from 44 percent in 1965 to 34 percent in 1968, with replacement by the white-collar workers.) In the early 1970s blue-collar workers became more inclined to play a more independent role based on the awareness of their strength and new sociopolitical opportunities.

THE NEW SOCIAL CONSCIOUSNESS

The social consciousness of the Polish blue-collar workers has been influenced by factors that stimulate their aspirations for better material well-being, social egalitarianism, fair treatment at work, possibilities to enter higher social strata, smooth organization of work, and extensive development of state-sponsored social services. I have here in mind two basic factors. The first is that the industrialization of the country had made a giant step forward under the conditions brought about by the Polish People's Republic. The second is that the totalitarian structure had hitherto negated the possibility of free development of truly class-bound institutions, which would be oriented to the needs of a given class, would serve that class, and would be directed by it. The existence of the working-class "youth" and its considerable recruitment from peasant elements does not explain anything, if we disregard the matter of an institutional superstructure.

"The overwhelming majority of contemporary Polish workers entered professional life with no knowledge of the past and the struggle of the workers for their own class interests" (Wacowska 1972, p. 162). This is not, however, the main reason for weak class consciousness. Other factors seem to explain the phenomenon much more convincingly. First of all, very clear common interest must appear, and then a chance for achieving the aims by means of a common effort, before class consciousness can truly mature. Good perspectives for individual advancement never give rise to class consciousness—quite the contrary, they are a hindrance. Moreover, in conditions of constant Party and police surveillance, it was (and still is to a considerable extent) risky to proclaim class consciousness—unless it was at the wish of the Party and in accordance with its totalitarian interests.

Studies that I undertook with a group of my students in several Polish steel foundries during the first half of the 1960s (Matejko 1965), as well as my frequent contacts with blue-collar workers during my studies of housing conditions during the 1950s (Matejko 1959), have convinced me that, as among the intelligentsia, so also among blue-collar workers, a style of individual dealing with the regime has been accepted. One exception is that in the working milieu, this has been a struggle based on concrete realities. The mechanism of indoctrination that Czeslaw Milosz so excellently presented (1953) never really existed among blue-collar workers, except in cases involving people who were consciously striving to rise above this milieu and to enter the ranks of "the higher classes."

Becoming a member of the Party was, and still is to a large extent, a practical matter. Being in circumstances of socioeconomical inferiority, it was necessary to clutch at the means that would permit the strengthening of one's position. The Party pretends not to notice that its blue-collar members go to church, baptize their children, and manifest a low level of interest in the official ideology. The Party needs them as a labor force and is more interested in their external loyalty than in anything else.

But blue-collar workers have to a significant extent learned to individually play the same game that the Party plays with respect to them. While interviewing workers and their families regarding housing (Matejko 1959), I was able to see at firsthand how quickly and easily the lower classes learned to use to their personal advantage the same phraseology that those at the top of the ladder considered as a cunning tool for subjugating the masses. Especially during the 1950s, all kinds of applications to the authorities for housing, raises, and other benefits were full of pseudo-ideological platitudes meant to convince the authorities that the suppliant knew how matters stood and what should be said.

This individual game was meaningful to the extent that it was necessary in order to survive and that there was something concrete to attain by it. At that time the rapid tempo of industrialization provided quite meaningful opportunities for people at the bottom of the ladder. The Party gave the lower classes access to many attractive positions by getting rid of the politically uncertain element that had

112

previously occupied them. If we consider the destitution of Polish villages before the war, and the more general destitution of the World War II years, we can understand that any amelioration of personal circumstances, especially among the lower classes, carried weight and facilitated the growth of mutual tolerance between these classes and the regime. This was of course no more than a marriage of convenience. People of the lower classes had none of the conditions found in the democratic West that would lead them to organize pressure groups. They had to make pacts with the authorities one by one, to accept the phraseology set down by the political establishment and give guarantees of their own political passivity. For this, however, they were compensated by the authorities with something concrete, such as good employment, a place to live, an occasional coupon for some attractive product, or at least not being imprisoned.

During the period immediately after World War II the intelligentsia was bankrupt politically, socially, and economically, and it could not be counted as a useful partner. And one could not, after all, take seriously the possibility of an armed uprising against authorities who were backed by the power of the USSR. The only remaining alternative was some sort of limited personal comfort, or "small stabilization." Vladyslaw Gomulka treated this alternative as the basis for his internal policy and thereby at first gained some popularity among the masses, but could not give "small stabilization" a realistic shape. As the years passed, aspirations grew, the fear of Stalinist times receded, and yet there was no visible improvement of material well-being. Moreover, the nation's leader continued to preach a policy of tightening the belt.

Data from sociological studies of Gomulka's Poland clearly show the blue-collar workers to be discontented not only with their modest material circumstances but also with the chaos prevailing in places of employment. It was not until the long-lasting top-level struggles between various groups interested in succeeding Gomulka had ripened that such a phenomenon as the big strikes in December 1970 became possible.

Ewa Wacowska is not right in claiming that "the relevant causes of the contemporary Polish proletariat's class loneliness are their lack of organization, their objectively low cultural level, their dearth of broader social aspirations and their passivity" (1972, p. 166). First of all, it is difficult even to speak of a class in the Marxist sense of the word when the fundamental raison d'être of a regime is to bar the masses from independent self-organization, from establishing their own associations and institutions, and from exerting group pressure on the ruling elite. The social aspirations of the workers are expressed above all in a concerted effort to raise their children to a higher level. Activity is manifested in attempts to achieve at least some semblance of stabilization. In his article "The Flood" (Zycie Warszawy, no. 133, 4-5 June 1972), Wieslaw Gornicki is dismayed with the typical disgust of a member of the elite at how the Polish masses were buying everything they possibly could in East Germany after the opening of the border. A trip to East Germany is one of the few chances for concrete initiative accessible to the lower Polish classes.

Although it existed before World War II, there is no longer a barrier between the working classes and other social groups. Sociological data show that all these groups have become significantly intermingled. Much of the contemporary intelligentsia has recent blue-collar worker or peasant origins. This is particularly true in the clerical occupations, technicians and engineers, paramedical personnel, and the military. The distance between workers and other groups has become far smaller than before World War II. A very significant segment of peasant village residents are actually workers.

The unspoken agreement between the man in the street and the government boils down to the former not expressing himself on political matters to the first person who comes along (especially not to Polish journalists) and the government, in turn, leaving him in peace. Wherever and whenever this unspoken agreement has been temporarily suspended (Poznan 1956, the Baltic coast 1970), the Polish proletariat has immediately begun to say very concrete things about matters of true import to it.

For the intelligentsia youth, political freedom was and is a primary need, whereas for the blue-collar workers it is only a secondary need. When the latter are trying to gain an advantage that is of primary importance to them, they do not want to, and cannot, begin by striving for something that will immediately prejudice the authorities against them.

To Polish blue-collar workers and farmers, especially, informal family ties are of enormous importance. Many workers' families have relatives and friends widely scattered throughout the bureaucracy, Party, and police and military apparatus of the Polish People's Republic. These influential friends can be very helpful, but only on the condition that they do not jeopardize their own position by supporting somebody who is politically dangerous, who talks too much or unthinkingly criticizes the people's authority.

The supposed "political apathy" of the blue-collar workers is thus primarily an element of the game for survival, for ameliorating one's standard of living, and for guaranteeing one's children a better future; they are simply careful not to destroy any advantageous contacts of an informal nature. Also, the blue-collar workers' families are as a rule so occupied with their work and their worries over everyday survival (this applies in particular to families that cultivate a small plot of land apart from their regular employment) that they have no time and energy left for reading and thinking. As in the West, television frees people from cultural self-initiative.

It would be a great mistake not to appreciate what Polish blue-collar workers have gained in People's Poland, though these gains are due not so much to the Communist political system as to the intensive industrialization of the country. The main difference between the younger and older generations of blue-collar workers is that the former value these achievements less and less, taking them for granted and desiring more. Thus it will be continually more difficult for the government to retain good relationships with the blue-collar workers without deciding on very basic reforms.

Whenever reforms were made, even such modest and illusory one as the introduction of "workers' councils" in 1956, this by no means led to bitter conflict between the workers and other classes. Rather, a common front of the entire personnel of a given workplace was formed against the top level bureaucracy. This formation of front so dismayed the ruling elite that it tried to incite the workers against the intelligentsia. For example, "specialists" in workers' self-management, brought in by the Party, tried to convince the blue-collar workers that the intelligentsia was taking over control of the workers' councils. In reality, however, the true function of the "workers' councils" was to improve the economics of industries. The blue-collar workers trustingly chose engineers and economists as their representatives in the "workers' council" because they were best suited to deal with matters of an economic and administrative nature than were professionals of the intelligentsia. The important role of the intelligentsia in these councils was such a threat to the Party that formal restrictions of the number of white-collar workers in the composition of the councils were introduced (Matejko 1973c).

6

FROM LOWER STRATA TO
THE MANAGERIAL ESTABLISHMENT

Immediately after World War II the Party was eager to have specialists from the traditional intelligentsia in executive positions, because they were badly needed for the reconstruction of the economy and administration. However, from the very start in 1945 there was a tendency to upgrade people from lower social strata to higher positions. Being dependent upon the establishment for everything they had achieved, upgraded people were much more loyal and politically reliable than the intelligentsia. During the period 1949-55 the tendency to upgrade became the rule even though it led to a general decline of qualifications. In a sample of 40 enterprises studied by Halina Najduchowska (1969b), the percentage of executives with higher technical education fell from 50 to less than 33 during 1948-1949.

The doctrinaire Marxist approach to economic matters was introduced in Poland on a major scale at the end of the 1940s and the new kind of executives started their careers. They were promoted not on the basis of their professional qualifications but on their unreserved committment to the Party. Most of the well-known Polish economists were shocked at what was happening to the economy. "Do not believe that socialism is so far removed from common sense as you appear to think", Edward Lipinski argued then, but nobody listened to him (Gella 1970, p. 196). The whole array of newly appointed executives blindly followed orders coming from the Party headquarters, and thus secured their future careers.

It was during those years that executives became the equivalent of apparatchiks. The Party established an institutionalized register, called the nomenclature, of reliable people chosen to fill all executive positions throughout the country. It became common practice to move these people from one executive slot to another, according to the changing plans and whims of top Party officials. Executives included in the nomenclature enjoyed relative security, in the sense that it was unusual to fire them. As long as they were politically reliable and committed to the current Party line, they could be sure of some kind of executive position.

This practice was discontinued to some extent in 1956; but the process, once started, was not reversible under the existing political conditions. The establishment was vitally interested in promoting people who would be totally reliable. At the same time, people from lower strata who were advancing educationally and socially searched for better positions for themselves, their friends, and their relatives.

According to data on 1,541 executives in 1965, only 20 percent were from the white-collar stratum (Najduchowska 1969a). This was much less than in most of the Western countries. "Approximately 60 percent of the samples of the business elite in Britain, the Netherlands, Sweden and the United States have businessmen as fathers" (Lipset and Bendix 1967, p. 40). Only about 50 percent of Polish executives who came from lower social strata had any higher education; quite a number were transferred from the ranks of apparatchiks in the Party, army, or secret police.

As in other Communist countries, with the progress toward higher levels of industrialization in Poland, there has been more and more emphasis on formal qualifications.

> With the emergent emphasis on industrial efficiency the
> tendency has been to appoint men to positions of authority
> and responsibility more on the basis of their formal qual-
> ifications than simply as a reward for political loyalty.
> The combination of a Party card and higher qualifications
> would appear to be the best guarantee of social advance-
> ment, and possession of the former is coming to rely
> more and more on prior posession of the latter. The new
> men who have flocked to join the Party do so to cultivate
> their careers, and only rarely out of ideological con-
> viction (Parkin 1969).

The 1965 survey of 1,541 industrial executives (manufacturing, light industry, chemistry, mining, power, foodstuffs) showed that the most common practice was to recruit them from the ranks of technical personnel. Some 60 percent were originally from the workers' class (Najduchowska 1969a, p. 195). About 66 percent had a technical education and about 16 percent had an economic education. This means that most of those executives were trained in technical disciplines (39 percent were graduates and 18 percent had secondary vocational education) and only a very few had some background in the humanities. According to data from 1964, engineers constituted

33 percent of all graduates employed in the nationalized Polish economy (the same was true in 1970/71). However, there was still a need for graduate engineers, because 20 percent of the positions that should have been occupied by them were held by people with lower qualifications.

Technical competence counts most as a criterion for appointment to executive positions—in addition, of course, to political competence. Leon Smolinski is quite right in saying:

> While Polish economists have made major contributions
> to the theory of economic planning and development, their
> influence on the actual practice of economic planning and
> management in Poland has remained rather limited. In
> practice, economic decisions were often left to engineers
> and technicians who ignored economic optimality criteria
> and profitability (1971, p. 25).

For engineers, being upgraded to managerial positions almost always results in the neglect of professional qualifications. Instead of pursuing what they learned in technical colleges, engineers commit themselves entirely to administrative tasks for which they were never professionally trained (Pasieczny 1968). This is the main reason why promotion to managerial ranks is not particularly attractive to engineers. Of 215 of them surveyed by Anna Grzelak (1965), only 10 percent said they would choose a job that would open the way to managerial promotion, while 71 percent expressed a preference for technically interesting jobs. On the other hand, 28 percent were interested in production as a career. This is closely related to the type of professional training given at technical universities. A study of adaptation of young engineers to their first job, done in 1960 by the author, shows that most of them were not prepared to assume any managerial responsibilities (Matejko 1962).

There is an antimanagement bias among young engineers, in the sense that they equate management with bureaucracy in the worst sense of the word. They prefer to move into design and construction offices even if it entails a drop in salary (Kolankiewicz 1973, p. 215). But the Party is becoming more and more aware that management positions must be occupied by people with specific qualifications and not by mere political appointees.

> Studies of enterprise directors in Poland have indicated a
> growth in their prestige during the 1960s. This growth is
> attributed partly to the rising qualifications of directors
> and partly to a wider recognition of the skills required in
> industrial management (Kolankiewicz 1973, p. 226).

There is still not enough realistic information reaching the policy-makers. There is also a dichotomy between commitment to the Party and to one's profession.

EXPOSURE TO CONTRADICTORY PRESSURES

As a distinct social category within the society, executives are exposed to the sociocultural trends and influences that dominate the national scene. It seems fully justified to say that at the moment Poland is culturally dominated by the intelligentsia more than before World War II. Even now, though almost totally incorporated into the political establishment, executives are still under the pressure of intellectual values. Political leaders, including executives, "are to some degree interpenetrated by traditional intellectuals, but the latter have rather limited influence on political decisions" (Szczepanski 1962, p. 419).

Although isolated from the rest of the population, executives are still exposed to informal pressures and influences. The values and norms of the intelligentsia play the main role in this respect: traditions of intellectual sincerity and tolerance, genuine political and cultural interests, strong emphasis on honor—as well as pretentiousness, no sense of reality, distaste for working merely in order to earn money, and no appreciation for business and calculation.

Under the bureaucratic model of communism, executives have not had real opportunity to develop their own ethics and their own sociocultural identity. It is significant that in the last few years the Soviet Union has tended to treat management as a separate problem, and not just as one of the issues of Party functioning. The necessity to appreciate the sociological and psychological aspects of management was emphasized by D. M. Gwiszani (1966), and since then it became politically acceptable to deal with them.

Because of the progressive ritualization and formalization of the official ideology in Poland, there has not been any real commitment to it. Under the pressure of the ruling Party elite, suspicious of any potential rivalry, there has been no opportunity for independent social forces and institutions to develop their own sociocultural patterns. The Catholic Church, the most dangerous rival, has always been kept far from the power structure in which executives are located.

However, in promoting education, art and culture, science, and mass media, the ruling Party had to accept the services of the intelligentsia and was unable to redirect the new members of the intelligentsia from workers' and peasants' ranks. In their leisure time executives have to follow the existing patterns, which were originated by the intelligentsia. The social gatherings they arrange are attended by members of the intelligentsia. Children of executives often choose careers that follow the ideals and values of the intelligentsia. In order to impress their friends and acquaintances, executives have to pay at least some lip service to typical values of the intelligentsia. Subject to the constant pressure of two opposite patterns—the orthodox pattern of Party dogmatism and the liberal pattern of intellectual tolerance—executives develop tactics based on evasion, procrastination, and even nihilism in order to survive and succeed.

There is a growing role ambiquity of Polish executives in industry and public administration. Their future behavior depends very much on their ability to find an adequate place between the ruling Party elite and the rest of the population, especially blue-collar workers and the intelligentsia. The Party elite hold all power, but the intelligentsia dominates the intellectual and spiritual life of the country. Executives are in between. They are treated by the Party elite as apparatchiks and are evaluated according to their political loyalty, successful attainment of Party goals, and general contribution to the Party. However, at the same time executives are to a growing extent professionals, mostly engineers and technicians. As professionals they share status incongruence with the intelligentsia. As people with growing social and cultural ambitions, they seek acceptance by the people with whom they socialize: engineers, medical doctors, scientists, journalists. Being responsible for the enterprises they manage, executives are becoming more and more aware that the whole system badly needs substantial reforms.

The executive has several good reasons to be suspicious of intellectuals. First of all, unlike intellectuals, he avoids the various utopias that, according to L. S. Feuer, "illuminate the unconscious stirrings and direction of the intellectuals" (1964, p. 88). Second, he does not share the doubts and frustrations of the intellectuals. Third, he suspects them of superiority complexes and, to some extent, of authoritarianism. Fourth, it is very difficult for him to appreciate a way of thinking that does not culminate in action. Fifth, his sense of reality prevents him from becoming too involved in abstract concepts.

However, the main obstacle built into the role of executives in Poland is related more to the low intellectual level of the ruling elite than to conflicts with intellectuals. Before World War II, the Communist Party in Poland was insignificant and not sufficiently influential to attract well-educated people (Polonsky 1972). The Party was illegal in Poland, and the few committed intellectuals fled to the Soviet Union, where almost all of them became victims of the great purge arranged by Stalin, who was especially suspicious of Polish Communists. Those who formed the new elite that took power under Soviet guidance in 1944-45 consisted mostly of either low-rank local agitators and leaders or new careerists who were seeking personal gains. In both cases the level of education and sophistication was very low. Even more important, these people developed a vested interest that discouraged significant change later. "In a party apparatus composed of some 7,000 officials, in 1964 only 1,275 and even by 1968 only around 2,000 had completed their higher education" (Bromke 1971, p. 486).

THE SOCIOPOLITICAL MODEL OF THE FACTORY

According to the Soviet model, as applied to Polish industry, the individual factory is a basic unit of collective production. Its purpose consists in fulfilling the tasks prescribed by the national plan. Its basic motivation is assumed to be rooted in the common will of working people organized by the Party and by the state authorities. According to the Party ideology, broader social interests should always prevail over particular interests. All occupants of responsible posts are expected to represent and to defend, if necessary, the broader interests. By contributing to the national and international welfare, the collective of the factory should fulfill its basic social obligation: to serve the Communist polity. For the individual the meaning of his life is to repay the social debt that he owes to the Party and to the state.

There is no place within this formal model for egoism and conflicts of interests. All people are expected to follow the same line in order to establish a politically oriented sociomoral unity. Everybody is expected to manifest his moral involvement. If one merely submits to the coercion (alienative involvement) or looks for benefits (calculative involvement), then one is considered unreliable.

It is not sufficient for executives, as well as for factory manual workers and employees, to do no more than blindly follow the orders of higher authorities. Nobody is free from error, and therefore everybody should be on his guard to see whether conditions of maximum efficiency are being attained. By exhibiting initiative, all organizational bodies must control one another and prevent waste. All sorts of problems supposedly can be corrected by the initiative of the masses. The same applies to the social obligation of all citizens to expose and condemn the wrongdoing of class enemies.

All resources and all types of basic data are kept under the central control of top authorities who steer the whole system. The factories are supplied with resources according to the priority of their tasks. Quantitatively and qualitatively better work should make it possible, according to the formal model, to save resources and thus to contribute to common well-being.

The principle of secrecy that permeates the economy makes it difficult for an executive to predict what kind of expectations he may have to satisfy in the future. By being well informed he may be able to prepare for future situations, and thus data dealing with the bureaucratic apparatus are in great demand by executives. For people in executive positions it has become more profitable to keep an eye on all such data rather than to concentrate on the fulfillment of tasks, because in a new bureaucratic configuration, present tasks may lose their importance and a commitment to them would prove troublesome.

Technological progress is considered to be one of the basic aspects of development, and the state invests large sums of money and tremendous effort to promote it. However, with a low level of wages and salaries there is not enough economic incentive for enterprises to replace people with machines. Furthermore, the bureaucratic structure puts much more emphasis on security than on technological progress. It is often much more profitable for factory management to follow proven traditional methods than to risk innovations (Feiwel 1971a, p. 76)—except, of course, in showcase projects, where the state creates specially favorable conditions for the particular factory. In most other cases the risk taken by management and by the crew in introducing technological innovations is too high and the potential rewards too small. By playing it safe, managers may be accused by the Party of conservatism but they do not risk their jobs or their security.

With the constantly growing educational and cultural standards of the labor force, there is also a growing demand for improvement in the supply of modern tools and machines. According to surveys, inadequate work organization is a primary source of employment dissatisfaction. The development of the technical basis is much slower than that of technical aspirations among the young generation.

The Party is vitally interested in effectively controlling all important positions in enterprises, particularly the managerial positions. According to data from 1960, 75 percent of all industrial enterprises in Poland had Party memberships ranging from 9 to 21 percent (with an average of 13-17 percent). Manual workers in the industrial, transport, and building sectors constituted 66 percent of memberships. However, there is a positive correlation between the power of a position within the hierarchy and Party membership. People who occupy leading positions are vitally interested in securing their authority by becoming members of the Party. As for the remaining positions, "the Party membership is relatively highest among foremen, followed by office staff, with engineers and technicians in the third place, and skilled and unskilled workers in fourth and fifth place respectively" (Bauman 1962, pp. 53-54). It is quite obvious that the strongest appeal of the Party is to people who want to overcome their status incongruence by overt Party militancy. According to research data, approximately 12.5 percent of all Party members are activists (they constitute 2 percent of all factory employees); half of them are engineers, technicians, office workers, and foremen—people who have to justify by activism their relatively privileged position. The same applies to education: "The Party militants in the production enterprise are recruited mainly from the more highly educated members of the factory personnel" (Bauman 1962, p. 60).

Party membership has literally become a necessity for people in managerial positions. How much power would an executive not belonging to the Party have? How would he be able to bargain with higher authorities, struggle for both private and collective favors, or defend his subordinates against external pressures and inconveniences? The Party membership card provides some security for anybody who is committed to power and who wants to exercise it actively. In a few cases people who do not belong to the Party have managed to survive in top positions because of their superior capabilities. However, even they have to secure basic acceptance by the Party. Sometimes they are propaganda examples that the Party card supposedly is not the only criterion of promotion.

THE TRUE MANAGERIAL SITUATION

Under the Soviet type of economic centralization, managers have an obvious desire for easy plans; they search for organizational slack, bargain for easier conditions of plan fulfillment, adjust utilization norms downward, distort data in their reports to higher authorities, overstate resource and manpower requirements, hoard materials, and distort costs and prices (Richman 1965, pp. 150-78). Executives remain almost entirely within the framework of a rigid bureaucracy, and so far there is little hope of their becoming a real enterpreneurial class with strong achievement motivation (Feiwel 1965; Kolaja 1960; Rosner 1957; Rawin 1965). Unfortunately, managerial passivity, authoritarianism, neglect of human-relations skill, and orientation toward security more than toward goal achievement place Eastern Europe in some respects closer to developing countries (Neghandi and Prasad 1971) than to the capitalist developed countries. The problem lies not so much in a lack of local managerial talent as in the inherent weakness of a sociopolitical system that places a premium on organizational conservatism. In this respect Poland shares the fate of all the societies presently within the Soviet bloc (Brzezinski 1970, pp. 123-94; Bauman 1971a, pp. 45-53). According to this type of economic model, the command originates in the Central Committee of the Party, goes down to the ministries, then to the industrial corporations (which are responsible for particular groups of enterprises), and finally to an individual enterprise. The communication upward is cumbersome and highly ineffective because all administrative levels above the enterprise select and even distort information data according to their own vested interests.

Corporations (associations) are under strong pressure from both sides: ministries and central Party authorities, on the one hand, and enterprises, on the other. At the top there is a tendency to treat the corporations' staffs as mere objects of manipulation. At the bottom there are constant attempts to bargain for benefits and privileges. Under such conditions it is very difficult for people in corporations to establish their own authority and to play an active role as middlemen. It seems easier to limit one's own responsibility to a simple transfer of orders down the hierarchy. The legal system of managing enterprises is so rigid that executives quite often have to rely on informal or even illegal means to carry out their formal tasks. Petty bribery, exchanges of services, dependence more on private connections and informal agreements than on formal channels, and mutual loyalty in making illegal arrangements have all become very common (Feiwel 1965; Richman 1965; Kurczewski and Frieske 1973). Within the organizational infrastructure there is plenty of room for unfair practices and mutual exploitation, and the public interest is often entirely neglected.

Production plans are drawn up on the basis of bargaining between the enterprise and higher levels of supervision that have their own vested interest in extending their scope of control.

> Since 1965, the stress has been on the association [corporation] as the basic planning, managing, and coordinating unit. There also was mention of the necessity of ensuring enterprises' conditions for "flexible activity," but in the main the identification of such conditions was left to be decided by the associations. Thus, the association (within the limits of its own autonomy) could determine the degree of independence of the enterprise (Feiwel 1971b, p. 23).

For executives the only solution is to strengthen their own bargaining power versus the higher authorities by not revealing actual resources. Managers hoard stock because the supply is quite often erratic, and generally unreliable.

> Inventory accumulation in Poland (as in the Soviet Union) is well above Western standards. Stocks of raw materials, semifinished and finished products (not counting

those held by [the] private sector and in strategic stock
piles) are about one-half of the (marxian) "national
income" (Brzeski 1967, p. 189).

Occasional reforms undertaken by the political establishment
in Poland are oriented toward stimulating management to make better
use of available resources. However, all these reforms have so far
not involved the crucial issue of autonomy and freedom of decision
on the local executive level.

The specific task premium system inherently contains
the seeds of self-destruction. Its very flexibility in the
hands of the central planner and those of associations
[corporations] could lead to depriving it of a consistent
incentive effect (Feiwel 1971b, p. 251).

Several factors constantly aggravate the current situation at
the managerial level. The structure of foreign trade does not encourage enough contacts with markets outside the Soviet bloc. Cooperation between various enterprises does not work satisfactorily.
Employees who are continually progressing in terms of education,
cultural sophistication, and equality need more consideration. The
traditional toughness of apparatchiks is meeting, to a growing extent,
not only with effective resistance but even ridicule and open contempt.
While becoming a fully industrialized country, Poland is, like Czechoslovakia, providing ample evidence that the authoritarian model of
Soviet Communism is not only immoral but also inefficient. In conditions of full employment and with a growing problem of young people
who cannot find enough attractive jobs, it does not make much sense
to leave a large portion of production facilities for 67 percent of the
time (see Table 6.1). The efforts of the higher authorities to convince the enterprises that they should employ more people on the
afternoon and night shifts have so far not been successful enough.
The second and the third shifts are not adequately utilized. Of
the total working time of Polish industrial wage earners employed
directly in production in 1972, 65 percent was spent on the morning
shift, 25 percent on the afternoon shift, and only 10 on the third
nightly shift. Only in a few industries (coal, ferrous and nonferrous
metallurgy, textiles) was a little more than half of the working time
spent on the second and third shifts. It would be possible to hire
more people without greatly increasing costs, but the rigid bureaucratic setup is extremely slow both with its own innovations and in
giving the green light to rank-and-file initiatives.
Most Polish enterprises are small enough to allow the achievement of meaningful social cohesion. The crystallization of autonomous

TABLE 6.1

Distribution of Industrial Blue-Collar Workers in
Czechoslovakia, East Germany, and Poland on
Various Shifts, 1970
(percentage)

	Morning Shift	Afternoon Shift	Night Shift
Czechoslovakia	74	20	6
G.D.R.	75	16	9
Poland	62	27	11

Sources: Statisticka 1971, p. 255.; Rocznik 1972, p. 187; Statistisches Jahrbuch 1972, p. 140.

and self-governing work communities would stimulate loyalty, stability of employment, better utilization of work time, and the development of a collective entrepreneurship. In their current form the trade unions are not able to do anything meaningful in this respect.

The main issue is still what sort of new organizational structures to introduce in order to bring all working people closer to the urgent economic goals.

It is a real problem of the socialist economy to motivate staff and management to formulate and achieve realistic social needs for their enterprise. The experience of years has proved that this can be achieved neither by directives nor by intensifying central control. If "self-control" or an automatic interior mechanism, which continually corrects any deviations from the "balance" with "social" does not act, then no outside control can do it (Lipinski 1968, p. 293).

Trade unions are expected by the Party to mobilize workers and employees for the fulfillment of production quotas, to organize cultural and social activities, and to administer recreation centers and sports. Trade unions embrace 95 percent of all workers and employees, but they are unable to defend the vital interests of their membership.

In their majority [trade union authorities] have taken,
with respect to the state administration, the position of
a client instead of a partner . . . . On the other hand, the
bureaucratic leadership of trade unions has eliminated
democratic principles from daily practice. Subservient
and loyalistic functionaries have been much better accepted
than energetic, critical and courageous people (Kucharski
1971, p. 4).

Among chairmen of local trade union committees located at
workplaces, until recently only 11 percent were less than 30 years
old; among members of executive committees of individual unions,
only 0.6 percent; and among chairmen of regional trade union boards,
only one person. (Urban 1971).
A survey taken in 1966 and 1967 in seven industrial enterprises
showed that blue-collar workers joining socialist work competitions,
sponsored officially by the Party, expect from them such practical
outcomes as higher work output (59 percent of all surveyed workers),
better wages (51 percent), bonuses (37 percent), and improvement
of qualifications (22 percent). In reality, however, workers become
disillusioned with what is actually offered to them. They quite often
view officially sponsored competition as just one more of the managerial devices that are beyond their control. Most of the surveyed
workers expressed deep distrust of the way management and local
Party authorities distribute rewards (Nicki 1969, pp. 203-24).

THE DIALECTICS OF MANAGING ENTERPRISES

Industrial executives, as people having administrative and
managerial authority, play such an important role in all more or
less developed societies that it seems quite obvious why they have
become an object of special interest for sociologists. There is a
growing need for cross-cultural comparative studies of management
in various countries (Haire et al. 1966; Webber 1969; Harbison and
Myers 1959; Negandhi and Prasad 1971) Unfortunately, we do not
yet know enough about the dynamic aspects of managerial roles.
Problems of management should be approached not only in terms of
its basic functions and structures but also in terms of conflicts, the
solving of which constitutes the daily activity of any manager.
There are everywhere dialectic contradictions common to the
processes of managing people and institutions. On the one hand, the
manager is responsible for integrating his own organizational unit
into the broader institutional context; but on the other hand, it would
be dangerous for him to neglect his own autonomy. Subordinates have

to be incorporated into a cohesive team, but the danger of conformity should be avoided. Order has to be maintained, but it must not lead to lack of internal competition and mutual inspiration. Stability is very welcome, but not to the degree of preventing substantial growth. Effectiveness of management necessitates some unity of command, but decentralization of power also has great advantages. The success of a manager depends upon solving all these contradictory demands in his daily work of stimulating subordinates and coordinating their activities.

It is precisely this agglomeration of contradictions that makes management particularly difficult. Under the Soviet type of communism, loyalty to the Party and organizational efficiency do not go easily together.

> The effort to guarantee both efficiency and loyalty produces ambivalent and contradictory organizational pressures. The drive for efficiency leads to emphasis on one-man management and reinforcement of the authority and prerequisites of the managerial class. The anxiety about loyalty induces strenuous efforts to assimilate the technical and managerial intelligentsia into the Party and involves reliance on Party and police controls to hold the power of the managerial elite in check (Fainsod 1963, pp. 503-04).

Checks and restraints imposed upon executives in the Soviet-style system make their position particularly difficult, and role ambivalence and role strains become notably evident. Therefore, organizational theory may benefit substantially from an analysis of these problems as they appear in Communist societies. In Poland the Communist system, as well as certain local sociocultural traditions and patterns, are of particular importance in this respect.

In general the Communist system in Poland has preserved the bureaucratic model taken over from the state capitalism that was quite influential in that country before World War II. There have been some corrections, but they are of secondary importance. The only basic difference consists in elevating the Party structure above the bureaucratic structure. The Party pushes for progress and assigns difficult tasks. The bureaucratic structure puts a premium on security and stability. Within the bureaucracy it is easier to do little and to risk nothing than to do much and run the risk that something will happen that deviates from the existing set of regulations. In order to create some show effects and to secure their own positions, bureaucrats constantly contrive regulations. Instead of taking risks by making administrative decisions, they hide behind the veil of regulations, even if these regulations do not help to fulfill the given tasks. As a result, in order to achieve anything, it is necessary either to look for indirect ways of dealing with matters or to transgress the existing legal order and rely on power. To achieve its goals the Party is forced to constantly imbalance the bureaucratic status quo by applying its power directly. The law is only for the weak and underprivileged, who do not have direct access to power centers. There is nothing basically cynical about this situation, because the Party supports only actions that seem beneficial to the Party goals. It is up to petitioners to ably and cleverly present their proposals so that they seem to be to the advantage of the Party (Feiwel 1965).

The behavior of an executive is greatly influenced by the contradictory expectations of his superiors. On the one hand, they expect him to cooperate closely with all kinds of institutionalized bodies: the local Party organization, the local trade union committee, the workers' council. On the other, he is not allowed to share his responsibility, and his decisions are to be of an authoritarian nature. If anything goes wrong, only he is held responsible. As a result, most executives develop a specific style of management based on a contradiction between collective and authoritarian approaches (Kiezun 1969). The typical executive attends numerous meetings and continually consults with his political and professional partners, but the real purpose of all these activities consists primarily in manipulating those concerned according to the executive's own will and interests. He knows what the higher authorities expect him to do, but it would not be to his advantage to reveal this information. While pretending to consult with his collaborators, he imposes his own goals upon them. Moreover, consultation provides a means by which to share at least part of the responsibility with them. Should trouble arise, it is extremely helpful to be able to reveal that the wrong view was shared by a larger number of people. Being under common accusation, the collaborators would then have to support the executive in order to protect themselves.

In the highly centralized Soviet-type economy, executives have to develop the peculiar ability of bargaining without bringing the real issue into the open. With respect to central authorities there is the problem of obtaining "the smallest possible target of production for the largest possible allocation of manpower, raw materials, and investment funds" (Swaniewicz 1968, p. 472). When dealing with his employees the executive is faced with the problem of satisfying their growing expectations with the scarce resources available, so that distribution of them will secure maximum subordination and commitment. In relation to other executives and their enterprises, the executive must try to obtain cooperation even if they do not have any particular interest in the quotas imposed by the central plan (Berliner 1957; Granick 1950).

129

In order to achieve his goals and to appear successful, the executive has to rely on clever manipulation; for example, the workers' councils in Poland arose at least to some extent out of the inability of executives to bargain effectively with their superiors in corporations, ministries, and Party bodies. Appointed by the higher levels of the state and Party bureaucracy, the executive was very limited in his opportunities to trying to acquire more favorable conditions for his enterprise. By establishing workers' councils it was possible to exert pressure on the higher authorities without exposing the executive and the local Party secretary to repression. Representatives elected to a workers' council are not directly dependent on the authorities above the enterprise and are, therefore, able to show some courage and initiative in defending the vital interests of their enterprise. Chairmen of workers' councils are members of advisory committees at the higher administrative level and thus can be quite helpful to executives in the struggle for a better position of the enterprise versus the central authorities (Morawski 1969, pp. 249-52).

Executives and leaders of workers' councils are vitally interested in cooperatively opposing higher echelons of the bureaucracy. It therefore is necessary to look on workers' councils more as local pressure groups designed to strengthen the position of executives than as actual self-government of workers. It is significant in this respect that, in public opinion polls conducted in 1961, blue-collar workers whose interests were being represented by workers' councils answered in many cases (41 percent of the respondents in electronics and 47 percent in manufacturing) that these councils were in fact representative of the interests of executives. Only 8 percent of the respondents in electronics and 5 percent in manufacturing felt that workers' councils really represented the interests of the manual working class (Wesolowski 1962).

Among the primary causes of waste in Polish factories are projects that appear to contribute to the social welfare but in fact serve individual or group interests. For example, the Party supports inventiveness among blue-collar workers and inventors receive special bonuses, but at the same time factories have their own development engineers who are expected to improve production and are paid for it. It is advantageous for engineers to make secret agreements with blue-collar workers to present their own projects in the name of the latter and then to divide the reward, since the bonus for blue-collar inventors is much higher than for engineers who are merely doing what they are paid to do. Another common occurrence is collaboration between inventors and bureaucrats. The latter share in a bonus because it may be the only way for an inventor to have his original project approved. By sharing the reward with a bureaucrat he considerably diminishes his own gain, but by proceeding otherwise he would not be able to gain acceptance for his project.

Informal relations provide the only solution in a situation marked by inconsistency between the strong pressure of the Party to produce and the strong resistance of the bureaucracy to innovation. The Party does not want to give up bureaucracy and thus allow the existing "law and order" to collapse, for the monopolistic position of the Party is buttressed by the bureaucratic order. However, the Party does not want to forgo its ambitions of fast economic and social growth. Even though the bureaucratic machine is usually able to produce some show effects that may satisfy the Party bureaucrats, international competition is always a factor and the Party cannot, therefore, accept any manifest slowing of progress. In such a situation the extensive development of informal relationships, sometimes accepted by the Party and at other times condemned or even persecuted, has become the only solution.

THE NATURE OF EXECUTIVE WORK

In general, executives work from 10 to 12 or even 14 hours per day, sometimes even longer (especially industrial executives), which means two or more hours longer than regular office hours. Their daily effort is split into many activities, often 60 or more, that do not balance one another (S. Kowalewski 1967, pp. 28, 31). Most of their activities are very short (7 to 10 minutes) and do not allow them to focus their attention. Executives are busy with details of administering their units and of preventing the organizational order from collapsing. The manager who does not spend all his time and effort on current issues almost unavoidably exposes himself to the accusation of being lazy and negligent. The only way of avoiding suspicion is to spend as much time as possible in the office, at the expense of family and private life.

Subordinates expect their supervisor to take as much formal responsibility as possible. Because of the low salaries, executives are not able to gain substantially by taking risks; and the heavy responsibility put on them discourages any initiative and puts a premium on playing safe. This leads to a situation in which the executive has to spend most of his time controlling his subordinates, to whom he is not able to pass full responsibility (and who are not interested in it), and being in contact with various political or bureaucratic authorities.

Under the constant pressure of deciding on issues forced upon him either by subordinates or by superiors, the executive has little opportunity to prepare and to conduct actions originating with him. Instead of steering the enterprise, he is constantly acted upon by events. People below him avoid taking responsibility, and therefore they overburden the executive with petty issues that he cannot brush off because he is personally responsible to political authorities for all shortcomings, even minor ones. By manifesting intensive activity, he constructs a defense against possible accusations of negligence or laziness.

A study of local bank executives conducted in 1964 and 1967 by Witold Kiezun shows a marked bureaucratic rigidity in decision-making. Executives are personally responsible for the fulfillment of many detailed directives that perpetually flow from higher levels of the centralized authority, but they do not have the time or resources to do so. The only reasonable solution is to pay lip service to most of the directives, follow some of them, and construct effective defense mechanisms to excuse the neglect of others (Kiezun 1968; 1968-69; 1969).

Executives are so busy with the bureaucratic aspects of their work that they do not have much time left for the social. According to a time-budget study conducted in 1958-60, executives in some industries spent only 4 percent of their time in dealing with the problems of employees. And yet, according to research data, executives spend from 33 to 66 percent of their time at conferences, with only a small part of their work time devoted to effective work in their own offices (Rupinski and Taubwurcel 1961, pp. 65-69). Much effort is dissipated on meeting various people, more than 40 per day. For conceptual work there is less than an hour per day, and for studying only a few minutes.

Data on span of control show that there is a common tendency to narrow this span to only a few people, especially in the state administration. Of the supervisors surveyed by Jan Dzida, 80 percent agreed that the multiplication of organizational units offers a good excuse for paying more to the people who supervise those units (Dzida 1969, pp. 220-21).

The prestige of office personnel in Poland is so low (Sarapata, ed. 1965a, p. 200) and there is such a marked tendency for people to move from the state administration to other kinds of institutions, that in order to retain them, it is necessary to artificially upgrade their salaries by creating new supervisory positions. It is quite common for good typists or secretaries to be retained by putting them in charge of more or less fictitious organizational units. In 22 regional offices of the state administration (voievodship people's councils), 84 percent of 415 supervisors studied formally had from 2 to 8 direct subordinates, but 37 percent cooperated with 9 to 30 subordinates who remained under their real control. On the other hand, 48 percent of all supervisors believed that their potential span of control was from 9 to 30 subordinates (the remaining 52 percent evaluated their potential span of control as from 2 to 8 subordinates) (Dzida 1969).

Being under the pressure of the Party and state bosses, the executive has to be quite tough in dealing with his subordinates. However, in order to succeed he needs their cooperation, and thus it is not to his advantage to discourage them. On lower managerial levels there is a widespread understanding that subordinates should be consulted. Eighty percent of the foremen surveyed in one of the Polish industrial enterprises in 1966 were in favor of offering workers the right of consultation in decisionmaking on a local level. There is also a common feeling that the current system of rewards puts too much emphasis on the quantity rather than on the quality of work and that subordinates therefore have little incentive to become concretely involved in management; they are too busy earning money, working rapidly and thereby neglecting all other commitments. A study conducted by Krystyna Bursche and Anna Grzelak in a Warsaw industrial plant shows that reward of good work was less pronounced than penalization of bad work, which naturally led to manifest dissatisfaction among workers (Bursche and Grzelak 1969, pp. 147-73).

EXECUTIVES VERSUS INTELLECTUALS
AND POLITICIANS

According to the official view, also shared by at least some Polish sociologists, "the relationship to the means of production is the same for all citizens. And if there appear differences in income, nature of work, prestige, opportunities and political attitudes, these are not determined by this relationship" (Wesolowski 1969a, p. 127). It seems impossible to agree with this. There is no justification for assuming the basic equality of all citizens versus the means of production as long as there are basic power inequalities. Official apologists of the system tend to miss the basic distinction between the formal status of citizens and their real power. Even though a minister or an executive may have lower social prestige in Poland than a teacher or a university professor, it does not mean that he is less powerful. In circumstances of a very high degree of power concentrations it seems quite naive to persist in maintaining that in socialist society there is only one criterion that determines the share of the individual in the social product: the quantity and quality of the work accomplished (Wesolowski 1969a, p. 134).

Power has become this sole criterion. Wlodzimierz Wesolowski admits that, for example, political directors as a group responsible for elaboration of the whole wage system may seem to be in a position that opposes the interests of other groups (Wesolowski 1969a, p. 140). However, following his assumption about the decomposition of the attributes of status in a socialist society, he entirely ignores the existence of even the most fundamental inequalities based on political and administrative power. Jan Szczepanski expresses the same view:

> The multidimensional character of the stratification should be emphasized. . . . The multidimensional strati- fication will persist for a long time (1970, pp. 144, 145).

It should be emphasized that even such orthodox Marxist eco- nomists as Bronislaw Minc are beginning to be more aware of con- flicting interests related to the unequal distribution of power. "Busi- ness executives and top decision makers share some common inter- ests which are based on fulfilling managerial functions. However, there are also some conflicting interests between these two groups" (Minc, 1967, pp. 20, 21). According to Minc, the reconciliation of these differing interests is of crucial importance for the functioning of the economy. Several leading Polish economists, such as Edward Lipinski, have argued strongly for paying more consideration to the necessity of freedom of initiative on the enterprise level. They expect a considerable improvement of the socialist economy from limiting the power of top Party and state bureaucrats in relation to the business executives who run enterprises.

Executives as a specific category of the state bureaucracy act within the framework of the "transfer culture" (to use the terminology suggested by Charles Johnson 1970), as opposed to the "goal culture" represented by the top political leaders, ideologues, and agitators. The basic issue for executives is how, and not what or, even less, why. By paying no more than lip service to ideological goals and by taking seriously only what is currently "practical," executives contribute heavily to the dominance of "transfer culture" over "goal culture." There is no longer room for ardent revolutionaries among the practically minded servants and executives of the state and Party bureaucracy, and the erosion of ideology has led to a situation in which the machine is functioning without basic guidelines.

Data on prestige in the eyes of the Polish population of teachers, scientists, journalists, engineers, and steelworkers show that there is obvious disagreement about the status of executives. Some people rank them very high and others put them relatively low.

According to data on 127 business executives (industry, con- struction, community services, trade) gathered in 1964 by Adam Sarapata, Polish executives, in comparison with their counterparts in Britain, West Germany, Italy, the United States, France, and Sweden, feel much less secure in their positions and far more limited in achieving some self-actualization (even though their ambitions in this respect are lower than in other countries), and put greater emphasis on gaining more autonomy (Sarapata 1970). The expectations of Polish executives are clearly shaped, but they are far from satisfied. Even though a comparative study (1959-68) done by the Polish Center of Public Opinion Polls shows some progress in improving the social prestige of executives, they are still far from having an established social position. Without a reform that gives local industrial executives much more power, their position will remain shaky and ambiguous.

What kind of reform is possible in the Polish economy under the current political conditions is always an open question. It must be remembered that bureaucracy and privately owned agriculture provide considerable room for the petite bourgeois mentality. Thus the same question that was acute under the relaxed economic policy of the early 1920s in Soviet Russia still exists for orthodox Marxists: how long the Communist government, which was bound to represent the ideal of the class of industrial workers, could survive before being engulfed in this petite bourgeois sea (Swaniewicz 1969, p. 73).

The same factors that pushed Soviet Marxists to their dramatic intervention in agriculture now prevent top Polish Party officials from committing themselves to any widespread reform of the overall economy in the sense of giving more freedom to local initiative. It is a long-established tradition of communism that leaders should be tough in dealing with all aspirations toward growing consumption among the masses. On the other hand, according to Andrzej Brzeski:

> Given the rising capital-output ratios, the maintenance of high growth rates has become difficult. Eventually, the communist economies must settle down to a lower tempo, unless, of course, they succeed in appreciably accelerating technical progress. In this context East European attempts to expand trade with the west and solicit Western credit acquire special poignancy (1971a, p. 289).

RESISTANCE TO THE CURRENT MANAGERIAL MODEL

Among East European intellectuals there are many who are very critical of the existing model of a highly centralized administrative command that is monopolized by the top of the hierarchy. It is particularly valid for Eastern Europe. It is quite obvious to local critics of the state bureaucracies that are imposed upon the nationalized economics of East European societies that growing needs cannot be effectively satisfied without more freedom. Initiative is discouraged. Contributions are not rewarded. Decisions are based

135

on distorted and belated information. Feedback does not work. Administrative means become ends in themselves. Improvements are piecemeal. Detailed interference in the running of enterprises reduces them to mere bureaucratic offices. "Desperate clinging to old methods of administration or government in the face of a new situation which demands that changes be brought [about] leads to the application of peremptory pressures on the one hand, and resistance and crisis on the other" (Lipinski 1971a, p. 3).

Many Polish specialists in organization have been aware for several years of the functional disorders brought about by the bureaucratic centralization of power.

> The danger that officials, as intermediaries in the wielding [of] power, might tear themselves away from those who really hold it, and the danger that the official will not notice the living person behind the document, bring about, as a reaction, three closely interrelated phenomena: formalization, organizational centralization, and excessive inspection. These phenomena should, therefore, be treated as unavoidable correlates of the indispensability of bureaucratism in the modern world (Zieleniewski 1968/69, p. 33).

In 1966 there were 84,000 legal regulations that dealt with the framework of executive decisions. In the Polish economy more than 100,000 persons are directly employed in planning, and if one adds to this number all those who assist in preparing plans, approximately one out of every 26 gainfully employed persons is involved in planning (Szczepanski 1964b; Madej 1963, pp. 31-37).

In the hands of bureaucrats, technical progress becomes yet another manipulative device for stimulating the orientation of people more toward show effects than toward real efficiency. For example, in mining, application of modern equipment is dictated by bureaucratic commands supported by attractive bonuses established mainly for managers and technical personnel. Instead of looking for real economic effects, local "supporters" of technical progress create artificial conditions in which new equipment provides short-term pseudo-attractive effects but in reality does harm to the long-term interests of the enterprise (Kraus 1968). In 1970, of all television and radio sets delivered to dealers, 31 percent were rejected by the wholesalers. Of the sets delivered to the retail stores, 25 percent of the televisions and about 16 percent of the radios had to be repaired before being sold. All sets sold had to be repaired under guarantee: every television set about three times and every radio set about once (Kilbach 1971, p. 5).

In Poland, economists and sociologists who favor a relaxation of the authoritarian system of management are quite numerous. Stefan Kurowski (1971) is outspoken in arguing for activation of the market, introduction of competition among enterprises, and stimulation of a businesslike orientation among managers. Edward Lipinski has on many occasions expressed his view that it is necessary to leave much freedom to industrial managers instead of limiting their initiative. On the other hand, he maintains, "The socialization of private property can only be made a reality by the participation of every member of the community in the business of decision-making. Only thus can the worker cease to be an isolated and alienated individual, subordinated to forces which he himself has created" (Lipinski 1971b, p. 129). The late Oskar Lange was for granting autonomy to enterprises and managers even if only within the framework of "mobile" central planning (Kowalik 1971, p. 13). According to Jan Szczepanski, bureaucratic commands that flow from the top "blur the responsibility for bad organization, defects, wastage, stifle all initiative, submerge the changes of rational management in a flood of unnecessary activity which is either demanded by the regulations or by the need to maneuver around them" (from an article published in the Warsaw newspaper, Zycie Warszawy in 1971). According to Adam Podgorecki, formalism is one of the main faults. It consists of a "proliferation of standing orders, out of all proportion to the actual objectives of the institution, which by deterring management from taking any legitimate risk curbs all initiative" (from an article published in Zycie Warszawy in 1971).

The main issue of all eventual reforms is how to transform industrial corporations and workplaces from administrative units into real enterprises able to sponsor entrepreneurship. Szymon Jakubowicz (1971) suggests a highly elastic grouping of nationalized enterprises into corporations, centralized or decentralized depending upon particular economic necessities.

The ruling elite is afraid to relax central planning, and even more so to eliminate it. According to the view widely held by members of the political elites, a market economy would lead to monopoly by the most successful enterprises, growth of inequalities, and, finally, to the abandonment of socialism. Some influential economists support this view. In Poland, Josef Pajestka says, "The whole point of socialist planning is rationality on a national scale, that is to arrive at the options which represent the general socioeconomic optimum over a longer time period. Such rationality cannot be achieved without safeguarding the proper role of central planning and making sure it is performed as well as it conceivably can be" (1971, p. 11). Pajestka belongs to the group of influential Party economists who wish to improve the whole system, but only within the limits of the same kind of benevolent autocracy. According to them, power "should belong to those who, by virtue of their grasp of the whole brief (that is to say, their command of the essential facts, their ability to proceed on them, their mastery of the broader issues and their positive motivation) can do the job best" (Pajestka 1971, p. 15). In practice this always means the preservation of total power and decisionmaking in the hands of the same people who joined the current political establishment a number of years ago, and do not want to resign from power and privileges. They regard themselves as those who "can do the job best."

In the early 1970s considerable progress in extending their freedom of decision was achieved by the executives who run the corporations. The number of central directives decreased. According to the officially held view:

> . . . it should result in a growth of initiative of enterprises, stimulation of their output, increase in productivity and cost reduction due to improvements in organization of work, better utilization of production facilities and speedier introduction of new technology (Zabkowicz 1969, p. 23).

This may lead to a much higher status and broader scope of decisionmaking for corporation executives. However, under the current system of personal dependence by the executive on political authorities, which so far has not been changed to any extent, it seems doubtful that executives would show real interest in looking for more independence in making their decisions. It is much safer for them to pass on final decisions to the higher echelons of administrative and political power. Only a very substantial increase of financial incentives would overcome this widespread tendency to play it safe.

The problem of economic reform in Poland, and in Eastern Europe in general, is the issue of democracy versus autocracy. The bureaucratic elite has its stake in preserving the centralized model, the maintenance of which ensures its survival. The masses, on the other hand, are increasingly interested in consumption and leisure that may be provided only under conditions of a decentralized model. However, large segments of the population are suspicious of any reform that may endanger their relatively stable, even if unsatisfactory, position. There is constantly growing evidence for the inability of the current economic system to deal effectively with problems that arise at a higher stage of development. It is becoming obvious that modern economy cannot flourish under the arbitrary rule of top decisionmakers who do not wish to accept any limits imposed on them by the market and the law.

The economic reform started under Gomulka in the late 1960s could not succeed because it did not involve the well-established rule of the apparatchiks. R. Selucky is right in saying:

> . . . although the Polish reform was successful at first, the ruling bureaucratic elite succeeded in the course of a few years to return the country's political and economic life back to the well-travelled track of the directive system. In addition to the strong pressure of the Soviet Union and other East European countries on the Polish leadership, in addition also to the strength of the Polish bureaucratic elite and the personal qualities of its foremost representative, one of the further causes of the degeneration of the Polish reform was the fact that the democratic changes in the economy and in politics were not based on any new, qualitatively different economic basis of market relations and that the new elements of management were merely affixed to the old institutional forms and to the bureaucratic power structure. The degeneration of the Polish reform serves to this day as a warning signal against an overestimating of partial economic reforms of the Soviet or East German type, and even against an overestimation of the current Hungarian reform (1970).

One additional point must be taken into consideration. Coming mostly from lower social strata, Polish executives are still, at least to some extent, under the influence of the peasant mentality. There is a "limited goods orientation" that does not permit many of them to overcome their narrow-mindedness in dealing with public affairs. Following the assumption common among peasants that all of the desired things in life "exist in finite quantity and are always in short supply" (Forster 1965, p. 296), Polish executives of lower-class extraction tend to be conservative and extremely anxious about the scope of their control. The impingement of the Party on executives contributes substantially to their constant insecurity. The only way of preventing others from undermining one's own position is to keep them as far as possible from one's own interests. Envy and distrust are quite common among executives. Even though they are expected to cooperate with one another within the framework of the centrally planned economy, they constantly suspect one another of ill will. There is thus little hope that executives will become an effective and important pressure group.

CHAPTER
7

THE INTELLIGENTSIA
AS A CULTURAL ELITE

When considering the intelligensia in Eastern Europe, and particularly in Poland, one should have in mind the relative value of such
terms as "intelligentsia" and the traditional elitist social position of
the social stratum about which we are talking. As members of the
educated stratum of society "who have an interest in ideas and a certain degree of consciousness of themselves as a social stratum"
(Theodorson and Theodorson 1969, p. 210), people from the intelligentsia share with the ruling establishment a concern for major problems of society. It is especially valid for the intellectuals who are,
or who pretend to be, creative, and for the leaders of the class as a
whole.

One has to agree with Alexander Hertz (1951) when he says
that the term "intelligentsia," and by the same token the subject it
describes, fits better in Slav civilizations than in those of the Anglo-
Saxon world. The traditional relatively high social status of people
accepted as members of the intelligentsia has its sources in the East
European societies with their strong feudal background, their economic
backwardness lasting until the recent period of Communist industrialization, and the privileges deriving from possessing any education beyond the elementary level (Hertz 1942). The gradual disappearance
of those factors tends to make some Marxist-oriented sociologists
assume that the intelligentsia as a distinct social stratum is in a
period of gradual decline. J. J. Wiatr says, "The very notion of
'intelligentsia', currently in the underdeveloped countries but somewhat alien to the speech habits of the western nations, becomes increasingly nebulous in the Poland of the second half of the 20th century; and it is more than probable that the type of stratification in
which the 'intelligentsia' has occupied a specified position will slowly
disappear" (Wiatr 1962, p. 14).

When considering the future of the intelligentsia as a separate social stratum, we have to keep in mind its traditional functions and particular position in the total society. In both those respects the Polish intelligentsia has some unique features that justify its relatively high social esteem, an active or even leading role in the life of the nation, and a special sociopolitical responsibility. Szczepanski points out that by "remaining closely linked with the nobility and the upper middle classes, who comprised the repository of the traditional values, the Polish intelligentsia was not alienated culturally from the nation, as was the Russian, since it cultivated values accepted by the whole nation. . . . It fulfilled an important social role which it regarded as a national duty, viz., to keep alive the national traditions, to develop the values of the national culture, to educate the new generations, for the struggle for national goals. It maintained and developed the language, literature, arts and science, it created social and political ideas, it searched for possibilities and analyzed social forces within the nation which would be decisive for regaining political independence" (Szczepanski 1969, pp. 34-35; see also Szczepanski 1962; Pipes 1961). All these circumstances are of crucial importance for understanding the social situation of the intelligentsia in contemporary Polish society. Taking them into consideration, it seems premature to assume that the intelligentsia as a social stratum is close to social decline.

THE GENTRY ORIGIN OF THE POLISH INTELLIGENTSIA

The fact that so many members of the intelligentsia originally came from the gentry had far-reaching implications. Of those who were born in the period 1760-1880 and who are mentioned in biographical dictionaries, 60 percent were from the gentry and only 10 percent from the bourgeoisie. Most practiced intellectual professions—scientists (21 percent), writers and journalists (18 percent), or artists (14 percent)—and only a few were in practical professions—physicians (10 percent), engineers (3 percent), or lawyers (3 percent). About 90 percent were Catholic, and conservatives and democratic liberals were equally represented. Half took active part in national insurrections and conspiracies that resulted in repression. A great majority traveled to other countries, many were forced to leave the country, and 20 percent died outside of Polish territory (Szczepanski 1960b, pp. 133-39).

The oppression that Poland has experienced because of the growth of Prussia and Russia since the 18th century to a large extent shaped the mentality of the Polish intelligentsia. As Adam Bromke sees it:

The discrepancy between Poland's potential and actual
position in the international sphere has generated a tension between the political order as people think it ought
to be and as it is. In short, Poles have been divided into
political idealists and political realists (Bromke 1967,
p. 2).

Romanticism and positivism are both self-defeating if pushed to their
extremes.

The end of the moderate versions of both programs is
essentially the same: to cope with the security dilemma
by advancing Poland's interest vis-à-vis its more powerful neighbors. . . . Each of them represents values which
in the long run are indispensable for the survival of a
nation—particularly a nation placed in as difficult a position as Poland. Political idealism emphasizes the need
for cultivating the high morale of the people, while political realism stresses the necessity of developing the
human and material resources of the country. As such,
in the long run, romanticism and positivism are not only
compatible but actually largely complementary (Bromke
1967, p. 253).

However, it seems that the tradition of the Polish intelligentsia
was not oriented toward a skillful oscillation between moderate versions of political idealism and political realism but, rather, to romanticism. The idea of shaking off the yoke of the East or of the West,
regardless of human costs, was always very tempting for the young
generation of the gentry or intelligentsia, especially if defeatism was
currently overshadowed by a feeling of strength. Aleksander Gella
points out, "The championing of social freedom and national independence became not only a basic characteristic of the Polish intelligentsia
but also helped to determine its character and destiny. In a nation
without institutions of formal political leadership, the intelligentsia
acquired an actual, though informal, position of national leadership
and strong charismatic feelings" (Gella 1971b, p. 13).

The idea of honor, inherited from the gentry, stimulated personal and social aspirations among the intelligentsia that, however,
were very difficult, if not impossible, to fulfill under foreign rule
and the change from feudalism to capitalism. Furthermore, as Andrzej
Zajaczkowski says, "The member of the intelligentsia defends himself against the inferiority complex, and the concommitant passivity,
by trying to assure himself how good he is, by promoting the affec-
tionate style of life, showing broad sociopolitical and cultural interests,

by suggesting that exactly he only is really well-mannered, cultured and patriotic. . . . (Zajaczkowski 1962, p. 26; see also Zajaczkowski 1961). Such pretensions saved the intelligentsia from social, economic, and moral hardships. On the other hand, they led to snobbishness. In Poland the cultural elite has traditionally enjoyed a social esteem quite often higher than the real social contribution of its individual members (Rawin 1968, p. 362). However, elegance, refinement, and good manners were not enough to bring success in the new capitalist world. Other people who possessed entirely new qualifications, and in addition quite often did not have much in common with the Polish noble heritage, managed to gain power.

Social revolution, independence, or preferably both became the common dreams of the intelligentsia. World War I provided the opportunity to pursue these dreams to an unexpected extent. As Solomon Rawin explains, "It was only in independent Poland that conditions arose for crystallization of the intelligentsia identity as the nation's new elite. . . . Throughout the interwar period, the special right of the intelligentsia to shape the new nationhood was hardly challenged. . . . Poland became 'an intelligentsia-dominated society' and there was hardly an area of public endeavor which did not bear the imprint of the intelligentsia's presence" (Rawin 1968, p. 362).

Many new employment opportunities that had previously been limited to foreigners (mostly Russians and Germans) became available to members of the intelligentsia, who had aspirations and pretensions inherited from the gentry. "The ideal of the intelligentsia was not a competent professional man, but a 'cultured man,' participating widely in the nation's cultural heritage, a man with knowledge of history, literature, the arts, and good manners" (Szczepanski 1962, p. 408). This does not mean, however, that the general level of white-collar workers grew adequately during the interwar period. In 1931 (the second and last Polish interwar census) only 55 percent of non-manual workers had at least a high school diploma (Bartnicki and Czajkowski 1936). On the other hand, many graduates found it impossible, or at least very difficult, to obtain gainful employment. Therefore, a considerable proportion of the young intelligentsia experienced frustration that led them either to servility toward the establishment or to radical orientations, both left and right (Blit 1965).

The "governance of souls" belonged in the period 1918-39 primarily to that part of the intelligentsia in public service, education, and culture. The nucleus of the intelligentsia, the professionals, constituted only 2 percent of the total population. Only 10 percent of white-collar workers had higher education, but in the institutions of higher education there were 7.5 times more students of white-collar descent than would be justified by their proportion of the total population. Between 20 and 25 percent of white-collar workers came from

143

lower classes; the rest either originated from the white-collar class or came from other privileged groups. The fact that more than 50 percent of the intelligentsia depended on the state led to discrimination. Among the professionals, Jews represented over 50 percent, but among white-collar workers in general only 14 percent—little more than in the total population. There was a tendency to employ very few Jews in the civil service (Zarnowski 1973, pp. 189-227).

The Polish intelligentsia maintained social aspirations relatively higher than those of the intelligentsia in several other Slavic countries—Bohemia, Slovakia, Bulgaria—where the intelligentsia came mostly from the countryside and claimed to be related predominantly to the peasants and to their specific folk culture. The Polish intelligentsia has played an exceptionally active role in social, cultural, and political fields. There were practically no Nazi supporters among the Polish intelligentsia; and the left-wing orientation of a considerable part of it was another reason why the Nazis decided to adopt an extermination policy to prevent the intelligentsia from reviving and reassuming the leading position in Polish society.

The close traditional relation of the Polish intelligentsia to the gentry, and the attractiveness of the social pattern of a nobleman transformed into an intellectual, have been emphasized and vividly criticized by those intellectuals who have wanted to associate the intelligentsia with the lower social strata. Jozef Chalasinski argues that the close relation with the gentry has considerably weakened the interest of the intelligentsia in economic problems, and this has had unfortunate repercussions on the total life of the nation. The intelligentsia's admiration of the societal patterns created by the gentry and the simulation of its way of thinking have, as Chalasinski (1946) maintains, directed the attention of the intelligentsia more toward superficial intellectualism than toward really responsible social activity.

THE INTELLIGENTSIA AFTER 1945

The assumption of power by Communists completely changed the position of the intelligentsia in Poland. The ruling Party started almost immediately after World War II to educate a new intelligentsia that would be unquestionably loyal, commited to the Communist cause, and easily manipulated. The number of people with secondary or higher education grew from about 100,000 immediately after the war to 2.5 million in 1960 and close to 4 million in 1970 (655,000 with higher education and 3.198 million with secondary education). However, the role of the intelligentsia changed to a large extent, as described by Szczepanski (1962): "The functions of creating philosophical and political ideas, shaping public opinion, and establishing value criteria are now taken over by the political party . . . . The new group of political leaders who form the very core of the people's intelligentsia and occupy leading positions of power apparatus, industry, and the mass organizations provide the national leadership. They are to some degree interpenetrated by traditional intellectuals, but the latter have rather limited influence on political decisions" (pp. 418-19).

In comparison with the prewar period, the intelligentsia lost economically, politically, and socially. There was a clear diminution of social distance between it and the traditionally lower strata such that "the intelligentsia seemed to discard some elements of its elitist outlook and embraced some clearly plebeian notions" (Rawin 1968, p. 369). It does not necessarily mean the total rejection of the elitist heritage. The new arrivals in the ranks of intelligentsia have a plebeian background but nonplebeian aspirations. East European communism, and particularly Polish communism, has so far failed to establish moral and cultural patterns competitive with those that the intelligentsia borrowed from the gentry or created itself.

The massive influx into the intelligentsia from the ranks of blue-collar workers and peasants was substantially stimulated by the change in the prewar selective character of secondary and higher education. The free education system introduced by the new regime thus become the basic source of structural change in the white-collar stratum. Among graduates of all secondary schools and colleges during the first 15 years after World War II, about 35 percent came from wage-earning families and 20 percent from peasant families, as compared with the interwar period, when the graduates came predominantly from the privileged social strata. According to J. J. Wiatr (1964), "80 to 90 percent of the university-trained intelligentsia today are products of the changes which took place in People's Poland."

The establishment of the new political system was accompanied by a growing demand for white-collar workers to man the new institutions of a planned economy. Especially at the beginning, the new regime was very eager to promote people from the lower strata into the white-collar ranks, regarding them as more reliable politically. The massive social advancement was, however, related primarily to the rapid industrialization of the country. It was accompanied by a drastic income redistribution, expressed in a 26 percent reduction of the real incomes of nonmanual workers during the period 1937-60. In the same period of time the real income of manual workers increased by 75 percent (Kalecki 1964).

The decline of the relative economic position of the intelligentsia versus other social strata has been accompanied by parallel changes in the social structure of the power elite. Although the nonmanual workers constitute a majority of all members of the ruling Polish

United Workers' Party, the percentage of people from lower strata occupying prominent political and administrative positions is relatively high.

These circumstances are typical for all countries of the Soviet bloc. However, in Poland, belonging to the intelligentsia and adopting its social and cultural patterns seems to have retained much more attractiveness than in Czechoslovakia, for example. There is a strong tendency among the members of the working class, as well as among peasants, to expect their children to join the professions of the intelligentsia. (Sarapata and Wesolowski 1961).

What in the past was only a dream came to be reality after World War II for a considerable part of the offspring of workers and peasants: "The barriers and differences dividing Polish society before the war have been almost completely abolished in the twenty years since the war as a result of intensive migrations, industrialization, democratization of social relations, and new policies in the field of education, housing, wages, etc." (Sarapata 1966a, pp. 26-27). More than half the engineers and technicians, as well as administrative and office workers, had been manual workers at some stage in their life. Over 20 percent of teachers, engineers, journalists, and doctors were of working-class background. Movement to and from the working class was so intense that, according to estimates made by Adam Sarapata, in no more than 30 percent of families was there a third working-class generation.

The growing economy has required college-trained persons, particularly those with technical education. However, in several branches of employment the demand for highly qualified personnel has considerably exceeded the supply; for example, physicists, mechanical, electrical, and chemical engineers, and economists (Charkiewicz 1966). As Janusz Tymowski said, in the early 1960s "the drafting of a long-range plan for 1961-1980 brought out the fact that the number of graduates needed by the economy would have to rise from the 270,000 employed in 1960 to approximately 800,000 in 1980. To meet this demand the universities will have to produce at the very least three times as many graduates as at present" (Tymowski 1963, p. 7).

PRESENT STATUS OF THE INTELLIGENTSIA

Rising standards and the shift in emphasis away from the humanities and toward technical and related professions favor basic changes in the concept of the intelligentsia. Not high school, but college, education becomes the necessary condition of being classified among the intelligentsia. Income level has lost much of its significance because of a relatively small differ nce in the average incomes of blue-collar and white-collar workers.

It is not material well-being that now basically differentiates the members of the intelligentsia from other social strata or stimulates the latter to advance into the ranks of the former. A certain traditional distaste for manual work plays an important role. People often prefer to earn less as white-collar workers, even when they have the opportunity to achieve a higher standard of living. From time to time governmental institutions try to get rid of excess office workers by transferring them (after state-supported occupational retraining) into the factories, but a considerable number of the transferred people sooner or later return to white-collar occupations.

The attractive social status of the intelligentsia, the social and cultural patterns cultivated by it, the social myth of moral and intellectual leadership, the solidarity of people who hold certain common cultural and moral values—all of these support the existence of the intelligentsia. Studies on college graduates carried out under the direction of Jan Szczepanski have revealed a relatively fast acculturation by newcomers from the lower social strata into the intelligentsia (Szczepanski, ed. 1959-60). It is astonishing how quickly the newcomers come to treat the traditional values of the intelligentsia as their own.

One explanation of this is the virtual lack in Poland of a middle class with a traditional emphasis on material well-being. In the Communist economy there is no opportunity to make a fortune safely. Owning an apartment or a small house, one car, and regular vacation travel abroad are the upper limits of material well-being accepted by law and by society. Anything more is hazardous and worthless in the circumstances of relatively tight formal and informal social control. People do not like others to be much richer than they are, and it is quite easy to levy sanctions against anybody whose high standard of living seems to be unjustified by his official source of income. Private businessmen are rare and their profession has a relatively low social esteem; their cleverness in achieving high profits is not treated as a virtue, but as a way of cheating customers and the state.

Instead of traditional middle-class values, which were always weak in Polish society, there are in Poland the values of the intelligentsia. The promotion of cultural and societal interests is relatively free and easy. The generous support given by the state to mass culture (Kloskowska 1964) enables almost everybody to attend the theater, to buy books, to visit resorts, and to participate in several sports. The intelligentsia not only is a chief customer of cultural services but virtually controls them. There is always considerable tension between the members of the creative intelligentsia and the state bureaucrats. However, the real influence of the intelligentsia in running the cultural and social institutions seems to be in many instances much greater than in those countries in which the commercialization of culture predominates.

There are some common interests of Party or state officials and the cultural intelligentsia, even if tensions between them are quite obvious and evident.

> Although party functionaires in their official declarations speak about the working class as the vanguard of society and the most important class in present-day Poland, they are well aware of the fact that without the consent and co-operation and the participation of the intelligentsia no full development of a country's resources is possible. Also, whatever social pressures may exist in East European countries, a serious conflict will erupt only when a significant part of the intelligentsia breaks its alliance with the ruling communist bureaucracy and channels the forces of change into definite political action. The policy of the political leadership therefore, in spite of occasional displays of mistrust and aversion towards intellectuals, is to reward those members of the creative intelligentsia who fully co-operate, while keeping in check the more restless, "unreliable" elements. The writers are the neuralgic point of the intelligentsia because they have a privileged position in socialist society. . . . The non-privileged classes are separated from the creative intelligentsia by a vast gap deriving from differences in income, status and style of life, a fact which makes the intelligentsia in the eyes of the masses look like the ally or the client of the ruling bureaucracy (Gömöri 1973, pp. 154-55, 161).

It is a specific mixture of privilege and professional ambitions that pushes the intelligentsia into opposition to the regime. For example, the ambition of a writer is, according to Gömöri, "to transcend the limitations of society including those imposed on society by the prevailing power structure, giving him a loyalty to the dialectics of change rather than to any political party" (1973, p. 158). On the other hand, the intelligentsia is too dependent on the Party and state officials to attempt an alliance with other classes that would be oriented against the status quo. The intellectuals will thunder against the "dictatorship of the numbskulls," but they will not go beyond signing protests and denouncing one another in private for being too loyal to the regime. In many respects the intellectuals continue to play the role of the "conscience of the nation" (Mond 1973, p. 132).

The intelligentsia's real participation and professional involvement are not on the same level as its position in the power structure. The total subordination of all social strata, including the intelligentsia, is in the nature of Soviet-style communism. However, the traditional claim to spiritual and social (if not political) responsibility tends to make those who belong to the intelligentsia—especially writers, scientists, and journalists—take an independent position on problems dealing with the functioning of institutions of vital importance to the whole society. A prominent sociologist, Stanislaw Ossowski, when discussing the relation between Marxism and scientific creativity in socialist society, wrote: "The fact that a man is a scholar does not free him from the discipline of his profession, nor from obedience as a citizen. But in certain circumstances professional discipline requires him to be disobedient . . . . If he is obedient, if he changes his views when ordered to do so, or if his thinking is not in agreement with his words, then he is neglectful of his duty, just as an engineer neglects his duty if for the sake of peace and quiet, or for the sake of profit, or out of sheer laziness or meanness he builds with hollow bricks instead of ferro-concrete, or uses wood instead of granite." According to his views, "The scientist is a man for whom disobedience of thought is a professional obligation. His social function is to question. In this respect he must obey neither the synod, nor the committee, nor the cabinet minister, nor Caesar, nor God" (Ossowski 1957; Nowak 1963).

THE CONSCIOUSNESS OF A STATUS INCONGRUENCE

The social consciousness of the present-day intelligentsia is a controversial issue among Polish sociologists. Jozef Chalasinski (1958) maintains that the postwar attempt to create a new class-conscious intelligentsia failed because this social stratum has not acquired a really plebeian character. A quite different view is represented by Ryszard Turski (1961) and J. J. Wiatr (1965). They emphasize the present smaller distance between the intelligentsia, on the one hand, and blue-collar workers and peasants, on the other; the massive social advancement of the representatives of lower social strata into the ranks of the intelligentsia; and the integrative social function of Marxist ideology and of the social policy of the Communist state. Wiatr concludes, on the basis of the available sociological data, that "particularly the young engineering and technical intelligentsia today constitute that part of the personnel which is most quickly joining the party and becoming politically active" (Wiatr 1964; Bauman 1962). A survey dealing with attitudes of Warsaw students showed

149

a general acceptance of the socialist political and economic system, even if among the subjects there is a fairly general dislike for the more heroic versions of socialism. The idea that the present generation should be sacrificed for the well-being and happiness of future generations was quite alien to the students of Warsaw. "An interesting characteristic of student thinking is the lack of enthusiasm towards participation in all institutionalized forms of public life, especially all such forms which might be connected with participation in political power . . . . Feeling this lack of interest for the more institutionalized forms of political activity, but at the same time experiencing the need for being useful to society, the students endeavor to satisfy these needs in different forms of activities on a limited scale, by being useful to their own small professional or social circle without taking part in wider public life. Others give up altogether the idea of satisfying this need (Nowak 1962, pp. 94-95).

The state of mind of the Warsaw students surveyed by Nowak exemplifies contradictions that are quite common, and not only for the young generation of the intelligentsia. Generally speaking, the Polish intelligentsia has been quite successful professionally in the period since World War II. Among the high school graduates studied by A. Borucki (the data deal with one high school situated in an industrial town), only 7 percent were in subordinate positions at the time of the interview and 64 percent held managerial or executive positions. In comparison with the prewar period, there is now much greater opportunity and a stronger tendency to change jobs in order to earn more money, to find greater work satisfaction, or to obtain occupational advancement. However, according to data gathered by Borucki, there is also a marked interdependence between approval of the sociopolitical changes that occurred in Poland after World War II and success in professional advancement (Borucki 1962).

Yet professional success of the present day intelligentsia compared with that before World War II is accompanied by a considerable decline in the material standard of living and also—at least in several instances—by a decline of political influence. The young generation of college-educated people in several branches of social and economic life has, with the passage of time, found it to be more and more difficult to obtain responsible positions because they are occupied by members of the establishment, quite often less educated but with much more seniority in the particular office or factory. Attractive positions have become less available than at the beginning of the period of rapid industrialization. The housing problem also is quite difficult for the young generation with its modest average income, great needs, and sometimes unrealistic expectations. The traditions typical of the intelligentsia, as well as their relative well-being during school years stir up ambitions that quite often lead to disillusionment with the reality of daily working and living conditions.

The conviction that the intelligentsia is a leading social stratum, and therefore deserves certain privileges, is even now quite strong among its members. According to a survey conducted in 1961, the demand for increased equality in the social structure was much stronger among blue-collar workers than among the intelligentsia. This was determined by answers to the question "How would you like to see social differences in Poland in the future?" Fifty-three percent of skilled workers voted for the total disappearance of differences, but only 38 percent of respondents from free professions and the creative intelligentsia. "On the one hand, the population as a whole is under the strong influence of the egalitarian ideals of socialism with the demand for transformation of the social structure in the direction of the abolition of social differences. On the other hand, the well known sociological mechanisms continue to operate and they cause a decrease in the attractiveness of egalitarian ideals with the increase of social and economic position . . . " (Nowak 1964, pp. 52-53). This truth is valid not only with regard to the intelligentsia. A survey of blue collar-workers in Warsaw by A. Malewski in the 1950s showed that the idea of narrowing the wage gap was much less acceptable to better-paid workers than to those in the lower income brackets.

The claim of certain privileges by the intelligentsia finds support in the current conviction that members of some professions (such as teachers and university professors) are underpaid. A study of the Warsaw population dealing with the occupational hierarchy revealed that several professions belonging to the intelligentsia enjoy much higher prestige than their actual position in the hierarchy of financial remuneration would indicate. The social responsibility of these professions deserves, according to general public opinion, a better material situation for their occupants than exists at the present time (Sarapata and Wesolowski 1961).

On the other hand, even on the level of official doctrine there has been a much greater tendency in the 1960s to accept a relativistic viewpoint regarding egalitarianism. Socialism can be given various interpretations, Jerzy Wiatr, one of the best-known Polish Marxist sociologists, comments; and emphasis can be placed either on the equality of opportunity or on genuinely equal conditions of life. And the difference in views and attitudes reflects more or less directly the disparity in the objective situation and interests of the various strata. Every major social group, and thus every stratum of socialist society, tends to accept opinions that conform with its interests and to reject those that are incompatible with them. . . . Contradictions tend to grow when, as a result of the actually existing economic situation and the restricted volume of goods, their distribution becomes insidious and difficult. . . . Egalitarianism in poverty is a wrong solution, for it leads to economic backwardness and is detrimental to the interest of the masses (Wiatr 1962, pp. 10-11).

THE BASIC DILEMMA

All factors and circumstances discussed so far do not provide a full explanation of the social consciousness of the present-day Polish intelligentsia. It is necessary to bring into the picture the specific role of the tiny intellectual, moral, and artistic elite in governance of souls (Gella 1971b). Being located in a crucial place between an illiterate mass of peasants, a few manual workers, local burghers of German or Jewish origin, and foreign occupying forces, in the 19th century the Polish intelligentsia crystallized a peculiar feeling of national mission and responsibility. For the survival of the captive nation, it was of crucial importance who would decide the moral identification of the Polish masses: foreigners vitally interested in subduing Poles to German, Austrian, or Russian identity, or Polish leaders.

The governance of souls became of such crucial importance among the leading circles of the Polish intelligentsia that even now much may be explained by that phrase. People have gained appeal by becoming martyrs or at least seeming to do so. For a scientist, writer, or journalist it has paid to suffer persecution because it has been the safest way to gain nationwide social visibility and recognition. Much personal manipulation has been oriented toward the "governance of souls" and building one's own monument in the social memory of the intelligentsia.

One of the basic paradoxes of communism is numerically in-creasing the intelligentsia, on the one hand, and, on the other, making it impossible for the intelligentsia to fulfill its fundamental raison d'être. A single rigid and formalized ideology and an extensive cen-tralization of authority do not permit the intelligentsia to freely exer-cise the "governance of souls" by formulating and implementing the national vision (whether nationalist or universalist). The role of the intelligentsia is in principle one of servitude with respect to the ruling elite. This is the root cause of the chronic impotence that has long been a problem for the Russian intelligentsia, and is at present com-mon among the Polish intelligentsia. A continual inner struggle be-tween the alternatives of self-condemnation and of blaming everything on the regime is characteristic of people confronted with the necessity to act but who cannot. The fabrication of myths for one's own or for someone else's use is an attempt to resolve this conflict. A typical case would be a journalist or a pseudo sociologist dreaming of a happy and carefree workers' class in People's Poland (Matejko 1972a).

One of the difficulties of governing a society absolutistically is the unavoidable fading away of the borderline between reality and fantasy. The masses of intellectuals, experts, and artists who make their living by fabricating cultural and scientific artifacts produce such a number of them that the power holders cannot fail to lose themselves in the mist of mythology veiling reality. The intelligentsia's pro-regime and tightly regime-controlled activity takes on, in the final analysis, a subversive character, regardless of the creators' intentions.

However, a correction in the direction of reality is effected in the everyday activity of that part of the intelligentsia that fulfills concrete human needs. Probably their best representative is the medical profession, which treats its patients seriously and tries to tangibly reduce their suffering. That is why a doctor in a hospital is one of the worst-paid state employees, and why the entire public health service suffers from chronic underinvestment.

Divorcing mythology from the activity of the intelligentsia depends not only on the democratization of the sociopolitical system but also, to a large extent, on the liberation of the intelligentsia's class consciousness. There is parochialism, envy, almost exaggerated hospitality (especially with respect to guests from abroad), adulation of anything from the West, and patriotic bigotry. The social advance en masse to the ranks of the intelligentsia accentuated this mixture even more by introducing materialistic greed and the lack of scruples in the struggle for more—in the form or cars or better and bigger apartments.

The search for status, and a feeling of instability regarding its social position, is one of the most characteristic features of the present-day Polish intelligentsia. It is necessary to relate this problem to the more general question of the still uncrystallized social stratification of modern Polish society.

> All available theoretical and empirical data show that the upheavals in Polish class structure undermined the old system of social stratification, but the construction of the new system did not keep pace with the rapid metamorphosis in the composition of social classes and in the web of their mutual relations. I doubt if we are at all justified in speaking of social stratification in present-day Poland. Manifold value standards intertwine here in highly unexpected ways. In such conditions any coherent image of social stratification can only be the product of statistical operations and does not correspond to real attitudes and behavioral manifestations or hierarchical appraisal. Two traditional values which had formerly been the main thread in the texture of social stratification—the values of "money" and "noble birth"—still compete with the new values, partly popularized by official propaganda and partly gaining acceptance as a result

of their great instrumental significance, such as "social utility" and "participation in power" (Bauman 1966, p. 538).

We should keep in mind the fluid character of Polish social stratification when analyzing the sources of status incongruence among the intelligentsia. The search for status in such a situation also means the search for social stability, for crystallization of a new structure adequate to the present economic, social, and political conditions. Present-day Poland represents a society in transition, seeking a satisfying new balance of several new social powers created and developed by Communist industrialization. The search for status among the intelligentsia is very important, in view of the growing objective importance in modern society of strategic elites consisting of college-educated experts (Keller 1963).

Looking for its place in modern Polish society, the intelligentsia also looks for a new social identity. The basic ideological values of the gentry, noble birth, equality, and landowning, which for a long time influenced the intelligentsia's way of thinking, have lost their attractive power. The "well-brought-up man" described by Florian Znaniecki (1935) and typical of the traditional intelligentsia (Chalasinski 1962) no longer fulfills the ambitions and needs of the young generation. The members of this generation "think rationally in terms of expediency and utility, eagerly seek reliable means to prescribed goals, are ready to devote all their energy to the tasks they are entrusted to fulfill. They are expedient, efficient, industrious, full of initiative, and rather ruthless in pushing forward what is to be done. They are able to guarantee conditions indispensable to organizing rapid economic growth" (Bauman 1966, p. 540). The personality pattern prevalent among the present-day intelligentsia has been shaped by the realities of the new social system but is not like the ideal socialist man, "who subordinates his individual desires to the general objectives of society and to the principles governing society as a whole, and expects that society will remunerate him with a just share of the social income" (Szczepanski 1964b, p. 15).

The present status incongruence of the Polish intelligentsia, though a source of tension and frustration, at the same time plays an important role as a stimulus to search for a new personality pattern and a new social role that will make possible a successful adaption to a society in transition.

154

8

THE WHITE-COLLAR
MOSAIC

With the general growth of the white-collar workers' stratum, characteristic of a rapidly expanding economy, there is also a constant increase in its internal differentiation. One may divide the intelligentsia, as does Jan Szczepanski, according to social function (creators of culture, organizers, specialists), occupation and education (engineers, humanists, administrators), and income and power (influential and relatively well-paid elite, medium-paid and noninfluential specialists) (Szczepanski 1960b, pp. 33-44). It seems that with the passing of time, the intellectual elite becomes differentiated as a real core of the group and the lower ranks of white-collar workers separate from the intelligentsia, creating a new social stratum, the pseudo-middle class.

This progressive differentiation of the intelligentsia makes it more difficult to treat the class as a unit. Various categories of white-collar workers often have little in common with one another. In order to illustrate existing differences, several groups of white collar workers will be characterized: clerks, teachers, technical cadres, architects, journalists, artists and actors, students, and academic staff. Naturally this review does not cover the entire spectrum of the Polish intelligentsia. However, it does seem broad enough for one to grasp the major trends in the various categories of what was traditionally considered the intelligentsia. The availability of empirical data from sociological studies was a primary factor in making the selection.

CLERKS

Communism is primarily in need of clerks; technicians and all the other strata of white-collar workers are of secondary importance.

The state machine tends to give a bureaucratic content to every kind of job. Also, the Party shows deep appreciation for technology, not so much because of its crucial importance for Party ideology as because of its contribution to the fulfillment of Party goals.

Immediately after World War II there was such a demand for white-collar workers (22 percent of the total population was killed by the Nazis, and the victims were mostly Jews and intelligentsia) that all sorts of candidates were admitted to salaried posts, especially since it was in the interests of the Party to have loyal and reliable people socially advanced from lower ranks in industry.

As can be seen in Table 8.1, socialist industrialization has been accompanied by a rapid growth of the middle-level and lower-level white-collar workers, most of them office workers. Many do not have even a high school education. According to a survey carried out by Krystyna Lutynska in 1960 in Lodz, Poland's second largest city, covering workers in lower office positions, only 45 percent of the respondents had completed their secondary education, and only 30 percent came from families belonging to the intelligentsia. The percentage of office workers of blue-collar origins was especially high among industrial employees (70 percent). The number of industrial respondents whose spouses were gainfully employed was higher (43 percent) than elsewhere; the same applies to the percentage (nearly 70) of people without secondary education.

TABLE 8.1

Social Structure of Polish White-
Collar Workers, 1921-60
(thousands)

	1921	1931	1939	1960
Higher stratum: intellectuals, managers, experts	210 (1.4)	255 (1.8)	310 (2.0)	700
Middle stratum	240 ⎱	355 ⎱	430 ⎱	1,800
Lower stratum: foremen,	⎰ (2.2)	⎰ (2.9)	⎰ (3.7)	
salesmen	75	105	120	
Total	525	715	860	2,500

Sources: Żarnowski 1964; Szczepanski, ed. 1965.

Directly after the war the ranks of office workers were filled by people who before 1939 had belonged to the lowest and the highest classes of society. The office workers therefore form a mixture of widely divergent social strata and classes. This category is like a melting pot in which we find office workers of widely differing intellectual and cultural levels derived from a wide range of classes and social strata, and representing different cultural patterns, ways of life, etc. (Lutynska 1965, p. 266).

The expanding industrial bureaucracy played a great role in opening up opportunities for advancement of former office workers into the white-collar ranks. Branches studied by Lutynska have a considerable percentage of people of blue-collar origin; for instance, in government more than half the office workers are children of working-class fathers (and half have less than a secondary education). Only in certain fields, such as banking, is there a predominance of people belonging traditionally to the intelligentsia and having at least a secondary education.

The social esteem of the office worker is relatively low because of the traditional red tape, the low educational level, the emphasis placed on production, and a general underestimation of the social and economic importance of administrative work. According to a public opinion survey conducted in Warsaw in 1958, the office clerk was placed in one of the lowest positions, based on social prestige, job security, and material rewards—much lower than the average skilled blue-collar worker (Sarapata and Wesolowski 1961).

Office workers are quite aware of the relatively low level of their professionalization. "A view particularly common among office workers is that their work, that is, office work, is not a skilled job, and that they are not skilled workers. For many of them this is the cause of much disappointment and dislike for their work. Many of them feel underprivileged and wronged, and have an inferiority complex with regard to other comparable occupations" (Lutynska 1964, p. 81).

They say that as compared with teachers, doctors, engineers, and even skilled workers, they have no skilled occupation at all. This conviction is a very strong one, and is connected with a feeling of injustice and social wrong, as well as with the feeling that office work is of no good to anyone, that it is meaningless and is of no importance to the community, since it cannot be said to be real work, and what is more important, is not productive. Practically none of the respondents would like their children

157

to take up office work, and nearly every respondent said
he would like to change his job (Lutynska 1967, pp. 265-66).

A study of accountants shows that there is a widespread feeling
among them that employees representing other occupations underestimate and deprecate accountants:

> an underestimation of the role and importance of his [the
> accountant's] profession leads to a lowering of the satis-
> faction derived from his job, and, as a result, unfavorably
> affects his will to work and attitude towards it. A situa-
> tion of this kind is conducive, in the case of ambitious ac-
> countants, to a decrease, and sometimes even to the total
> disappearance of the ideological stimulus to work, a
> factor of considerable importance for work productivity
> (Michon 1964).

Mutual understanding and mutual esteem among accountants and the
remaining staff is hampered by the fact that the accounting staff has
to perform a directive and controlling function given to it by the
authorities outside the institutions in which they work. The accounting
staff is responsible directly to these authorities but at the same time
has strong common interests with the rest of the staff in its own institution. As a result, it is in an ambivalent position, aggravated even
more by the relatively low level of salaries. The accountant quite
often has under his indirect control people earning much higher
salaries than he; they also are more educated. In relation to them
he is in an ambiguous position, which makes mutual understanding
even more difficult. The routinization of work and a feeling of monot-
ony are additional factors strengthening negative attitudes toward
accounting.

In the Polish society there is a common distaste for clerks as
the bulwark of the highly bureaucratized state machine. "Lower-
echelon employees become the scapegoats of any and all shortcomings
and deficiencies in the present order. They are blamed for 'bureaucratic' distortions, and the populace very often holds them responsible
for any inconveniences, shortages of goods, and so forth" (Szczepanski
1970, p. 123). Therefore, advance into the clerical ranks is no longer
attractive for the young generation of blue-collar descent. Clerical
occupations have become distasteful even more to workers than to
the intelligentsia. This fact contributes substantially to the general
dissatisfaction of clerks with their professional image.

The clerical staff is to a large extent made responsible for the
inefficiency and inhumanity of bureaucracy. However, most of them

do not really have anything to say. Two-thirds of lower and middle clerical positions, even in industry, are occupied by low-paid women. There is among clerks a very considerable percentage of people with relatively low education and of manual-worker descent. Their incomes are much lower than those of technicians and quite often below the wages of workers. In 1972, in the entire nationalized industry, the administrative and clerical staff, including managers, averaged 2,805 zloty per month, the same as blue-collar workers but much less than the 4,193 zloty of the technical personnel (Concise 1973, p. 95).

There is a common feeling among the clerical staff in industry and in other branches that their position is inferior, that they are grossly underpaid, and that it is not worthwhile to be a clerk. For example, of the trade employees (sales clerks as well as store managers) surveyed by Jerzy Altkorn, about 70 percent would not like their children to enter the same profession; this was valid in almost the same degree for their sons as for their daughters. Only 24 percent of sales clerks and 33 percent of store managers said that they would choose the same profession if they had another chance (Altkorn 1963, pp. 29, 37).

For clerks, and even more so for their supervisors, the practical solution is to strengthen their position by joining the Party. There is therefore a great eagerness of people from the clerical and administrative ranks to be accepted into the Party. However, the Workers' Party is endangered by this inflow of bureaucrats who are widely disliked or even hated by the masses. Thus, from time to time there is a purge of Party ranks in which mostly clerks suffer by being fired and losing their privileges.

TEACHERS

Status incongruity is especially common among office workers, but it also appears in several other white-collar professions, especially in those whose occupants only recently entered the ranks of the intelligentsia. The profession of primary school teacher is a case in point because it has changed considerably since the end of World War II. The rapid development of a free education system has created a great demand for teaching personnel. The number of teachers in primary schools increased from 66,600 in 1946-47 (76,600 in the public schools in 1937-38) to 214,000 in 1972-73. But the opening of opportunities to enter other occupations has considerably diminished the attractiveness of the teaching profession; in addition, salaries are relatively low and the responsibilities disproportionally large.

During the interwar period the majority of teachers were recruited from the urban population, but now most of them are of peasant background. There is also an increasing number of women among teachers. Both these facts mean that at the present time the primary teacher's occupation is attractive primarily to those social categories with limited opportunities to obtain better-paying jobs. "New opportunities whereby people can gain an education and fulfill their ambitions and the relatively easy entrance into other more attractive occupations have led to a situation where relatively few pupils attending the primary and secondary schools at present choose teaching as a profession " (Woskowski 1964).

Programs of additional education and involvement in political activity give the primary school teachers an opportunity to improve their status, which is declining relative to professions that are growing in importance as the industrialization process continues. Many teachers try to supplement their education by taking training courses.

> Education is one of the principal means whereby the
> teacher can climb the ladder of promotion. The result
> is that headmasters on the average have a higher level
> of education than rank and file teachers. Teachers with
> higher qualifications mostly work in the towns, in schools
> with a higher level of organization. In the rural areas,
> the teacher with a university education is still the ex-
> ception (Woskowski 1964, p. 86).

The political participation of primary school teachers is relatively higher than in many other professions. In a sample of teachers studied by J. Woskowski in 1959-61, 22 percent were members of political parties (16 percent belonging to the Polish United Workers' Party, 5 percent to the United Peasants' Party, and 1 percent to the Democratic Party). Many teachers take active part in local government and in various social, cultural, and athletic associations. The percentage of religious believers seems to be lower (about 40 percent) than in other professions. The primary school teacher is expected to represent the official doctrine, especially in the countryside, where there are relatively few government officials and where he is predisposed to be a member of the local elite. However, he is simultaneously in a relatively worse social and material position than the occupants of many professions that are growing very rapidly both in the towns and in the countryside. There are also controversial issues on which the primary school teacher has to take a stand, risking his prestige with either a considerable part of the population or the authorities.

Given the framework of official goals and principles sponsored by the Party, Polish teachers, as agents of socialization, represent a particularly interesting and illuminating case of status incongruence, as well as of cognitive dissonance. Since religion in Poland is at odds with the official ideology, and yet most of the Polish population probably still believes in God, teachers are under pressure from both sides. They are expected by their employer to conform to official policy, but at the same time they do not want to be on bad terms with the parents of their pupils.

On the basis of data and insights gathered in Poland during the period 1965-68, Joseph R. Fiszman concluded that there is a substantial gap between the official intent and the real performance of Polish teachers. Secondary school teachers favor the position of the Church rather than that of the Party, even if they tend to be loyalistic. "Young Poles seem to have assimilated values and styles that they associate with "Modernity' which, while secularizing (inasmuch as these are frowned upon by the traditionalist Church), are also quite removed from Socialist ideals" (Fiszman 1972, p. 312). Teachers of peasant-farmer and rural backgrounds are still quite resistant to the official values.

> This, despite the fact that youth of peasant-farmer back-
> ground, along with working-class youth, are accorded, at
> least in theory, various allowances upon entering second-
> ary and higher education and, once there, enjoy certain
> tangible privileges, and despite the fact that on the whole,
> the economic and social status of the peasantry has under-
> gone improvement under the new system. . . . The re-
> curring failure to involve the very youngest of the
> teachers (and student-teachers) in the complex of sys-
> temic values, norms, and goals may call into question
> the ability of the system to affect a greater degree of
> socialization in the future, which would enable it to
> achieve its goals more effectively (Fiszman 1972, pp.
> 135, 313).

Fiszman looks at Polish teachers as a group that, for socio-economic and sociocultural reasons, is unable or unwilling to fulfill the expectations of the political establishment. Teachers feel deprived of prestige and adequate material compensation. The local authorities utilize them for administrative and sociopolitical tasks that represent a heavy, additional burden.

While the general public in Poland still holds teachers in high esteem, their position in the local community is at least ambiguous, if not unfavorable. Within the larger professional-educational establishment as well, the teacher is in a much more inferior position than he was before World War II. Secondary school teachers in interwar Poland were relatively well paid. Some of them were very active in the intellectual and political life of the country. There was some mobility between their ranks and the ranks of the academic staff. Now the gap seems to be greater than before because of the large differences in credentials, institutional affiliation, geographical locations, income, and degree of freedom from cross pressures. Concentrated in large cities, the academic staff in general enjoys more freedom from local interference of a political nature than do the elementary and secondary school teachers, who are widely dispersed in rural and urban communities.

The recruitment of the teaching profession is far from being satisfactory. A substantial portion of the candidates for the teaching profession are young people who failed to achieve something more socially attractive, such as a professional career based on academic credentials. The prestige of teachers in the local community is not sufficiently high to impress pupils or their parents. The majority of teachers in Poland have inferiority feelings. Many among them think of themselves as "professional failures, since they do not possess the credentials which lead to greater professional recognition" (Fiszman 1972, p. 318).

The status and role ambiguity experienced by Polish teachers is especially evident in provincial communities, On one hand, they are expected by the authorities to be obedient agents of the system and to socialize pupils according to the Marxist-Leninist doctrine. Any devotion to religion entails political and economic risks, especially if the local Party and state officials are very doctrinaire. On the other hand, the teacher must cooperate with the pupils and their parents. There are informal community pressures that serve to intimidate or at least restrain the Party loyalist. Especially in localities outside the big cities, devotion to religion represents an escape or rescue from the drabness of daily existence. The teacher experiences problems similar to those of the other local people, and there is a natural tendency to share at least some common beliefs with them. There is a substantial difference in this respect between teachers and officials. The latter enjoy much more power and privilege, and therefore they can (or even must) isolate themselves from the rest of the local community.

The ambiguous position of teachers, especially teachers in small towns and rural communities, has much to do with the fierce ideological struggle in Poland between the ruling Communist Party and the Roman Catholic Church. For the common man religion may quite often present the only spiritual resource in the struggle of daily life. But there is also an obvious difference in orientation and experience between the blue-collar worker who earns his living by manual work and the relatively privileged people who served for years as obedient servants of the Stalinist establishment and now enjoy above-average salaries and generous fringe benefits.

The problems of Polish teachers are obviously related to the crisis of state socialism.

> The student seems to perceive his teacher as a sort of operative, a bit timid and generally loyal to the system who, in order to gain favour in the eyes of superiors, tends to discriminate in the classroom in favour of students of working-class or peasant background, or in favour of children whose parents hold high administrative or political posts (Fiszman 1972, pp. 41-42).

It is typical for totalitarianism to utilize teachers as "operatives" for manipulating youth to the advantage of the ruling elite. Yet Fiszman states that in Poland, "Resentments born of economic frustration and status anxieties are easily aggravated and could be turned against those who are perceived to be privileged or 'better off'" (Fiszman 1972, p. 81). This is typical of all sociopolitical situations characterized by widespread social injustice.

TECHNICAL CADRES

In the period 1958-71 the number of people with higher education employed in the Polish nationalized economy grew from 240,000 to 535,000 (women from 67,000 to 199,000), and the number of people with a secondary professional education grew from 439,000 to 1,401,000 (women from 225,000 to 737,000) (Rocznik 1972, p. 116). A large part of them are engineers and technicians. From a small privileged group during the interwar period (5,000 in 1921 and less than 15,000 in 1939), engineers have become very numerous. Employment of engineering and technical personnel in the nationalized industry doubled in the period 1960-71, and the membership of technical professional associations more than doubled.

The growing professionalization of the Polish intelligentsia emphasizes greater identification with the profession than loyalty to the employer. Among graduate chemists studied by Zolzislaw Kowalewski who were working in establishments governed by the Ministry of Chemical Industry, 33 percent showed complete identification with the profession and 38.6 percent showed partial identification; but among the same respondents 10.1 percent felt that they were not partners of the enterprise and 37.2 percent had a passive attitude toward the employing institution. Almost half of all respondents had unsatisfactory housing conditions, which, together with low salaries, was a major source of complaints. Appreciation of material prosperity and of social status was the basic driving force for 66 percent of all the chemists studied by Zdzislaw Kowalewski 1962). In a centralized economy the direct employer has rather limited resources for satisfying the needs for better housing and higher salaries. This is one of the basic reasons for relatively high labor turnover; people go from one workplace to another in search of higher income and better living conditions.

Engineers prefer construction bureaus or research and development institutes over employment in industry. In the case of a sample studied by Anna Grzelak (1965), 66 percent of the surveyed engineers mentioned poor human relations and 50 percent mentioned poor work organization as serious shortcomings of their workplaces. This was so characteristic of the political and managerial system that engineers felt helpless in dealing with such problems. In Zdzislaw Kowalewski's study (1962) of chemical engineers, 50 percent did not believe that they could improve the situation by their own actions or did not want to act, and only 10 percent felt personally responsible for what happened in their workplace. A survey of engineers employed in heavy industry in Warsaw showed a very high level of dissatisfaction with the organization of work (81 percent), with salaries (77 percent), with attention paid by the employer to the interests of his subordinates (72 percent), with prospects for promotion (60 percent), and with the atmosphere (51 percent). Among engineers who wanted to change their jobs, 70 percent were in enterprises, 62 percent were in design bureaus, and 58 percent were in research institutes. A negative evaluation of work organization was given by 81 percent of engineers in industrial enterprises and 68.5 percent of engineers in design offices and institutes. A very positive opinion about organization was expressed only by 3 percent of engineers in enterprises and 4 percent of engineers in bureaus and institutes. In comparison with these aspects, the climate of human relations was evaluated more favorably. This means that it was primarily the formal organization imposed by the higher authorities that caused dissatisfaction (Hozer 1970, p. 156).

In the circumstances of constantly being pressured by an ossified and dehumanized formal organization imposed arbitrarily from outside of one's own workplace, the only rescue may be provided by friends. Engineers surveyed by Jan Hozer were asked who among others would defend their interests if necessary. Twelve percent said the management of their factories, 10 percent said the Party (or other political institutions managed by it), 16 percent said professional associations, 18 percent said that nobody would help them, and the largest portion, 41 percent, said their friends. This means that informal ties play a much more important role than any formalized safeguards (Hozer 1969, p. 119).

It is significant that dissatisfaction with the formal organization existed even among engineers in managerial positions (see Table 8.2). There was some reduction, but the drop did not seem great enough to change the picture greatly. Under the current highly centralized system of management, all engineers in workplaces, whether occupying managerial positions or not, felt dissatisfied.

The same data, related to engineers employed in 1963 in heavy industry, show some basic differences in opinions about the current system of incentives. People who held managerial positions appeared to be more pessimistic (see Table 8.3). Almost 50 percent of all surveyed engineers were employed in research development centers and almost 33 percent in factories (Hozer 1969, pp. 118, 136, 137).

A study of engineers in the electrotechnical industry led L. Pasieczny to conclude that the currently applied "system of financial rewards in general does not stimulate a motivation which would favour technical progress" (Pasieczny 1968, p. 352).

The dissatisfaction among engineers does not mean, however, that they withdraw from commitment to the Party. Many of them advanced socially under the new regime, and they have to pay in a political sense for their promotion. According to data from a 1965 sampling of nine industrial enterprises located in various parts of the country, 65 percent of the technical personnel originally came from the lower social strata (24 percent from peasants and 41 percent from blue-collar workers). Second, the technical personnel are not very far from the blue-collar workers in their basic characteristics and thus do not practice the "splendid isolation" that prevented the traditional intelligentsia from committing themselves to the ruling class. Third, in Poland political activity increases with higher position in the hierarchy. Among engineers and technicians 33 percent are activists, among foremen, 20 percent; among clerical staff, about 15 percent; among skilled workers, about 9 percent; and among unskilled workers, 4 percent (Krall 1970). The technical specialists employed directly in production and management have found it very useful to join the Party. In 1967 over 40 percent of all employed engineers were Party members—many more in production than in design or research and development.

> As party membership becomes more necessary for both
> occupational as well as political reasons at higher levels
> of production management, at lower levels it becomes
> less necessary. Thus if one does not want to enter man-
> agement, then one does not have to become a party mem-
> ber and a process of self-selection occurs by which those
> wanting promotion to management in factories know that
> it entails joining the party at some time. (Kolankiewicz
> 1973, p. 209).

TABLE 8.2

Evaluation of Salaries and Other Material Benefits by
Managerial and Nonmanagerial Engineers

	Positive Evaluation of Current Material Rewards (percent)	
	Managerial	Nonmanagerial
Smooth work	50	18
Technical progress	49	34
Quality improvement	48	33
Cost improvement	40	24
Quantity improvement	39	13
Inventiveness	34	20
Saving of materials	33	22
Operation toward export	32	20
Higher work efficiency	29	11

Source: Hozer 1969, p. 137.

TABLE 8.3

Dissatisfaction of Engineers with Working Conditions
(percent)

Subject of Dissatisfaction	Supervisors				Execu- tives
	Nonmana- gerial	Sec- tion	Depart- ment	Branch	
Salaries	85	82	68	43	52
Work organization	77	84	80	75	57
Consideration for employees	77	76	63	56	18
Opportunities for promotion	71	58	60	36	9
Accommodation and safety	58	54	53	53	39
Pace of work	57	65	63	59	45
Work climate	43	50	51	49	30
Merit rating	39	38	37	28	25
Autonomy	32	24	28	24	24
Relations with superiors	21	23	27	23	18
Work Hours	18	21	30	20	36
Relations with subordinates	4	4	8	4	4
Relations with colleagues	3	4	6	2	7
Conditions of commuting	44	45	29	40	14

Source: Hozer 1969, p. 136.

TABLE 8.4

Social Characteristics of Manual
Workers and Technical Staff
(percent per category)

Characteristic	Manual Workers	Technical Staff
Age 25–40	65	83
Middle or higher education	10	98
Peasant descent	22	24
Worker descent	54	41
Married	92	85
Working Wives	46	68
Wife with secondary or higher education	14	47
Closest friends among engineers or technicians	5	61
Seniority of less than 10 years at present workplace	29	55
Satisfaction with work	55	34
Active interest in changing employer	12	25
Membership in Polish United Workers' Party	31	43
Monthly income over 3,000 zloty	4	23
Regular reading for pleasure	25	44
Regular theater attendance	8	18

Source: Preiss 1967.

People educated under the rule of the present regime are less reluctant than their fathers to join the Party and to gain concrete advantages from it. As long as the percentage of young people ideologically committed to religion is decreasing and the number of people who are not concerned about any ideology is growing (Nowak 1962; Pawelczynska and Nowak 1962; Jozefowicz et al. 1958a, 1958b; Nowak 1960; Kasinska 1970; Wilder 1964), there are no reservations about becoming active in the Party, especially if it seems necessary to support one's professional career. This explains why the percentage of Party militants "is highest among comparatively young engineers and technicians, who have been Party members for 6-10 years, and who have been working for 3-5 years in the same place of employment, and who have a fairly high level of education" (Bauman 1962, p. 64).

Polish engineers and technicians tend to follow a purely pragmatic approach in their orientation toward the Party. In order to achieve something, it is necessary to gain personal acceptance by the Party; commitment to the Party seems no more than practical. Such an interpretation is consistent with the contemporary Polish utilitarian approach to principles. According to survey data from 1970, only 23 percent of Poles felt that one should always follow moral principles, 40 percent declared themselves for flexibility in that respect, and 30 percent took a purely pragmatic approach (7 percent did not answer). In another survey the majority of respondents said they preferred good human relations over effective work (Podgorecki 1971b; 1964; 1966a.

According to data from public opinion polls conducted in 1970, principles evidently count less than the achievement of practical goals in Polish society. Only 22 percent of those surveyed in this respect said they were oriented primarily toward principles, while the rest of the sample was more or less practically oriented (Podgorecki and Kojder 1972, p. 27). The changes in this respect correlate with urbanization and industrialization. It is very significant that farmers committed themselves to the moralistic orientation much more than any other occupational group. The data from public opinion polls also show that Poles are much more individualistically oriented than socially oriented, and that this orientation is slowly changing under the impact of modernization. People become more socially oriented with rise of education, position in the occupational hierarchy, engagement in the social and political activities, and promotion to more responsible jobs (Podgorecki and Kojder 1972, p. 35).

On the other hand, there is an evident tendency in the young generation to give priority to concrete tasks over political loyalties and commitments. Among students surveyed about their ideals, more than half declared themselves for work commitment but only 19 percent declared themselves for loyalty to the state authorities (13 percent among students of worker descent) and only 14 percent declared their political commitment (Przeclawska and Sawa 1971, p. 11).

It seems possible to generalize that the evident growth of importance in Polish society of specialists such as graduate engineers has a very substantial impact on the changes in its ethos. People become more practical, less vulnerable to ideological manipulation, much more utilitarian and task-oriented. Joining the Party ranks becomes a purely practical issue with no substantial ideological consequences. By entering the Party ranks, engineers strengthen its economic and administrative power but also contribute to the progressive dilution of its doctrinal content.

ARCHITECTS

The principal outlet for architectural activity in Poland is within the framework of the 260 designing agencies, which employ a total of 82,000 people (1972). It is common knowledge that these agencies— as servants of the construction industry, to a great extent subordinated to that industry's rigorous demands—have brought a methodology to the field of architecture considerably different from the traditional one. An effective harmonizing of the construction bureaucracy's requirements with the creative demands of designing has come to be of particular importance. The construction sector, being significantly limited in its resources and rather conservative, forces the designing agencies "to treat designing as if it were production. From this arises the inappropriate application of the same yardsticks to the organization of designing as are applied to industrial production . . ." (Buszko 1967, p. 21). As a result, designing agencies limit the creative aptitude of designers to a considerably greater extent than they facilitate the development of such aptitude.

> The material stimuli applied in designing agencies do not encourage designers to seek innovative solutions. . . . The lack of suitably high rewards for innovative solutions, the tension of design deadlines, the endlessness of design outline approval, the difficulties of overcoming resistance to novelties, and the heavy work load, incommensurately rewarded, connected with the constant quest for remuneration all discourage the designer from introducing technological and economic advances" (Pirog 1966, p. 64).

There is comparatively little room in the Polish economy for consciously undertaken, calculated risk; this often leads to errors that result from the lack of opportunity to gain experience from small mistakes. Designing agencies are thus neither capable of nor prone to experimentation, for which they have no resources, no suitable legal framework, nor even a sufficiently wide margin of freedom in self-initiative.

Designing, as practiced within the framework of existing design agencies, is becoming more and more anonymous; the creator is losing control over his work. Architect's supervision is turning into more or less an illusion.

This state of affairs is only partly connected with the change in the architect's role in modern construction: from a patron to a director coordinating the activities of various specialists. The main cause lies in the peculiar institutionalization of an architects' work, which makes it an impersonal product of agency X, and not the product of a particular person or a particular group of people.

Work teams in designing agencies, like research teams (Matejko 1973a), are as a rule small, and are based on individual efforts integrated and coordinated by a group leader. As in scientific research, there is considerable professionalization; there is also support personnel with considerably lower qualifications (in this case, draftsmen and others). Group collaboration by representatives of various specializations is often hampered by the inability to find a common language.

The institutional community of a designing or a construction agency usually consists of three employment categories: the engineering and technical personnel (54,000 people in 1971), the administrative personnel 19,000 in 1971), and the support personnel (about 3,500 in 1971).

There is a social distance between these various categories that has an obvious material basis. On the average, the engineering and technical personnel earn much more (6,000 zloty per month in 1972) than the rest of the workers (3,300 zloty per month in administration and 2,200 zloty for support personnel per month in 1971), and it is fully conscious that the agency depends on its work, and it is furthermore capable of looking after its own interests.

The engineering and technical personnel work in studios that usually have quite a bit of independence as far as taking on contracts and settling accounts are concerned. Employees' remuneration is related to the type of contract that the studio obtains. Much depends on the astuteness of the studio's director and on the extent of his personal contacts. As a result there are often considerable differences between particular studios in the amount of the average remuneration to their employees.

Within particular studios there is a differentiation of social position that is not necessarily linked to the differentiation of rank. This results from the fact that in a creative milieu, professional criteria are usually placed above administrative and institutional criteria.

The director, especially in larger studios, does not occupy the highest position socially; in fact, since he does not participate directly in the designing, his subordinates often consider him to be less important than the senior designers. His domain is the drawing up of contracts, the evaluation of documentation costs, deadlines, and bargaining for his studio's designs with the agency management.

Professional authority is always in the hands of the senior designers—the group leaders. Groups that collaborate to produce a design are usually found in larger studios and consist of one or two designers, some assistants, and a draftsman in addition to the senior designer.

The team leaders or principal designers are the hub of the studio; they establish its work trends, they inform the studio director about production quotas and how many contracts their group can take on (contracts that the studio director then must find), they divide bonuses among the group members, and they make recommendations for promotion.

Professional bonds among groups of designers or technical consultants are to be found not only within a given studio but also between studios, because of the necessity for collaboration among experts representing complementary specializations. This collaboration must take place on the levels of both formal and informal organization. For example, any fundamental changes in a design, which are very troublesome to effect through formal channels, can be made with comparative ease and rapidity in an informal way if the professionals involved are social colleagues.

In studios there are often quite substantial antagonisms connected with differences of privilege, and thus at the same time with the possibility of raising one's employment income. Distances between particular ranks and conflicts arising from them seem to manifest themselves in studios with greater clarity than, for example, in scientific research groups. The amount of actual remuneration is known and is an important criterion of prestige—much more so than in academic circles. Ill feeling between group members is fed not only by differences of privilege but also by the restricted office space and tense work situations. In both of these respects, the average circumstances of engineering and technical personnel are worse than those of scientific personnel.

Involvement with current tasks is so extensive among architects in designing agencies that they have little time left to seek professional stimulation outside their everyday employment responsibilities. Studies carried out in 1965 showed that only a small percentage of designers and studio directors worked eight hours daily during the average workweek; the majority worked more (Pirog 1966). Of architects surveyed in 1959, 80 percent did professional work on Sundays and holidays for anywhere from four to ten hours (Szarfenberg 1966).

The prevailing conception of designing agencies shows a clear preference of productive qualifications to creative qualifications. Agencies are not interested in the creative stimulation of designers; and this is manifested by the dearth of organized exchange of experiences (both at home and abroad), by the lack of education for new

171

arrivals and reeducation of older personnel, and by the lack of stimuli for creative pursuits.

The comparatively high level of professional and cultural aspirations of architects, very closely linked with the intelligentsia tradition of the profession—according to studies in 1959, about 70 percent of architects came from the intelligentsia (Szarfenberg 1966)—is obviously incompatible with existing institutional and organizational conditions. There are few architects (4.7 percent, according to studies from 1965) in the management of designing agencies, whereas economists and lawyers are in the majority (12 percent did not have any profession at all). Architect-designers have comparatively little say in the organization of designing agencies (Pirog 1966).

The internal organization of designing agencies is based on administrative and bureaucratic criteria and by its very nature bypasses professional criteria. Creative needs by no means influence the structure and personnel composition of the studios, for the sole considerations are the needs of current administration. This gives rise to organizational rigidity, a numerical overgrowth of personnel beyond reasonable bounds, a poor attitude of the administrative support personnel, and the impossibility for designers to regroup themselves in answer to the dynamics of changing creative tasks. As a result the organization, instead of serving the creative needs of architecture, suppresses them by isolating itself from them and by coming to be an end in itself.

In the conception of designing agencies, institutional loyalty is placed far higher than professional loyalty. However, agencies do not have the resources to promote this institutional loyalty, for in their aspirations and values, architects and designers always remain professionals and do not become members of institutions. Conservation of this state of affairs is in the interests of designing agencies, since an ambitious architect-creator will always design better than an architect-bureaucrat, even if the former is not sufficiently subordinated.

The role of coordinator and director that falls to the lot of an architect requires a suitable level of autonomy for his professional position, and necessitates protecting him from pressure and giving him enough leeway to take responsibility for his work. In the final analysis, the designing agency as an institution is not capable of completely meeting the architect's professional needs. At present the responsibility for architectural bungling is diluted in impersonal institutional responsibility. Whenever there is nobody to take responsibility for a given piece of work from beginning to end, and at the same time to exert proper influence on the work, undesirable results are inevitable.

There is considerable truth in the universal grumbling of architect-designers that designing agencies are too conservative. This conservatism results from these agencies' being adjuncts to the construction industry. Instead of a creative interchange between architectural conceptions, investors' needs, and construction requirements, the latter at present has all the say. And in the designing agencies there are insufficient resources for propagating novelties and putting them into practice. Efforts aimed at preserving the status quo reign supreme.

JOURNALISTS

The Polish journalist looks upon himself as a member of the intelligentsia (Kupis 1966; Dziecielska 1967); he is connected by social and cultural ties with other members of this social stratum; and he is extremely interested in showing that he shares the traditional social values held by the intelligentsia. Freedom of self-expression, opportunity to achieve something socially valuable, professional autonomy, and opportunity to travel abroad and to learn something about the world outside are values appreciated by journalists.

Journalists are stimulated every day by their environment to accept the values mentioned above. A journalist does not want to be ashamed when comparing his own professional conduct with the conduct of people constituting his sociocultural reference group (his spouse, his friends and acquaintances). His professional activity is under constant scrutiny by these people, who read his articles, criticize him, and expect him not to be opportunistic, narrow-minded, or too materialistic. The fear of not being sufficiently appreciated by members of one's own social circle plays an important role in the motivation of the journalist.

In his job the newspaperman is continually under stress. Sometimes he feels the lack of someone on whose decision he can rely. Other people's opinions of his work are only relative and are not always convincing. The effects he achieves are ephemeral. It is not surprising, therefore, that the newspaperman's moods sometimes change from one extreme to another.

A pleasant atmosphere among the staff, inspired by the behavior of the editors, is therefore of particular importance. A friendly atmosphere in the office is an effective antidote to depression. The understanding and help of other people on the staff neutralize the stresses caused by the very character of the job, and may help to restore emotional balance.

The confidence felt by the staff in the assessment of their work by superiors who enjoy all-round authority (professional, administrative, and personal) facilitates self-analysis and helps people to take

173

a balanced view of their work. Freedom in the office encourages people to take a positive attitude toward their work and to attach appropriate weight to its ethical aspect.

A study of the journalistic staffs of two prominent Polish journals and two well-known newspapers, made in 1963, showed that the attractiveness of a particular working environment is evaluated by journalists and newspapermen not only on the basis of material reward but also according to the possibility of maintaining the intellectual, moral, and social standards held by the higher social strata of the intelligentsia. The management of a newspaper or of a journal has to take this into consideration if it wants to keep its employees and to promote a climate favorable to creativity. The employees expect their supervisors to preserve the internal freedom of the editorial staff from external pressures, to maintain high professional standards, and to take care of the basic material needs of the personnel; they also expect to have an opportunity to participate in important decisions.

Effective management of a journal or newspaper in Poland consists, according to the survey mentioned above, in effectively counterbalancing the external pressures with the professional and social aspirations of the personnel. In this respect the most effective managers are those with strong political positions and spend most of their time and effort in making the attitude of external authorities as favorable as possible toward the journal or newspaper. However, they have to simultaneously recognize the professional aspirations of their subordinates, to allow room for expression, not to take their own power too seriously, and to be friendly with publicists who enjoy high professional prestige.

The publicists form a professional elite in the best Polish newspapers and journals. They feel responsible for the good name of the journal or newspaper; they have a decisive voice in many internal and external affairs; they are the contact men between the journalists and other professions; they also have many connections with important political pressure groups. A good management is eager to cooperate with publicists, thus establishing its own power and avoiding unnecessary tensions. This means giving journalists autonomy within the editorial office and accepting professional values and prestige hierarchy. The alliance of management and of the elite consisting of publicists was typical for the journalistic teams studied, which showed very high indexes of work satisfaction and professional creativity (Matejko 1964b).

The journalistic team has been mentioned in order to emphasize two characteristics of Polish professionals. One of them is shared with professionals everywhere, and especially in the West: a strong predilection for professional autonomy. The other is much more unusual, even if not unique to Poland. It deals with the specific social role of the profession as a link between the individual and the intelligentsia, with its specific tradition and its myth of being the moral leader of the nation. In this last respect Polish journalists differ much from, for example, American journalists, whose frame of reference is in general much narrower, limited to their own profession or even to their own newsroom (Breed 1955).

On all the four papers studied, the staff members had very strong social and professional ambitions. They tended to look on journalism as a job calling for boldness, a job in which they should put forward and submit to public discussion such views of their own as would lead to wide controversy, and would inspire and compel others to revise their stereotyped ways of thinking and acting.

It is not suprising, then, that on the papers in our study the dominant role on the staff is played by the journalists. On both dailies they constitute a majority of the editorial staff and on both weeklies a very pronounced majority. They who set the tone of the paper, it is their opinions that count, and their values and aspirations as journalists count the most. As a result, all four papers are quality publications.

It often happens that newspapermen's ambitions extend beyond journalism to the creative, literary sphere as well because they have many and wide contacts with other people in the creative arts and the professions. There is a fairly sharp difference here between the newspapermen studied by us and the American newspapermen studied by W. Breed. The Americans live in a homogeneous circle that restricts their ambitions. The Poles live in a professionally mixed environment of intelligentsia and are under the pressure of its traditional values, norms, and patterns. The journalists want to raise their prestige to the level of those professions, and therefore try to make their work as creative as possible. They specialize, and try to secure a stable position not only in the own world of the press but also in the particular environment—artistic, legal, political—in which they are professionally interested. Hence the tendency for journalists to keep introducing new subjects that will be of interest to the public, and that will bring public approval not only to the paper but also to the people working on it.

A number of circumstances, both external and internal, determine what new topics are brought up and whether or not they see the light of day. Many factors—the authorities' approval or disapproval of the ideas put forward by the paper, limitations of space, the editor's encouraging or discouraging attitude toward the ideas submitted, commendation or lack of commendation by colleagues, the habits of readers—all affect the creative atmosphere in the newspaper office. In the case of the two weeklies in the survey, these factors had an inspiring effect and the same was to an extent true of the two daily papers, although they had much less scope for development.

In all four cases, however, circumstances were not up to the high social and professional aspirations of the staff. Their chances of finding space for their articles, of being able to execute bold new plans, of finding access to material (for example, through foreign travel), or of reporting an interesting subject were restricted, mostly by external considerations independent of the paper. Both the editors in charge and the journalists were well aware of the necessity of accepting restrictions from outside, and this awareness was one of the strong bonds between them.

On the other hand, the social and professional aspirations of the newspapermen were not restricted to any great extent by the relationships within the staff itself. Seldom was a journalist held back in his professional ambitions by pressure from his immediate superiors or by the general atmosphere in the office. Rather, both the attitude of the editors and the atmosphere among colleagues tended to provide inspiration, to arouse ambition, and to condemn the easy way out. In this respect the situation here was quite the opposite of that found in the American papers investigated by W. Breed (1955), where the atmosphere in the office clearly discouraged the newspapermen from taking an interest in wider affairs, and encouraged them to pursue success in the narrow field of sensational or local news. It must be remembered, however, that in Poland the newspapermen belonged to some of the leading papers in the country, whereas the newspapermen studied by W. Breed worked on smaller papers in the northeastern states.

The staff of the papers in our survey did not complain to any great extent of their ambitions being frustrated by authoritarianism on the part of the editors, by unjust favoritism of one group over another, by the low professional, intellectual, or moral level of other members of the staff (and the editors in particular), or by bad human relations in the office. Complaints were, of course, sometimes made, but infrequently.

The fact that the newspapermen in our survey have close links with other occupational groups undoubtedly makes it easier for them to keep well informed of readers' tastes and of the best way to influence them. All four papers in our survey clearly cater to the educated classes. When both writers and readers belong mostly to the intelligentsia, there is no difficulty in finding a common language. The occupational motivation of the newspapermen is based firmly on the wish to maintain the level of their paper and to keep raising it. They are usually sensitive to public opinion, which reaches them easily through social contacts. Clearly they are anxious not to lose the confidence of their readers but, rather, to increase that confidence by taking up topics of special importance to the wider public.

As an important medium of mass communication, a periodical, particularly a daily paper, must fulfill requirements of a political nature. Some of these matters are quite delicate. For instance, the paper is expected to show certain problems in a certain light, or to perform tasks of particular importance to the authorities. The editors, and especially the editor-in-chief, have the difficult task of passing on the authorities' suggestions and of inducing the staff to follow the official line. On the other hand, the editor-in-chief represents the staff to the authorities and voices its wishes. In both cases he must act as a cushion for the shocks that are inevitable with every change on the staff or in the content of the paper—changes that often have a very strong impact on the mood and professional morale of writers who take their work seriously.

On all the papers in our survey, the editor-in-chief keeps close contacts with government and Party authorities, which usually takes up a great deal of his time. Since he has many duties outside the office, he is sometimes unable to act effectively as head of the paper and be readily available to members of the staff who want his advice or decision. This is not beneficial to the paper, but it is of paramount importance that the editor-in-chief do a good job as liaison with the authorities.

The standards of the paper depend upon the talents and the enthusiasm of its editorial staff. Hence the atmosphere of the office must promote the individual and collective initiative. In all the offices investigated in our survey, both the editors and the other employees are interested in keeping up the level of the paper, which creates a bond of understanding between them and does a great deal to maintain a friendly atmosphere. The editor usually gives his staff a great deal of freedom, imposing minimal restrictions and avoiding bureaucratic methods. "You have to trust people," remarked the editor of one of these papers. "Let them assume full responsibility for their own work. . . . In running this paper I have learned the value of tolerance. I know that we have to do with a very sensitive organism."

Emphasis is placed on careful personnel selection and on the encouragement of strong job motivation. As a rule there are few changes of staff. It is a great honor for a newspaperman to be a member of the staff of any of these papers. Nearly 75 percent of the newspapermen involved have been working for the same paper for more than five years. Nearly 66 percent have been in the occupation for more than 10 years, and over 90 percent have been working as newspapermen for more than five years; yet only 20 percent are aged 45 or over. One-quarter are women, this proportion being the same as the national average in the occupation. Eighty percent belong to the intelligentsia by background. Newspapermen exceed the national monthly average earnings (3,175 zloty, according to a 1960 survey), but there is a considerable difference between the elite, such as the journalists and editors, and the rest of the staff. Approximately 60 percent of the elite and about 40 percent of the rest have an income of over 2,000 zloty per person in the family (1963). More than 40 percent of the elite and only 20 percent of the rest assess their own financial situation as better than average.

There is a very friendly atmosphere, although distance is respected, between the principal journalists and the rest of the staff. The editors usually enjoy considerable authority among their staff because they themselves are writers. In this study, we compared three different kinds of authority accorded by the staff to the editors: professional authority (as journalists), administrative authority (as superiors), and personal authority (as colleagues). In most cases these kinds of authority coincide (an important index of the functional value of the editors), which undoubtedly makes for stability of relationships on the paper's staff.

As a rule the formal organization of the office is simple, loose, and fairly elastic. Sometimes the sections are not even clearly defined. The same may be said about the assignment of responsibility. The organization is very pliable and the editor changes it as he goes along, as he thinks fit. This is possible because there is a distinctly crystallized informal organization within the office, welding people together and bringing order to the human relationships. This organization is obvious on all levels of the staffs of these papers but especially at the top, on the editorial level.

On these papers the editors have been a well-knit team for years. They are not only colleagues during office hours but friends as well. In the case of the two weeklies, for example, the people at the top form a solid group. In both cases the editor-in-chief leaves the everyday running of the paper to his deputy and to the editorial secretary, both of whom are his personal friends. These three people are at the helm of the paper and between them the responsibilities are fairly clearly delineated.

The dominant group on these papers is composed of the journalists (feature writers), who have been closely linked for years. They are closest to the editors, with whom they are connected both professionally and socially. Other categories of the staff (those who work in the city section or the telegraphists) form their own groups. These, however, are of much less significance. The proofreaders and office staff who are not journalists are really outsiders, although as a rule they are on polite terms with the newspapermen. Thus between the writers and the nonwriters, between the famous names and the employees unknown to the general public, between the editors and the rank-and-file employees, the fundamental barriers remain.

On all the surveyed papers, there is a division of responsibility. One person (the technical editor) looks after the everyday management of the work. Someone else looks after the financial side. One person is a constant source of new ideas. Another is regarded by the others as an authority on moral questions, and his opinion is sought whenever there is a dispute. One person is known to be always ready to organize help. Another acts as the paper's conscience, and openly expresses opinions even if they are displeasing to the authorities above. All these people are necessary if the social system on the paper is to function properly, for they help to lower tensions that might otherwise threaten the cohesion of the staff.

As far as the newspapers in our survey were concerned, it was obvious that the principle of minimum intervention was being applied: "Meddle as little as possible with the course of events, achieve your ends by interfering as little as possible, and wherever possible without your own intervention" (Kotarbinski 1955, p. 149). This principle is of particular significance when one is dealing with highly qualified people who know their jobs and know each other. The confidence shown by a superior in his subordinates encourages the team to show still more collective initiative, and frees the man in charge from having to push, urge, and control. In such circumstances the team effectively controls itself, and by itself produces the creative energy to push it along.

In this study considerable weight was attached to finding out how the staff of a newspaper regarded the job and its institutional framework. The newspapermen were asked about the attractions and drawbacks of their job, and the hierarchy of positive and negative traits shown below was obtained (these traits are given in order of the frequency with which they were mentioned).

Naturally the various categories of employees in the newspaper world assess their occupational situations differently. Journalists have much more cause for satisfaction than telegraphists, for example; some of the latter treat their job as a temporary stage, an unpleasant but necessary stepping-stone to something better on the professional ladder. But even among journalists, 40 percent said they had insufficient opportunities for creative expression, while more than 66 percent were dissatisfied with themselves (evidence of their tendency toward self-criticism). There is a general feeling of insecurity that is heightened by insufficient professional training (hence a certain amount of jealousy with regard to physicians and engineers) and by the exaggerated impressions of respondents that the occupation of newspaperman enjoys low prestige among the public.*

---

*According to a study made toward the end of 1958 by Wlodzimierz Wesolowski and Adam Sarapata on the opinions of Warsaw

Attractions of the Job

1. Attractive in itself because it offers an opportunity for wide contacts and for seeing life.   51%

2. It gives a large degree of personal freedom,
   much more than other office occupations (with
   which the newspaperman often compares his own).   24%

3. It gives an opportunity to do something useful for
   the community.   25%

Drawbacks of the Job

1. It is nerve-wracking, exhausting work involving
   constant tension.   34%

2. Neither the authorities nor the public really
   understands the character of newspaper work and
   its problems.   20%

3. It is poorly paid compared with the effort and
   qualifications required.   17%

4. It is marked by professional dilettantism as
   compared with the more specialized professions.   14%

5. It achieves little effect.   11%

6. It has no drawbacks.   4%

Newspapermen have fairly high social and professional aspirations, and their job does not offer them a field where they can find
sufficient stability, where they can feel completely secure and enjoy
the satisfaction of permanent achievement. As with the actor, the
newspaperman must always reassert his position by producing new
work that is soon forgotten. Even the most effective article has a
short life, especially an article published in a daily. Consequently,
the more ambitious journalist often tries to publish a book. This,

---

inhabitants, the newspaperman was ninth on the list of occupations
in regard to social prestige and financial rewards but eleventh on the
list in regard to job security (Sarapata and Wesolowski 1961).

however, calls for quite a different approach—first and foremost, concentration on a single subject, which is difficult for a man used to jumping from one subject to another. The social model of the literary man is an attractive one and is not too difficult for the newspaperman to achieve, compared with the roles of professor, politician, or social worker.

Among newspapermen and especially among journalists, there was considerable criticism of their own occupational group. Asked to mention the principal traits of newspapermen, the journalists mentioned mostly negative traits: superficiality (33 percent of the replies), conceit (16 percent), and cynicism and opportunism (12.5 percent). Positive traits, such as mental agility, sensitivity, and broad horizons were mentioned; but they came further down the scale (all these positive traits taken together were mentioned in only a little more than 33 percent of the replies). Newspapermen also took a rather pessimistic view of the prestige of their occupation both in the eyes of the public and in the eyes of the authorities.

This self-criticism should be interpreted in terms of the disparity between the newspapermen's aspirations and their actual social and occupational situation. The elite of the newspaper staffs (the editors and journalists) think the essence of their job is above all to inform readers and to intervene in the public interest (28 percent of the replies for each of these), and only to a lesser extent to form public opinion (26 percent) or to act as a link between the authorities and the public (10 percent). According to the journalists in our survey, the traits desirable in journalists are honesty and personal integrity (36 percent of the replies), and a well-informed mind and width of horizons (23 percent); further down the scale were agility of mind, talent and professional skill, easy rapport with people, and commitment to public issues (which together accounted for 41 percent of the replies).

According to the elite of the newspaper staff, external impositions are responsible for the difficulty of achieving these ideals. When asked about the conditions necessary for practicing the occupation of newspaperman as it should be, 75 percent of the respondents mentioned external conditions: satisfactory working conditions and pay, 29 percent; freedom of expression, 25 percent; good treatment by the authorities, 8 percent; good atmosphere in the office, 7 percent; public respect and understanding of the character of the job, 5 percent. Only about 25 percent mentioned the intellectual level (17 percent) and moral level (9 percent) of the newspapermen themselves.

ARTISTS AND ACTORS

In the development of many white-collar professions there are instances where professional aspirations and legitimate expectations of basic conditions for properly cultivating the profession have considerably outgrown the reality of a society that has quite limited internal resources. The artistic profession is a good example. Because of the support given by the Communist state to art schools, the number of artists tripled within a little more than a decade. Several institutions have been established to promote artistic creativity.

The annual number of graduates of institutions of higher artistic education has grown four times when comparing the academic year 1970/71 with that 1950/51. According to data for 1971/72, there were over 5,000 students enrolled in art schools on the academic level and 30,000 in art schools on the secondary education level (Rocznik 1972, pp. 469, 473). However, the demand for artistic products is still limited primarily to government purchases. The general public is not sufficiently well off to buy the goods created by artists, even though they are relatively much less expensive than those found in the West. There is also a problem of the artistic maturity of the population as potential customers.

All these factors make the situation of the artist ambiguous. On the one hand he is stimulated by professional ambition and by the pressure of his environment to strive for artistic values, which are treated as important national assets. Also, his social position is relatively high in a society lacking the prewar privileged strata that formerly were sponsors for "marginal people" like the artists. The artist now depends on his professional milieu not only occupationally and socially but also economically. To a large extent it is his colleagues who decide the stipend he eventually receives, his participation in exhibits, and his acceptance or nonacceptance. "The economic career and prestige status of an artist in society in great measure depends on his milieu, as often does his career in intellectual and artistic circles, and the degree of his professional satisfaction. The influence and power of the milieu is due on the one hand to its indispensability and attractiveness to the artist, and on the other, to the effective means of reprisal it possesses. The artist's dependence on his milieu is many-sided and it may be complete in the case of average talents" (Wallis 1964, p. 228).

The development of a centrally planned social system, with its expanded bureaucracy, does not necessarily diminish the social role of the more or less autonomous professional artistic groups. The bureaucrat has to depend on the opinions of experts shaped by their specific environments and cultivating their own professional values.

The social importance of strategic elites (Keller 1963) that consist of highly educated members of various substrata of the intelligentsia is far from negligible. The expanding economy needs experts, but this does not necessarily mean that the needs and expectations of the latter are fully met.

STUDENTS

The situation of the Polish higher educational system since the 1950s reveals both features that are universal and inherent in academic systems, and features that are particular to relatively poor countries, to countries in which the government is determined to use the universities as instruments of social and economic progress, in which the government aspires to achieve progress through comprehensive planning, and in which the government believes in the rightness of a uniformity of opinion as the foundation of its security and progress.

What is universal is the persistence of academic tradition, a persistence that is greatly fostered by the high prestige of universities, colleges, and the academic profession. The academic traditions are those arising from Alexander von Humboldt's reforms of the German universities at the beginning of the 19th century—the freedom of teaching and research, the unity of teaching and research, and academic self-government.

There are now more than twice as many institutions of higher education in Poland as there were before World War II. The number of students has grown from 14 per 10,000 population in 1937-38 to 57 in 1957-58 and 109 in 1972-73. From 1945 to 1965 four times more diplomas were awarded than during 1919-39.

This great expansion is a function of deliberate government policies deriving from the intention to increase the number of persons capable of filling higher administrative, technological, and managerial roles and the corresponding financial support to the institutions that produce such personnel; it is also a function of an increased demand for higher education by strata of the society that before World War II contributed only a tiny proportion of the students at Polish universities and colleges.

As in other countries, the possession of higher education has become one of the most important preconditions for entry into positions with greater authority, prestige, and remuneration. Naturally, as in other countries, it is not the sole precondition; membership in the Polish United Workers' Party is also of great importance.

Nonetheless, it is not just popular demand for higher education that determines the numbers attending universities and colleges in

Poland. The Polish government, believing that it needs higher education to meet the managerial and technological needs of the society it is seeking to create, attempts to plan its higher educational system in accordance with estimates of future "needs." The number of freshmen to be accepted is decided every year by central planning authorities on the basis of criteria that purport to take into consideration the long-term demand for specialists in particular branches, as well as the facilities and staffs of the school system. The decisions regarding the right number of places to provide are not, however, all-powerful, since they cannot control the vocational aspirations of young people. For example, in the last few years interest in medical careers has diminished considerably, apparently because of the relatively modest incomes of physicians and the hard work believed to be characteristic of their profession.

The power of the planners is also restricted by limitations on resources. Even if they wished to have more graduates, it would be difficult because of the limited academic staff and facilities. The availability of both is directly determined by the state, the only disposer of all resources; the demand for resources in fields other than higher education limits the planners' capacities in higher education. The rising cost of modern scientific equipment and the demand of university teachers for opportunities and means of doing research also affect the capacity of the planners to concentrate their resources on the output of technological and other highly qualified specialists. Since the Polish government is also committed to the furtherance of scientific research and to the development of technological research, it cannot disregard these demands, although they are difficult to harmonize with the planning of the output of high-level manpower.

Besides these variables, which are independent of and sometimes antithetical to higher education planning as a part of economic and social planning, there is faculty and departmental particularism, which leads to exaggerated demands and often bears little relation to intellectual or social needs. Some groups try to establish a monopolistic position. There are also conflicts between various occupational groups—between scientists and administrators, or between junior and senior staff—that are expressed in conflicting demands for resources. Finally, the effort to plan research—which is a different operation from the planning of higher education—quite apart from inherent difficulties, has to allow for the freedom of individual initiative and for idiosyncratic modes of dealing with scientific problems. Some of these difficulties are characteristic of any modern society that, expending much of its resources on higher education, attempts to obtain the best possible results; others are more typical of a centralized, one-party system of government committed to comprehensive planning, and others may be unique to Poland, which combines the first two characteristics with Polish traditions.

The Polish university system has a long tradition (Barycz 1957). The Jagiellonian University at Cracow, established in 1364, is the oldest. It was only in the 19th century, however, that Poland established its own university traditions. And since parts of Poland were occupied by Russia, Austria, and Prussia from 1795 to 1918, Polish universities existed only in a restricted area of the country. Only in the part occupied by Austria was higher education conducted in Polish. Students were in spirit and in background closely linked to the existing elites—aristocracy, gentry, bourgeoisie and the professional classes. Even during the interwar period when Poland regained its territorial integrity, the relatively small student body—50,000 in 1937-38 for a population of 35 million—was limited almost entirely to the offspring of socially privileged strata. The style of life and the expectations of Polish university students were shaped almost exclusively by the traditions of the gentry and of the intelligentsia. Good manners, broad cultural interests, strong feelings of honor and patriotism, indifference toward practical applications of knowledge, feelings of superiority over lower social strata, distaste for hard work, and a lively conviviality were important parts of the Polish academic ethos.

The present-day Polish students are in many respects quite different from their prewar predecessors. First of all, there are many more of them—361,000 in 1972-73, in a population of 33 million. Second, a considerable number of them come from the manual workers' stratum and the peasantry. Third, a large proportion (37 percent in 1972-73) attend evening courses or enroll for extramural studies, combining education with gainful employment. Certain other notable differences exist: for example, a very large proportion of the student body (36 percent) is in technological studies (see Table 8.5). The proportion of women students has increased in the period 1950-72 from 34 percent to 44 percent, and a very large proportion of students are sponsored by the state.

In 1967-68 all institutions of higher education admitted 45 percent of all candidates for the first year of studies: universities, 40 percent; technical colleges, 51 percent; agricultural colleges, 46 percent; schools of economics, 44 percent; schools of education, 52 percent; medical schools, 37 percent; schools of physical culture, 33.5 percent; schools of art, 32 percent. Some candidates not admitted enter the evening and extension programs. Probably for this reason the number of students participating in the fields mentioned above has grown especially fast—from 27,000 to 84,000 in 1971-72. The demand for places varies markedly from field to field. For example, in the 1960s psychology, archaeology, sociology, and English language and literature became very popular, and there were four, five, six, or more candidates for one place. The popularity of education, economics, medicine, pharmacology, mathematics, and physics,

TABLE 8.5

The Rate of Increase of Students in
Various Fields, 1937-66
(1937-38 = 100)

Technical sciences	1,132.1
Agricultural sciences	891.9
Mathematics and natural sciences	571.3
Economics and political science	472.0
Humanities	453.1
Medicine	398.7
Art	218.1
Law	173.6
Theology	139.3

Source: Compiled by the author from data in the Polish statistical yearbooks.

has considerably diminished. The trend is by no means linear. For example, the proportion of graduates in the humanities, law, and economics fell between 1937 and 1956 from 56.8 percent to 19.2 percent, but by 1966-67 it had risen to 34.6 percent.

Polish higher education has a high proportion of female students. The sex ratio among the urban population in the age group 20-24 is 105 females to 100 males (in rural population only 89 females to 100 males), but of all university daytime students 60 percent are women. They dominate in biology, philology, history, education, psychology, and library science. In medical schools, women constitute 66 percent of all students, and in teacher training the percentage is even higher. Considering graduates from all institutions of higher education, the proportion of women has grown from 31 percent in 1952-53 to 39 percent in 1966-67 and to 43 percent in 1970-71.

Despite the increased equality of opportunity in comparison with the interwar period, of all candidates for admission to higher education, 60 percent come from the white-collar strata, which constitute less than 25 percent of the gainfully employed. Among young people who completed their secondary education and came from peasant or worker strata, only 33-50 percent continue their studies up to the level of higher education. Thus the unequal extent to which the various social classes participate in higher education persists, even though higher education is free. The traditional orientations are still to be seen, for example, in the fact that interest in humanities is most pronounced among the offspring of those in the learned professions. The offspring of peasants and workers incline much more toward technical studies.

The government and Party authorities are sensitive about the origins of the student body. For example, the student demonstrations in March 1968 were said by the authorities to be the result of inadequate representation by peasants' and workers' offspring in the student body. In order to change this situation, certain privileges for those coming from worker and peasant backgrounds were considerably extended. For example, more scholarships are awarded and more points given to applicants for admission from these strata. Government and Party leaders are convinced that if they can change the balance between students of worker and peasant origin and students from the families of the intelligentsia, they will be able to diminish political criticism and dissatisfaction among students. It is possible, however, that they underestimate the great prestige in Poland of the social and cultural patterns created and maintained by the intelligentsia and the influence of these patterns on young persons from the lower social strata who enter the universities.

Forty percent of all daytime students have scholarships that are supposed to help support them while they are studying (there are no school fees). Of the students who have scholarships, 33 percent have only partial scholarships. Scholars are sponsored either by the school authorities (77 percent) or by factories and institutions interested in employing graduates—local authorities, state enterprises, cooperatives, banks, and others (23 percent) (Rocznik 1972, p. 489). About 25 percent of all daytime students live in student residences free of charge. Nevertheless, even those students who have full scholarships and live in residences need additional income. There are many extracurricular activities in which students would like to participate: drama societies, cinemas, sports, concerts, excursions, summer camps. Indeed, the student is expected to participate in them. The diffusion of West European and North American styles of life is quite significant in this respect. All this creates severe pressures, especially on students who do not have any substantial financial support from their families.

There are 88 separate institutions of higher education, including 10 universities, in Poland. Almost 20 percent of all students are in Warsaw. The four largest academic centers—Warsaw, Cracow, Poznan, and Wroclaw—have more than half of the entire student population (54 percent in 1971/72), as well as of all day students (55 percent in 1971/72).

The territorially unequal distribution of schools creates problems regarding the availability of educational facilities to people in various parts of the country and from various social strata. On the whole, candidates from the peasant and worker strata tend to come from provincial areas, whereas those from the white-collar strata are from big cities. As Jan Szczepanski points out, the number of applicants per 1,000 inhabitants is several times higher in Warsaw or large voivodship towns with one or more university schools than in rural areas. Some agricultural areas situated far from the center send fewer candidates than central voivodships with big university towns. Many village children are unable to obtain secondary education, since many secondary schools have no adequate boarding facilities; also, many families cannot afford to send their children to university towns because their income is too high to qualify for a grant but not high enough to support a son or daughter away from home (Szczepanski 1966, pp. 35-36).

The requirement of linking teaching to research work is widely acknowledged in Poland. However, this requirement is quite difficult to put into practice, especially when—as is the case in Poland and throughout the Communist countries—basic and applied research is to a large extent organizationally separated from higher education. W. Michajlow, the deputy minister of education, pointed out: "We rightly want teaching to be based on research work, but at the same time we know in advance that we will not be able to provide all centres and chairs [departments] with sufficient funds for their full development and ensure rapid and continuous modernization of the necessary apparatus (up to 10 percent of its annual value)" (Michajlow 1966, p. 16).

The second problem, which at present seems even more acute, is related to the question of how to reconcile specialized teaching with the formation of personalities. Education, in its broader sense, should "help young people to make the right decisions, draw them into the mainstream of social progress and encourage active participation in it" (Golanski 1966, p. 25). In the daily practice of teaching it is, however, quite difficult to find enough time and attention for anything beyond the basic curriculum. There is a general trend to the professionalization of education, which quite often narrows the outlook of the teachers as well as of the students. This is particularly true for technical and medical colleges.

The entrance examinations, which young people have to pass (after receiving a matriculation certificate from their secondary school) in order to be admitted to one of the higher education institutions, give priority to candidates with some inclination for the particular subject. After being admitted, the student concentrates on topics closely related to one particular field. It is, of course, necessary to make a specialist of him; but at the same time not enough room has been left over for breadth of education. The danger of overspecialization, of "trained incapacity," may be overcome only by broadening the curriculum, by exploring and developing new ways of teaching, and by widening the horizons of the teaching staff. Some improvements in all these respects have been introduced. For example, sociology has become a subject of instruction in technical colleges. However, much more needs to be done.

ACADEMIC STAFF

The academic staff is divided into two basic categories: senior staff, consisting of full professors, associate professors, and assistant professors (called docents and situated higher in the hierarchy in Poland than in the United States); and junior staff, consisting of adjuncts (with a doctorate or even a docent degree), senior assistants, and junior assistants. In addition to these two basic categories, there are posts found only in universities or research institutes. In the more academic institutions there are lecturers, tutors, persons who have special three-year grants in order to study for the doctorate, and trainees who have a master's degree and are appointed for one year, with a view to subsequent appointment to an assistantship. In institutes of applied research, there are senior research workers who may not have a doctorate but have been appointed because of their long experience and achievements, mostly of a practical character (Matejko, ed, 1967; Szlapczynski 1968).

The graduate student with a master's degree who is employed as an assistant must serve for a minimum of two years to be appointed to a senior assistantship. He has to work for from three to six years for his doctorate and may afterward be employed as an adjunct. He then has to write a new dissertation and pass a special examination for appointment as a docent. This takes another six years. After several years of teaching and research, some docents are appointed to an associate professorship.

According to the revised higher education bill of December 1968, the ministry responsible for education has the power to promote junior staff members with a doctorate (even without this degree in exceptional cases) to the post of assistant or associate professor without presenting the docent dissertation and taking the special examination. This is a very significant change from the previous state of affairs. The power of the state authorities in selecting candidates for professorial posts has thus been considerably extended. About 2,000 doctorates were awarded annually during the 1960s, whereas in 1955-60 only about 400 were awarded annually. In 1972, 2,801 doctorates were granted, 25 percent to women. The number of docent degrees has increased from 82 annually in 1956-60 to about 600 annually in 1969-71. In 1972, 518 docent degrees were granted, about 20 percent to women (Concise 1973, pp. 218-19).

There was a very serious shortage of academic staff in Poland after World War II; some institutions were understaffed for several years and the quality of the staff, especially in the professional schools, was inadequate. In the 1960s this situation improved considerably through the establishment of a large fellowship program and to the formal pressure of state and Party authorities. There were 38,000 teachers in institutions of higher education in 1972-73, compared with 19,000 in 1960-61. Nonetheless, in all technical colleges the average number of students per professor rose during the period 1960-68 from 64.6 to 92.4. In general, the ratio of professors to students is still inadequate (1:73 in the Mining and Foundry Academy, in Cracow, and 1:234 in the schools of engineering).

According to government plans, the size of the academic staff should rise considerably. The senior staff has so far grown more slowly than the junior staff. As a result, the average age of full and associate professors was 62 in 1960 and only a small percentage of all professors are in the 30-40 age bracket. The slow growth of the number of full and associate professors may be explained in part by the strength of the vested interests of the senior staff in restricting their own numbers and in part by the very cautious policy of the ministry, which until recently acted very slowly on recommendations for promotion.*

A more rapid expansion of the number of professors would be costly; but since their salaries are not high, the cost would not be extreme. Over half (56.4 percent) of all professors are in Warsaw. The capital is attractive for academic staff because it is the cultural, social, and political center of the country. Brilliant men tend to gravitate to Warsaw. This does not mean, however, that provincial universities and research centers are in general much inferior.

It is quite difficult for academic staff to move because of housing shortages and legal difficulties. The government authorities deliberately seek, as a matter of policy, to hold down the mobility of urban inhabitants. It is impossible to settle in big cities without special permission, which is quite difficult to obtain, especially for Warsaw. The relocation of academic staff and training within Poland is therefore so difficult that it is sometimes easier to study abroad.

---

*There were several changes in the name and scope of the state ministry responsible for the academic staff. For several years it was a special Ministry of Higher Education, which later was reunited with the Ministry of Elementary and Secondary Education. Since 1973 there has been one ministry responsible for education, science, and technology.

The structure of the academic staff reflects government policy in another way: there is a tendency for new appointments to be made increasingly in the natural sciences, medicine, and technology, while relatively few are made in the arts, thus freezing the traditionally top-heavy structure of the more conventional academic subjects; appointments in the junior grades go increasingly to the more "useful" subjects.

By contrast with the prewar period, the dominant position among academic staff, as among the entire Polish intelligentsia, has moved from students of humanities to those of technical and related professions. Of the 45,500 members of scientific societies at the end of 1971, only 33 percent were in the social sciences and 50 percent in the natural sciences and technology. The number of technical personnel (graduate engineers and technicians) who were members of their professional societies doubled in the 1960s (from 155,000 in 1960 to 327,000 in 1971). In 1971, 29 percent of all associate professor appointments were in technology, compared with only 7 percent in 1960. Of all doctorates given on the basis of a written thesis, those in technology grew from 10 percent in 1961 to 21 percent in 1971 (Rocznik 1972, pp. 451, 453, 449). In Poland it is now possible to obtain a doctorate either on the basis of a written thesis or without it.

Of the 42,000 scientific workers active in Poland in 1971 (46,000 in 1972), only 5 percent were full or associate professors, a large majority of them being concentrated in institutions of higher education. These institutions obviously dominate research even though the state spends much effort in promoting centers of applied research other than teaching institutions. Some changes, occurring gradually from the bottom, can be observed in the increase of women in scientific work (see Table 8.6). Women are much more numerous on the lower levels of the professional ladder than on the higher ones, for the professional advancement of women to the higher ranks is still slow.

Within departments and institutes the most promising students are encouraged to pursue an academic career. The performance of students at seminars and participation in research conducted by the professor or other senior staff members provide frequent opportunities for careful observation of candidates. Every department or institute has to apply to the university, and the university to the state ministry, for the provision of paid assistantships and paid three-year doctoral fellowships. If the ministry is sympathetic to the subject or to its professor, or if it believes that the subject satisfies social and economic "needs," it will strengthen that particular department or institute. The head will have at his disposal enough facilities to recruit the best students and to foster their first steps up the academic ladder. The personal relations of the head with university and ministerial authorities play an important part. If, for

TABLE 8.6

Percentage of Women on the Research and Teaching Staffs of Colleges, 1966

	Full Professor	Associate Professor	Assistant Professor	Adjunct	Assistant Junior	Assistant Senior
Total	5	7	15	28	33	36
General universities	5	12	23	32	35	39
Technical universities	2	3	4	13	20	24
Agricultural schools	4	7	10	25	36	36
Economic schools	—	6	7	19	27	29
Medical schools	6	13	20	45	45	45
Educational schools	—	10	17	34	39	29
Art schools	19	16	22	20	34	24
Number	33	94	293	1,674	2,019	1,011

Source: Compiled by the author from data of the Polish Ministry of Higher Education.

personal or political reasons, the ministry is unsympathetic to the professor, then it is likely to be difficult for him to make his organizational unit attractive to students by providing them with research and employment opportunities.

The roles of the institution's rector and of the state ministry are quite important at this stage of the academic career. It is for the rector and the ministry to decide who may enlarge his department or institute, or make provision for and give incentives to his protégés. The authorities of the particular faculty (the dean and the institute director) also have something to say in this respect, since the proposal to the rector and the ministry must have their approval and their decisions are guided by the same considerations as guide the rector and the ministry: the relative claims of other fields, institutes and departments; the "demand" for the subject or for trained personnel in it; and the good standing of the proposing professor. The ministry acts in close cooperation with the Science Commission of the Central Committee of the Polish United Workers' Party.

Promotion depends upon achievements in research (as evaluated by peers), the number and quality of serious publications, effectiveness in the supervision of doctoral students, active participation in administrative duties and political activities (especially in the Party cell at the university), and on popularity among colleagues. Every member of the senior staff is obliged to attend meetings of the faculty council regularly. He may be elected as a dean, pro-dean, or institute director and take on administrative duties. He may also become a representative of the faculty council on the university senate.

Ultimately and officially, all appointment and promotion decisions, especially those related to the senior staff, fall under the jurisdiction of the rector and the Minister of Education, Science, and Technology* who act on recommendations of the faculty council and senate of the particular institution. The minister is advised by the Education Council, which is a consultative body for all institutions and not only for universities and is made up of teachers elected by institutions or nominated by the minister. It discusses curricula, research proposals, the appointment of new senior staff members, and higher educational policy. The minister is formally required to take note of its recommendations but is not bound by them.

Polish academics, especially those of the young generation, manifest much interest in international contacts and are greatly

---

*Higher education used to be under the auspices of a separate Ministry of Higher Education. Starting in 1968, elementary and secondary education, science, and technology were gradually joined and one ministry took over all these fields.

concerned with the need to adhere to international standards. The academic tradition in Poland before World War II was closely related to Western traditions. Many of the professors were educated in the West, and they still maintain contacts with their foreign friends. Before 1914 close ties linked the Polish academic staff with the universities of Vienna, Paris, Berlin, St. Petersburg, and Dorpat. According to Joanna Matejko's study (1966) of the academic staff in Warsaw in the middle of the 19th century, 73 percent of the professors were educated outside Poland, mostly in Germany, Russia, France, and Austria. About 9 percent were foreigners.

After the end of World War II and until 1949, most university teachers were able to continue their earlier lines of interest and research techniques. However, the political and social changes introduced by the new regime began to influence the academic world as well. The main change of the period 1949-56 was the increased importance of Marxist doctrine in all schools, even medical and technical ones. Of fundamental importance were the role of the ruling Party authorities and of Party members in the making of academic policy and the substantial growth of centralization of the decision-making power in the allocation of material resources and personnel. The new policy regarding personnel favored persons who explicitly expressed Marxist views. A special school was established by the party for the sole purpose of training Marxist academics.

Under the new government that came to power in 1956, the political pressure on schools and their academic staff was reduced. Colleges and universities acquired greater autonomy, as did individual staff members. Disciplines condemned or seriously limited in 1949-56—sociology, praxiology, cybernetics, and psychology—were reinstated; free exchange of scientific information with Western countries was permitted; and there was considerable relaxation of the censorship of scientific publications.* This resulted in much greater opportunities for scientists and scholars to publish their writings; it also permitted the acceptance of scholarships by Polish scientific workers to study abroad. Finally, there was more financial support by the government for several branches of science that had previously been neglected, such as agricultural studies and chemistry.

---

*According to Polish law, in order to be printed and distributed, a publication must first be read by the government censors. After 1956 this censorship was considerably relaxed, especially for scientific publications. Books and articles published abroad in foreign languages must be reviewed by the state authorities, particularly when they deal with important problems and their publication might conceivably affect the vital interests of the state.

As a result, sociology, previously condemned, began to flourish and to encounter broad and very favorable public response. Among the senior staff in sociology, almost everyone had an opportunity to go abroad in order to obtain additional training, mostly to the United States under American scholarships and fellowships. In the period since 1956 several centers of sociological research and teaching have been established. Hundreds of books have been published in large editions—mostly from 5,000 to 10,000 copies—and quickly sold out. The same has happened with psychology, cybernetics, praxiology, and philosophy. The natural sciences had been much less damaged than the humanities in the period 1949-56, and they had less ground to make up.

The international connections of the academic staff, especially of the senior members, have grown greatly since 1956. Specialists in medicine, chemistry, technology, physics (especially nuclear physics), and sociology have traveled widely since then. Polish university and college libraries have acquired large holdings of foreign books, although since 1968 it has become more difficult to acquire American books because of the failure to renew the Polish-American agreement for the importation of books on easy terms. Foreign scientific books in Polish university libraries are generally available to both students and staff. Knowledge of English has begun to be common.

There have been significant changes in the popularity of certain foreign languages among academics and scientists. Before World War I, Russian, German, and (to some degree) French prevailed. During the interwar period the role of Russian diminished considerably. After World War II, two languages came to dominate the Polish scene: Russian, especially in technological subjects, and English in physics, biochemistry, sociology, economics, psychology, and management studies. The use of German is now slight.

The reentry of Polish academics into the international scientific and scholarly community raised their self-esteem and their level of aspirations; it also reinforced their attachment to the internal traditions of science and scholarship and has led to an increased demand for intellectual freedom and the denunciation of the bureaucratization of science, which they equate with incompetent interference in academic affairs. However, those with positions in the centralized system of administration are naturally inclined to treat scholars like other citizens and to deny them any academic privileges, however essential the latter are to ensure the effective conduct of scientific and scholarly activity. The state machinery claims, in this respect, to defend the egalitarian model of a socialist society against "elitist" tendencies.

By law any member of the academic staff may be suspended or transferred by the Ministry of Education. However, this legal power was exercised only in the spring of 1968, when a number of professors were suspended following the student demonstrations. The Ministry has to take into consideration, to some extent, the personal preferences of staff members when it wishes to make transfers. The relatively modest salaries and shortage of housing available for the transferred employees limit the decisionmaking powers of the Ministry to some degree.

According to Irena Nowakowska, members of the academic staff are characterized by fairly high tolerance, the need for freedom, and professional solidarity. "Involved are strong sentiments common to one's specific environment and feelings of having social ties with academic circles beyond national boundaries . . . also the consciousness of the pluralism of the academic world view. . . . In this sense it is possible to speak of the strong liberal sentiments of the [academic] milieu. This is related to the widespread regard, among both religious and non-religious academic workers, of religion as a completely private affair" (Nowakowska 1964).

Of 1,366 academic workers studied in 1959, 25 percent reported themselves as practicing believers, 15 percent as nonpracticing believers, 2 percent as anticlerical believers, 12 percent as tied to religious tradition, and 1 percent as having a personal religion. Of the remaining 45 percent, 8 percent were militant atheists, 22 percent were nonbelievers, and 11 percent were indifferent to religion. Technicians, agronomists, and foresters had the highest percentages of practicing believers (each about 34 percent) and biology had the lowest (12 percent). Almost 33 percent of the academic workers thought there was a contradiction between religious belief and science. Relatively many humanists and very few agronomists, foresters, and technicians thought so.

Nearly half of the children of physicians and technicians follow their fathers' professions. The children of foresters, agronomists, and lawyers also frequently follow their fathers' professions. Having a wife or husband in the same profession as one's own is most common among physicians, then among humanists, lawyers, agronomists, and foresters (Nowakowska 1964, p. 17).

The results of Polish surveys of the social status of the academic profession are not very different from those found by surveys in other countries, such as the United States, where academics and scientists are ranked near the top of the hierarchy of prestige (Reiss 1961).

On the average, persons engaged in academic and scientific activities earn slightly more than employees in other branches of the economy. In 1971, average monthly salaries were academic staff,

3,654 zloty; high school teachers, 2,872 zloty; elementary school teachers, 2,247 zloty (Rocznik 1972, p. 462). This does not mean, however, that they are satisfied with their earnings. Comparing themselves with their colleagues in other industrialized countries they feel that their regular income is too low. Of the teachers at one of the technological colleges, surveyed in 1966 by the Inter-University Center for Studies into Higher Education, only a small percentage felt satisfied with their salaries. Only 10 percent of all respondents thought that their salary enabled them to maintain a decent standard of living. Sixty percent thought it necessary to obtain additional income from teaching extramural courses, consultation, and writing. Many of those who did so thought it harmful to their main academic work. When they compared their own standard of living with that college colleagues who chose a nonacademic career, 41 percent thought it about the same, 26 percent being worse or much worse, 15 percent better, and only 1 percent much better. Twenty percent of the respondents felt they had achieved professional success or would have a chance to do so in at their present position, 42 percent were satisfied with their work even though they were not outstandingly successful, and only 6 percent felt that they were failures (Radzko and Majewska 1968, pp. 23-134).

The survey done by Andrzej Radzko and Barbara Majewska covered 407 departmental staff members of the Technical College in Warsaw. The purpose of the study was to determine the commitments of the departmental staff with respect to their duties. It was found that 60 percent of all staff members devoted an average of 20-40 hours to scientific work. The median was 25-30 hours. This would not have been so bad, but nearly half of the time was dispersed, which means much less efficiency. The basic reason for this dispersion was not only a lack of proper integration in teaching duties but, even more so, a commitment to administrative duties that diverted attention from research. Seventeen percent of staff members devoted 20 hours or more per week to these duties (Radzko and Majewska 1968).

In the Communist system there is an emphasis on the social and political activization of all members of the society. Among the academic staff, 53 percent of all respondents were active in this respect. What did this mean in terms of their time budget? Almost 27 percent of the respondents devoted from three to five hours per week to political and social activity, and 29 percent devoted from five to ten hours per week.

The respondents appeared to be nonconformists and were quite individualistically oriented. Forty-five percent of the young respondents (under 30 years of age) did not feel close to their departments. The reasons for being critical were manifold, and they appeared especially among the younger staff. Almost 33 percent of the respondents felt that their research tasks were not well defined. Only a small part of the younger staff (graduate students working for their master's and doctor's degrees) felt that they had good guidance from one specific patron in the professorial ranks. There were complains about the inadequacy of consultation, technical equipment, and technical or administrative help. Twenty-one percent of the respondents stated that they could not personally influence what happened in their departments. All these complaints, however, were much more related to inadequate management, material supply, and organization than to human relations. Eighty percent of the respondents stated that they had found a common language with their colleagues for handling professional questions.

The problems of managing departments and of relations between superiors and subordinates on the departmental level were treated with detailed attention in the study by Wanda Mlicka (1967). This research was carried out at the same technical college in 1966 and covered 80 staff members employed in 15 departments. According to the research data, most staff members accepted their superiors as people but were quite critical of their organizational performance. Forty percent of the respondents stated that their superiors did not pay adequate attention to what the subordinates were doing. Those who would have liked to have superiors who were simultaneously as good scientists as organizers and as human beings outnumbered the percentage of respondents who said that they had superiors with such qualities (45 percent versus 16 percent; see Table 8.7). Seventy-five percent of the respondents did not feel that the higher authorities had shown enough understanding for their scientific efforts.

There appeared to be a significant gradation in the fulfillment of aspirations according to professional status. Satisfaction was highest among full and associate professors (84 percent said that their expectations were fulfilled) and among assistant professors (70 percent of them were satisfied). Among the junior staff who had just obtained their master's degrees, 56 percent were satisfied; and among the junior staff with doctorates, 36 percent were satisfied. This means that the position of those in the middle was not stabilized and that their expectations were probably not realistic enough in terms of actual openings for attractive jobs and careers.

There were apparent contraditions between the dominant orientation of the respondents and the reality of their organizational setting. Data from the survey done by Andrzej Radzko and Barbara Majewska (1968) show that purely intellectual pursuits were a more common motivation than other pursuits, such as serving the community. People who were independent in choosing their study subjects developed better professionally than those who expected superiors to

TABLE 8.7

Perceived Characteristics of Department Heads and
the Preferences of Their Subordinates in a
Technological College

Characteristics	Perceived Characteristics (percentage)	Preferred Characteristics (percentage)
Scientific	5	8
Organizational	13	4
Personal	16	3
Scientific and organizational	5	10
Scientific and personal	35	25
Organizational and personal	10	5
Scientific, organizational, and personal	16	45
Number of respondents	62	73

Source: Mlicka 1967.

tell them what to do. The most common aspiration was to work in a friendly atmosphere and the least common was to have an administrative career. Women were almost equal in their aspirations with men. Theoretical interests appeared to be deeper than others.

All these data make evident the primarily intellectual and professional orientation of the respondents. In reality, however, organizational position quite often counted more than professional abilities. This might be one reason why people were interested in taking managerial positions without being personally committed to administration. By becoming head of a department, it was possible to obtain privileges crucial for pursuing professional goals: research money, travel money, attendance at important conferences, appointment of younger personnel for help in performing research authorized by the department head.

At the same time, involvement in administrative or political duties took so much time and effort that those in managerial positions were not able to pursue their professional careers. Something had to be sacrificed. Department heads either devoted themselves to administration and policymaking, thus neglecting their own profession, or they pretended to be administrators and pursued their professional interests. In both cases tensions appeared. Conscientious administrators became envious that their subordinates could devote more

199

time to their professional careers, while they had to spend their time on something which, in the long run, did not count professionally. On the other hand, subordinates did not show enough understanding of the difficulties that the superior had to face in order to satisfy their expectations. These expectations often became exaggerated. Department heads who pretended to be administrators neglected the interests of their departments for sake of their own interests. The departments became understaffed and undersupplied, nobody paid enough attention to the young people, and everything disintegrated.

The conditions under which young people work for their degrees were the subject of two studies. Henryk Szarras did a survey in 1964 among the junior academic staff employed in departments (1969, pp. 135-48). At that time there were 15,000 such people employed by institutions of higher education in Poland. According to data from 1966-67, there were 16,000 such people, of whom 57 percent had doctoral degrees and 31 percent were women. The ratio of students per junior academic staff member was 1:10.4 (13.4 if one includes extension students).

According to the study by Szarras, the working conditions of the junior staff varied widely. In general, however, they were unsatisfactory. Only 20 percent had their own office; 33 percent did not have their own desk or table in an office; 40 percent usually worked at home because of the scarcity of room at the department. The need for technical help was satisfied in only 66 percent of the cases, and 25 percent of staff members working on their doctorates complained that they did not have any support.

When asked to list improvements, 25 percent suggested that they be provided with better rooms in which to work, 25 percent proposed improved equipment, 17 percent more adequate auxiliary personnel, 10 percent better administration, and 7 percent better modes of supervising research. Private concerns, such as income and housing conditions, ranked rather low.

In 1966 Bogdan Cichomski interviewed 60 postgraduate younger staff members employed in three departments of a technical college (Cichomski 1967). Half of them were behind in their studies and two-thirds did not make enough progress. The policy emphasizing scientific degrees was only recently introduced into technical colleges, which previously pursued practical interests. According to the new regulations all junior staff members, including those in technical colleges, have to acquire doctoral degrees within a few years in order to retain their employment. Not having a tradition of doctoral studies and being involved in time-consuming activities of a practical nature (teaching, applied research for industry), the technicians found it quite difficult to progress in their doctoral studies. They were under pressure, and their busy superiors did not have the time or ability to help them in their studies.

All these surveys disclose that senior staff members are not thought to pay enough attention to their junior staff, who therefore believe that there is insufficient scientific stimulus as well as inadequate opportunity for them to share in the managing of the department.

The internal formal organization of the institutions of higher education in Poland has been traditionally built around (1) the dominant authority of the senior staff; (2) the privileges of the professors who head the departments or institutes; (3) extensive autonomy of the individual organizational unit (department, study and research team, laboratory, institute, faculty), and self-government of the faculties, which comprise several departments or institutes dealing with the same subject or related subjects. There are, however, some discrepancies between this framework and the actual functioning of the institution as one of the many units of a planned economy dominated by central authorities. It was these discrepancies that encouraged the state authorities to put through, at the end of the 1960s, the reform of higher educational institutions by concentrating all academic staff in institutes instead of traditional departments. The state and party authorities wanted to gain more power in locating and transferring the academic staff. The technocrat argued, quite rationally, that the traditional organization ossified the allocation of resources and made any shift quite difficult. The junior academic staff was also dissatisfied with the monopolization of crucial posts in science by people who were not always eager to sponsor younger colleagues.

In the 1960s there appeared a growing awareness in Poland that the traditional structure of universities creates serious obstacles for true multidisciplinary teamwork. "The structure of the universities in this part of Europe tends to be a petrified 19th century formation with not a few guild throwbacks. The lynch-pin is still the chair [small department]. Its compositions, traditions and habits of individual work do not, on the whole, make for the emergence of close-knit teams or for a balanced, all-round approach to research studies" (Golanski 1966, p. 29). The traditional isolationism of many small departments harmed the development of modern science, and there was extensive fragmentation of effort. For example, in 1964 at universities and technical, economic, and agricultural schools, almost 10,000 different research topics were investigated—while the entire senior academic staff in all those schools numbered only 2,500. "The narrow furrow ploughed by each chair is a barrier to the proper bringing-in of young academics whose advance must be related to a wider horizon" (Golanski 1966, p. 29). Every department (chair) had its own particularistic ambitions, which could be especially harmful in regard to the proper utilization of expensive and scarce equipment. There was rivalry among various schools, especially for the allocation of resources by the Ministry of Education. The corporate identity within any department, faculty, or school played an important role in this respect.

In general, however, the prestige of a particular school plays a much less important role in the Polish planned system of resource allocation than, for instance, in the United States, where there appears to be a free academic market. Scientists who have been able to establish themselves at a particular school may lose much moving to another school and beginning again. Of course, any move is quite difficult because of the fixed allocation of posts and resources. Therefore active and well-developed scientific teams exist outside Warsaw— for example, the excellent team of mathematicians in Wroclaw.

The prevailing criteria of academic success confer privileges on persons who are in charge of institutes or departments and laboratories attached to them. This is why there is strong pressure from the bottom to establish as many organizational units as possible, even if they are relatively small and weak. (Organizational diversification creates serious obstacles to interdisciplinary research, which is impeded by the separatism of small organizational units.) At the seven universities in 1966, there were 637 departments and 867 laboratories for 1,039 professors, which means that some of those organizational units were headed by junior staff members because of the shortage of senior staff. At the universities each department or laboratory had an average of only 0.7 professors and two junior staff members (assistants or adjuncts). In the technological colleges the equivalent figures were 0.55 and 2.5. While the total number of institutions of higher education more than doubled in 1937-66, from 32 to 76, the number of departments in these institutions grew 3.5 times, from 782 to 2,735. The rate of organizational differentiation was close to the rate of growth shown by the senior academic staff, which showed a fourfold increase during the same period.

The creation of a new department, institute, or laboratory depends upon a proposal by the institution and its acceptance by the rector and the Minister of Education, Science, and Technology. Bargaining between the staff and the authorities takes much time and effort. The authorities are under pressure from individual members of the academic staff who want new arrangements. The ministry, on the other hand, tries to adhere to its policy, which does not necessarily coincide with the expectations and desires of particular scientists or scholars. It is necessary to convince the university or college authorities, as well as the ministry, of the absolute necessity of establishing a new organizational unit. The prestige of prominent and influential scientists is usually very important in this respect. Therefore the possibility of introducing a new subject into the curriculum, as well as of establishing a new department or institute, depends very much on the support given by persons who are regarded by the Ministry as experts. Thus the rapid development of sociology after 1956—the Polish Sociological Association quadrupled its membership in the period 1961-71 to over 800—was much eased by the favorable opinion of this discipline prevailing among respectable scientists, such as the late Oskar Lange.

In recent years there has been growing dissatisfaction with the traditional internal fragmentation of higher educational institutions, which have become little more than loose federations of autonomous departments. This development of the tradition of academic self-government, although previously tolerated and even furthered by the Ministry of Education, which has countenanced it by the appointment of practically irremovable department heads, impedes the freedom of government and Party authorities who would like to have more power in the assignment and transfer of members of the academic staff. Those who regard comprehensive planning as feasible and desirable argue that the traditional autonomy resists the planned allocation of resources. The rank-and-file of academic staff, especially younger members, argue that decisionmaking powers in the universities are too strongly concentrated in the hands of full and associate professors.

Thus we see in Poland a situation similar to that in universities in the German Federal Republic and other West European countries where professorial autocracy and a great many small institutes hamper the emergence of new subjects, reinforce the inherited structure of specialization, and force younger scholars and scientists into an unwelcome and often repressive dependence on their institutional supervisors.

The pressure of central control receives its main counterbalance not from the university or college as a corporate entity, but from the department, institute, or faculty. Thus the coherence of the university or college is enfeebled and identification with it by its members is not strong. Nonetheless, there is now a widespread tendency for the individual members of the academic staff to unite and to form larger units with several professors. Within these new, larger structures there is room for research teams that are flexible in membership as well as in tasks. New institutes have been created to unite departments and to provide better facilities for them. These new organizational structures were first developed in technological colleges but have become common in universities. There is, of course, resistance by some of the academic staff to these new arrangements, which they fear will strengthen the administration of the institution or the Ministry of Education, Science, and Technology and thereby constrict their freedom of decision and action.

The internal self-government of Polish universities and colleges is conditioned by factors which do not generally appear in the universities of Western Europe and North America. The most important is the local unit of the ruling Polish United Workers' Party, the position of which has been considerably strengthened since 1968. In accordance with recent organizational changes, representatives of the local Party unit and those of the local trade union unit and youth organizations take an active part in the senate, faculty councils, and other academic bodies. Party activists are expected to pay special attention to all problems relating to students; and to facilitate this, committees to deal with student affairs have been created at university and faculty level. Two-thirds of the membership of these committees are made up of academic staff and one third of students.

The academic authorities are expected to be in constant touch with the Party unit and with other organizations in the institution. Vital problems are discussed at the meetings of the local Party unit (non-Party members are invited to attend some of these meetings), and the opinions expressed in these discussions must be taken very seriously by academic administrators when making the decisions that they are formally empowered to make. Academic bodies are not obliged to follow the main trend of Party opinion, but they usually do so in order not to create any serious tension between the Party and the university bodies.

Supplementary influences are brought to bear upon academic bodies by the local branches of the two other political parties that exist in Poland: the United Peasant Party and the Democratic Party. The local branches of the Trade Union of Teachers (which include all employees, both academic and nonacademic), the Polish Students Association, the League of Socialist Youth, the League of Democratic Youth, the League of Peasant Youth, student subject clubs, and local branches of scientific societies also exert influence proportional to their proximity to the Polish United Workers' Party. These various extra-academic influences offset to some extent the constitutionally established oligarchy of the professors.

Under the higher education law of December 1968, university administration was expected to become considerably strengthened. Even greater centralization appeared; rectors and deputy rectors, instead of being elected by the senate every three years, are appointed by the Minister of Education, Science, and Technology. The faculty deans and their deputy deans, instead of being elected by the faculty council, are appointed by the rector. On the other hand, the powers of rectors, deans, and institute directors are now somewhat larger than before. In order to help them in their daily business, new advisory committees have been established.

It is difficult to say now how much this new arrangement has been able to overcome the traditional weaknesses in the administration of universities. The lack of a well-qualified and properly motivated administrative staff has been one of the most important shortcomings.

At institutions of higher education, the ratio of academic staff to administrative staff and to maintenance and service staff in 1966 was 1:0.14 and 1:0.26. In this respect there was no significant difference between universities and technological colleges. The attempt to put a large part of the administrative burden on the self-governing academic bodies has not produced successful results. Senates, faculty councils, institute boards, and other academic bodies have the difficult task of making decisions on matters that are usually of only limited interest to the participants. The rectors, deans, and institute directors change every few years. Being committed primarily to their own scientific careers, they have been able and willing to devote only a limited amount of time and attention to administrative duties. Even if in many cases they take these duties seriously, they encounter the resistance of their professional colleagues and the weakness of their own secretariat. The continuity of effective administration has by no means been assured by this system.

The administrative changes in the late 1960s indicated the pressures building up against the traditional weakness of university and college administration. These pressures came not only from the government and Party, whose ideas of planning and organizational conformity were offended by this weakness, but also from the staff members, especially those of the younger generation, who had come to regard traditional academic administration as outmoded and ineffective.

As in bourgeois Europe and America, in Poland the professorial oligarchy is not well regarded by those below it in the hierarchy. The whole social atmosphere in Polish higher education has changed substantially since World War II. Relations between professors and younger staff members, as well as relations between academic staff and students, are more equalitarian than they used to be (Szczepanski 1963; 1964a). Nevertheless, the senior staff still has the upper hand. Ascendancy often depends not so much on popularity with the students, lively lecturing style, stimulating scientific ideas, or the patronage of students as upon scientific fame, prestige among government and Party authorities, and organizational savoir-faire. It is the senior staff who rule institutes, faculty councils, and the senate. Junior academic staff have some representatives on these bodies, but they are but few in number and do not ordinarily dare to voice their real opinions.

Variations from a strictly oligarchical structure within departments, institutes, and faculties depend mostly on the personal inclinations and abilities of the heads. In the previous traditional structure, up to the end of the 1960s, heads of autonomous departments possessed, at least in theory, great power, which in reality depended on their personal positions within the university social system—for example, how much acceptance the head of an institute or department had from different pressure groups. It quite often happened that heads of institutes and departments were more interested in their own studies than in exercising administrative power. In consequence they neglected their institutes or departments, and failed both to stimulate their subordinates and to coordinate the work of their juniors.

THE PERSONAL INFRASTRUCTURE

The fate of any society is not just the product of the interplay of historical factors and of formal structures regulating the general shape of mutual influence and exchange of goods and services. It is also to some extent dependent on the infrastructure of informal ties, personal relationships and life attitudes. Ludwik Krzywicki, one of the founders of Polish sociology, considered this infrastructure to be of particular importance and clearly differentiated between objectified ties (of a material nature) and personal ties between people of "common needs, emotions and ideals, evolved on the background of common instincts, mutual social influences and a growing consciousness of common goals" (Rychlinski 1938). It is worth asking what shape this structure of personal ties has taken in contemporary Poland, on what it depends, and to what extent it influences the fate of society.

In his excellent article "Proba Diagnozy," published in the now defunct Cultural Review (1957), Jan Szczepanski described Polish society as having a traditionally strong informal structure and a comparatively inefficient and only superficially established formal structure. Such a state of affairs is understandable in a nation that since the 18th century has had foreign structures imposed upon it by external force. Personal ties and loyalties remaining outside the framework of the foreign rule made it possible for Poles to survive, to make do, and to incorporate, wherever possible, their particular interests, whether personal, local, or national. Against a background of a common feeling of danger and the necessity of defending vital common interests, a tissue of very personal bonds, characterized by sentiment, was formed in Poland. This led to people's being at least not mutually indifferent. This tissue differentiates Poland, to her decided advantage, from those societies based on a highly developed division of labor in which mutual psychic and moral isolation dominates the sphere of public relations and profoundly permeates social and family life.

The infrastructure of social relations in Poland expresses not only the conflict between "tradition" and "modernity," but to a much larger extent it expresses the contradiction between the historically shaped aspirations of Poles and the relatively meager opportunities open to them. There is also the obvious contradiction between the gentry culture of Poland and the present-day uniform bureaucratic character of the formal organization. The nonexpression of feeling, fulfillment of obligations regardless of the social status of the other, focus of attention on performance, and devotion to the administrative hierarchy are still foreign to members of the Polish nation, which traditionally cultivated affection, diffuseness, particularism, ascription, and (to some extent) collectivity orientation—behavioral patterns closely related to traditionalism (Parsons 1951, pp. 51-67).

Religion has greatly influenced the Polish personal infrastructure. However, the strong and widespread commitment to religion in Poland is no longer of a traditionalistic nature but represents to a growing extent the spiritual resistance of Polish masses to the doctrine and practice of state socialism. People who feel alienated within the rigid and highly impersonalized bureaucracy find their religious faith as the only rescue. It is the historical paradox of Soviet-style communism that its shortcomings stimulate quite a large number of people in Poland to look to religion as the final answer.

It does not make much sense to apply to the Polish society such simple dichotomies as the "progressive" Marxists on the one side and the "conservative" Catholics on the other. Poles are not passive, erratic, and highly inconsistent people who vacillate between two opposing positions: the "superrational" Marxist elite and the traditionalist Roman Catholic hierarchy.

It is probably to a large extent the "irrationality" or even absurdity of state socialism that draws people to the churches even though they cannot gain materially. Devotion to religion in Poland is not as costly to the people as it is to people in the Soviet Union. However, Poles are bound to suffer materially, especially when occupying more attractive occupational positions. For many members of the intelligentsia, secularization is a must in order to obtain favors from the ruling elite. Party members who occupy white-collar positions are afraid to publicly attend churches. They go to another town in order to have a church wedding. Even if there is no open religious persecution in Poland, it seems quite obvious that the atheistic establishment tolerates Catholicism only for tactical reasons.

Of course, it is always an open question whether the Polish Catholic tradition served Poland well. Pawel Jasienica, in his excellent analysis of Poland in the 18th century (1972), blames the Roman Catholic Church for several serious historical faults. However, the unique freedom enjoyed by the Roman Catholic Church in Poland, in comparison with virtually all other Communist countries, makes it an institution of particular social and spiritual importance. The church and religion were loci of resistance to the totalitarian rule under Nazism and later under Stalinism.

It is probably because of religious tradition that in Poland friendship, and even more so love, is identified with sacrifice. One should give up one's own good, sacrifice oneself, give everything one has. Thus one can find mothers toiling in the households of their grown-up children without so much as a word of thanks (not to mention any sort of payment), lovers laying themselves open to various humiliations, money-lenders expecting neither interest nor even repayment of a loan, and guests treated to whatever can be bought—at serious danger to the household budget. A person who expects the repayment of a loan in the established time (or repayment at all) runs the risk of mortal resentment, as does someone who expects promises given while drinking vodka to be fulfilled, or even punctual appearance at an arranged meeting. The Poles' love for all kinds of fantasies must be recognized. "Bring out the red carpet when entertaining guests" and "Show that you are not a coward" are still Polish customs of behavior. One is not allowed to be down-to-earth, to calculate losses and gains, or to be afraid of risk. Especially in the eyes of women, one must play the part of a passionate daredevil who is not afraid of anything, is generous, and likes to speak his mind.

The problem is that the tradition of unmercenary friendship (or love) and romantic fantasy is increasingly inadequate for the social and political realities of People's Poland. First of all, the social composition of the groups that dictate codes of behavior has undergone considerable change. Instead of the postnobility intelligentsia (and in their national sense of honor), there is more of an element that has just advanced from the lower rungs of the social ladder. It puts a high value on middle-class realities and is often completely devoid of the scruples characteristic of the traditional Polish noble or intellectual. It is this element that is more prone to take than to give, to pretend to have moral values than to accept them, to act like an intellectual than to be one. Second, the clerical nature of bureaucratized Poland, filled with a crowd of people living above their means for only a few days after the first of each month, is not suited to sacrificing or to fantasy. The clerk, an individual completely dependent on the whims of his superiors, must be mercenary and careful. At the bottom of the Polish clerk's heart there can be often found the bluster of an 18th-century nobleman, but this bluster can be used at most for impressing others. Finally, through its industrialization, People's Poland has become highly formalized. Most matters cannot be arranged verbally, solely on the basis of the basis of the good will of the negotiators—especially in an economic and administrative system that is vulnerable to all kinds of maneuvers and evasions.

The dominance of personal ties in the society is quite attractive and even delightful in terms of warm human relationships, as long as it does not paralyze the formal (economic, administrative, and political structures) in their daily functioning. Having been under foreign rule for so long, Poles did not have the opportunity to create enough of their own administrators, entrepreneurs, managers, and politicians. They were forced to take a defensive attitude toward formal structures imposed upon them, not to benefit them but to dominate and exploit them.

Thus there is a long historical tradition in Poland of an evident contradiction between personal ties and the formal structure, a contradiction that is highly dysfunctional in terms of goal attainment. For in order to achieve any substantial economic growth, the infra-structure of personal ties must be harmonized with the structure of formal relations. There is a peculiar contradiction in such a harmonization: the principles of behavior and the life aspirations of informal human groups have a very important impact on the func-tioning of formal structures. However, this impact must be limited by the principle of common well-being. One cannot base everything on underhanded dealings, or favoritism, or putting friendship loyalty above employment loyalty, or always supporting one's friends and relatives against strangers. When the formal procedures for getting something done are no longer treated seriously by either the power-holders or the clients; when people laugh at somebody who tries to take the "normal" path of official activity; when the society becomes clearly divided between artful dodgers with "influence" and suckers who are their objects of exploitative manipulation, then it is difficult to seriously discuss any sort of authentic progress or reform. Then the society loses its fundamental sociomoral adhesives and becomes a loose horde of mutually estranged individuals, struggling with each other for everything and by every possible means, taking pleasure in tripping up others, and striving solely for personal advantages.

Formal structure can exert a lesser or greater influence on informal ties depending upon the level of its perfection. The configu-ration of employment relationships, to an important extent decides the configuration of personal relationships. Collaboration brings people closer to one another, even if this closeness is based only on conflicts. The policy of personnel choice and filling particular positions has certain informal effects. If, for example, responsible positions are filled exclusively with loyal Party members, then a sharply delineated differentiation between Party members and non-Party members will arise.

The formal structure has a particular influence on the infrastructure whenever the former reaches very deeply into the everyday life of the society, as it does in state socialism. Wherever and whenever, as in contemporary Eastern Europe, bureaucratization is a universal phenomenon, the formal network becomes a frame for informal networks of various types. Illnesses of the formal structure disease the infrastructure with a particular vigor. The rigor of enforcement and fear makes people inert not only as pawns of the bureaucracy, but also in their social life—unless an effective antidote to the official dogma is crystallized within the framework of the infrastructure. Where, however, the people have no hope, the emptiness of the official language finds its full reflection in the insipidness of personal contacts. People cease to have anything relevant to say to one another, they put up false fronts, they are full of pretense and mutual distaste. In the excellent short stories of Jerzy Urban (pseudonym Kibic), published regularly on the last page of the Polish popular magazine Kulisy, the same theme of profiting from another's emotions appears frequently. Somebody confides in someone else, wanting to trust the other on the basis of emotions, and is shamefully tricked, cheated, taken advantage of. As a consequence the matter reaches the courts, and it is there that Urban finds the inspiration for his stories.

POLAND UNDER STATE SOCIALISM

As J. R. Fiszman quite rightly points out, contemporary Poland is full of contrasts. Religion practiced openly can be found side by side with the orthodoxy of the Party. Workers and peasants advance socially en masse, but a goodly portion of the climbers end up in traditional, conservative positions. The intelligentsia has been forced into a subordinate role, but Poland is today even more intellectualistic than during the interwar period. Poles go through the motions of religious ritual, but they do not take religion quite seriously. The tradition of the nobility still has a strong effect on Polish customs. The ideals of state socialism still constitute the official ideology, but they have been sacrificed in favor of a bureaucracy proclaiming these ideals. The Church and the Party stand at opposite ends of the stick, but in serious crises they at least stay neutral toward one another (Fiszman, 1970, pp. 37-88).

It is worth adding to what Fiszman says that probably the sharpest contrasts are to be found in the economy. The Poles are comparatively well educated and culturally polished, yet the economy

of the country is very seriously lame. One cannot agree with Jan
Szczepanski (1971a, 1971b) and Aleksander Bochenski (1972) that this
is a deafening of the industrious majority by the lazy but loud-mouthed
minority. In Poland, more and more writers are trying to explain
why the Polish economy is not growing as fast as a decided majority
of the Polish society would have it. Bochenski's opinions are particularly noteworthy.

Aleksander Bochenski, a prominent Polish intellectual in the
conservative tradition, in 1972 published a very significant book on
the Polish mentality. His deep concern for the relatively low productivity in Poland, which makes any significant improvement of the
standard of living almost impossible, is worthy of appreciation.
Bochenski, who became well known after World War II through his
controversial book on the history of Polish political naiveté (1947),
looks to history in his explanation of why contemporary Poles do not
work industriously enough. In the conservative tradition, he criticizes
not only the egoism and frivolity of the gentry but also the whole
romantic heritage. He would like to see Poles much more rational,
less devoted to militarism, active in economics, dynamic, and serious
with respect to time and money. According to Bochenski, there has
not so far been enough room in the life of the Polish nation for positivism, enterpreneurship, and a truly responsible attitude toward one's
own life. A constructive economic orientation did not develop strongly
enough to influence the mentality of the masses even in the Polish
Roman Catholic Church. Among the Polish intelligentsia, it has become distasteful to pay serious attention to earning and saving money.
Instead of searching for something more risky and innovative, the
young member of the Polish intelligentsia simply settles down as a
clerk and waits for "better times" to present him with opportunities.
For the youth of lower social strata, the perspectives are very limited;
but when striving for better status, they take over the traditional values and preferences of the privileged few.

What has changed under communism? Bochenski makes it
quite clear that no matter what the circumstances, Poland's economic
potential will be of primary importance to its future. Unfortunately,
rewards are inadequately related to real productivity, and many
people gain money and promotions without working hard enough. According to Bochenski, there is not enough room in the economy for
initiative and personal responsibility connected with well-calculated
risk.

Bochenski is very careful not to condemn the establishment,
and his interpretation of why Poles do not work industriously enough
tends to be loyalistic. He praises the alliance with the Soviet Union
as the best guarantee of a better future. However, even within this
general framework, the message is quite clear: The formal structures

of contemporary Poland do not encourage liberation of the Polish mentality from the traditional status orientation. The bureaucracy that dominates in state socialism perpetuates hierarchic relations in workplaces. The concentration of decisionmaking power in the hands of a few Party and state administrators robs the masses of sufficient opportunity for initiative. Any quest for "economic rationalization" will not be of much help. The urge to increase efficiency is effectively undermined by the restricting and wasteful ways in which the competence of young people is used. The number of college graduates is growing, but there is no demand for their talent and enthusiasm.

Bochenski asks that the Polish people work more industriously and develop constructive attitudes. His conservative and loyalistic background prevents him from understanding to what extent human attitudes depend on organizational and structural circumstances. Data from Polish sociological studies prove conclusively that the main problem lies not with attitudes but with the highly inefficient nature of centralized decisionmaking under Soviet-style state socialism.

It is probably above all the ossified bureaucratic system, based on directives from above and the pressuring of and lack of confidence in subordinates, that is least suited to the Poles' mentality or to giving them an outlet for their initiative and resourcefulness. On the other hand, the private ownership economy did not give particularly encouraging results in interwar Poland and it has ceased to be a general solution.

A phenomenon of major importance in Poland is the proletarization of a vast majority of the society, including a large part of the peasantry. The earnings of the intelligentsia have decreased with respect to those of the interwar period, whereas the workers' earnings have gone up. The standard of living of the peasantry has significantly improved. However, all these classes have found themselves to be hired workers, for even the "independent" peasant deals mainly with the state and is at its mercy. The heaviness of the bureaucracy weighs on all these classes to an almost equal extent. They are all vitally interested in ameliorating their standard of living, in decreasing the oppression of control from above, in simplifying the administrative procedure, and in greater respect for citizens. The Polish economy is bound together by a complicated network of ties based on favoritism that begins at the top of the social ladder and reaches far down it (Matejko 1968; pp. 225-90; Dyoniziak 1967; Majchrzak 1965). Cliques distribute the better jobs among their members; they fight to extend their influence; and they develop well-planned strategies for appropriating a maximum for themselves.

The formal organization of workplaces is permeated with informal contacts and connections. The dichotomy of power—the Party and the state administration—is conducive to informal methods of settling matters. This can be observed even in science. Studies carried out by me and my team in the mid-1960s on the subject of the functioning of research and educational institutes brought to light informal mechanisms that otherwise honest people had to use in order to achieve anything (Matejko 1966c; 1970b; 1973a; Matejko, ed. 1967, 1968, 1969).

On the blue-collar workers' level, informal manipulation does not appear to a lesser extent than higher up. Its intensity depends on the nature of the workplace and the position. The scale of possibilities for misusing time paid for by the employer, as well as materials and tools, is very different in various employment positions and workplaces. Depending upon their personal relations with their superiors, supervised workers receive more or less advantageous occupations. Promotion also depends to a considerable extent on good relations with influential people situated higher up. One must find allies who might be of help. There are people in places of employment whose word counts for much (Party functionaries) and so it is worth linking oneself to them, doing them favors, in order to gain something in return.

For example, the concept of socialist competition among workers has this basis. Party and union activists are expected by their superiors to promote socialist competition as a device for achieving higher work efficiency. A group of workers (usually young) forms a socialist work brigade, which is then given certain special conditions facilitating the achievement of a greater productivity than other work teams. I studied such brigades at the beginning of the 1960s; and it is characteristic that one of them, the best in the area of study, consisted exclusively of people who were somehow blameworthy in the eyes of the law or the Party. Participation in the brigade was for them an opportunity for rehabilitation.

The mass movement of rationalizers and inventors functions similarly. Interesting studies carried out by one of my younger colleagues showed that favoritism lies at the foundation of this movement. A rationalizer or inventor must "share" his bonus with influential people in the place of employment if he wants his idea to be put into effect and not lost in somebody's drawer. Furthermore, technicians and engineers enter into secret agreements with blue-collar workers whereby the latter put their names to an idea and then they all share the bonus, which would otherwise be inaccessible to a white-collar employee or accessible with considerable difficulty (Matejko 1968, p. 288).

This informal network jeopardizes the success of any rational reform. Even the most sensible directives from above, as they wind their way to the bottom, are translated into the language of interests of particular cliques. The cliques are by nature conservative, obstructing novelties and supporting the status quo. Workplaces are full of struggles between cliques that have various bases. "Villagers" defend themselves against townfolk. Those from other parts of Poland carry on power struggles with the local people. Police functionaries who were relieved of their employment when the police apparatus was reduced and transferred to factories, help one another to secure better jobs. Every influential person tries to widen the sphere of his influence by buying people with various kinds of services, in return for which they are to be loyal to him. Every person of authority in Poland, even on the highest levels, has his hands tied by conflicting clique interests. Anyone who wants to achieve something must take these interests into consideration (Bauman, 1971; Matejko 1968, pp. 248-90).

The demoralization of employees by a bureaucracy is the fundamental social disease of contemporary Poland. It can be deduced from an enormous store of sociological data (public opinion studies, surveys of various social groups, studies based on interviews with selected people) that in almost all the socioprofessional groups that through their work participate in increasing the national income, there is considerable displeasure with the state of the economy. When asked by sociologists to express their opinions, Polish blue-collar workers complain not about employment and remuneration but about bad management that makes it impossible for them to work productively. Factors that make it impossible to achieve high productivity include the chronic insufficiency of materials and tools, bad coordination, irregular work tempo (especially rapid just before the deadline for filling a production quota), the production of goods for which there is no market demand, the disharmony of stimuli and actual productivity, selection of people for positions on the basis of criteria that have little in common with their professional usefulness, discouragement of constructive criticism, and an incessant disturbance of the existing structure of relationships (unjustified reorganizations). Even if the establishment supports initiatives that aim to raise the organizational standards of workplaces, these initiatives are condemned to failure unless and until sociopolitical sources of inefficiency are eliminated.

The principle of egalitarianism has become strongly entrenched in Eastern Europe. However, a by-product is the universal inability to define one's own position with respect to those of others. The principle of equality is incessantly contradicted by actual inequality. A working woman is formally equal to a man, but in reality the weight of household responsibilities and running from one shop to another falls primarily on her; in addition, a comparatively large female labor supply leads to unattractive and badly paid positions falling to the lot of women. Highly qualified professionals resent the contradiction between their expertise and their actual impotence in making practical decisions. Party intellectuals are worried by the fact that their non-Party colleagues are often better off than they—who, after all, sacrificed their consciences (the truly privileged class is numerically very small). Artful dodgers run extremely profitable businesses, but they can neither guarantee their looted goods and privileges nor transmit them to their children. As a result everybody, including Party officials, suffers from dissatisfaction and insecurity; and this makes it impossible for the sociopolitical system to achieve a balance. The internal instability of the system is conducive to the prevalence of a parasitic element, both among the intelligentsia and even more so among the Party elite. This element preys on people who work well, taking advantage of their work and loyalty by means of fear and compulsion, by organizing their own groups who occupy better positions and help one another.

Who is really responsible for all these shortcomings of state socialism in Eastern Europe? The general public, especially the intelligentsia, tends to blame the Party executives for corruption, misuse of their privileged position, and lack of moral responsibility.

In order to rule the society, the Party created personnel totally dedicated to it and gave it certain privileges, though these remain far below what executives in the West have. The size of this executive group is rather small, for the generally badly paid lower-rank managers can hardly be included in it. In return for permanent employment and privileges, the executives must give the Party more loyalty and work than is demanded from the intelligentsia. They often work a dozen or so hours daily; they are always on call; and they have to beware of internal office politics and of being replaced by somebody else. An executive is not supposed to live well, because people may think he has been stealing or because he may damage the authority of the Party (this is especially true for an executive working in the countryside). An executive should not have his own clear-cut opinion, for the Party may change its dogma and the loyalty of a dedicated Party member is primarily expressed through the repression of his ego. The family of an executive is also continually on show and must behave in such a way as not to draw the slightest criticism.

Thus the executive is considerably more restricted than anybody else, particularly the intellectual. The official newspaper of the Party is his daily reading material, along with Party periodicals and materials. If an executive dares to read other things (and he is not likely to have much desire and time for it), then they must be connected in some way with his professional responsibilities. There is always a suspicion that reading non-Party, and more so anti-Party, material can give an executive ideas and lead him to activity that may not quite be fractional but is at least not directly related to the realization of the Party's current goals.

It is the duty of the East European executive to love the Soviet Union—a very unattractive proposition, in view of the level of lectures and speeches about that country, the infrequency of trips to the USSR (even among Party functionaries), and the overwhelming competition of those experiences and material goods that various acquaintances (very often not Party members) bring back with them from trips to the West. I was always puzzled in Poland to see how little Party activists know about the Soviet Union, how little they read about it, and even how badly they speak the Russian language. This probably results from the fact that sympathy for the USSR is inversely proportional to direct dependence on it.

In Poland the snobbism of the intelligentsia is transferred to the executives to some extent and keeps them from proclaiming love for the USSR. Service in the Party machine and the rewards connected with it are one thing; but drinking vodka with members of the intelligentsia, who fill Poland and are in fact her content, is another. Even if hunting, the theater, concerts, and reading novels are not possible, then they at least form a threshold of desire and symbolize a higher standard.

Naturally, one can give thousands of examples of good will wasted by thoughtlessness or of outright bad will of the bureaucrats. For example, in Poland some teachers who had settled in an out-of-the-way village thought it would be a good idea to establish a local training center for farmers. The authorities supported the initiative, for it was very much along the lines of the current agricultural policy. However, the local officials were quickly put off by the idea when it turned out that the founders by no means intended to let notables from the area use the center's building and budget for expense-paid vacations. In order to get rid of the initiators and to put less devoted people in their place, they were accused of squandering of state funds. The accusation eventually proved to be groundless, but it was sufficient to accomplish what the notables wanted.

On the other hand, however, one can also point out many occurrences showing that people who are stubborn and know what they want, are able to force their ideas through. Among Polish working people, there are thousands of quiet heroes doggedly fighting for social amelioration despite a host of obstacles. The problem lies in creating an atmosphere that would guarantee them spiritual and social support, and not isolate them as "suckers" whom it is not worth taking seriously.

It is difficult to disagree with Wieslaw Gornicki when he blames hotheads and idlers for the country's unfavorable state of affairs (Zycie Warszawy, 13 April 1971). The hotheads' inertia and waste at the top, and the ignorance and laziness of the idlers at the bottom, excellently work complementarily in destroying all attempts at authentic reform.

THE POTENTIAL FOR INTERNAL REFORM

The prominent Polish dialectician Leszek Kolakowski (now in semiexile in Great Britain) has expressed faith in the "possibility of effective fragmentary and gradual pressure, carried out in a long-range perspective . . ." (Kolakowski, 1971b, pp. 16-17). The road from dictatorship of the bureaucracy to basic democratic freedoms is by its very nature long and quite hard. It cannot be greatly shortened and quickened without the risk of serious cataclysms in the Polish society. However, a condition for success in progress is a fundamental change in the structure of social forces that influence economic development. The basic question that must be asked today is what are the realistic chances for working people to organize themselves to present their vital interests, and as a result to have some impact on the future of the Polish society.

So far, these chances are rather small. Trade unions are still of almost no value. To be sure, with a bit of initiative, local union functionaries manage from time to time to obtain something for their rank and file, mainly by playing various bureaucratic machines against one another. But this is activity of socially marginal importance. More profound discussion in local Party organizations, does not develop, for the Party remains a completely centralized apparatus that does not really allow any internal democracy. Any hope for democratization of the Party is very small, for it would be necessary to fundamentally revise the philosophical and political premises on which the existence of the entire system is based. Without great upheavals, usually coming from outside, more serious transformations are quite improbable. The remaining institutions and social organizations of the Polish People's Republic—the State apparatus, the local and regional public authorities, the industrial associations—are so subservient to the Party that they cannot change without permission from above.

What, however, are the chances of change effected from below through active pressure by the masses? They should not be over-estimated, taking into account that a few days of revolt is one thing and the crystalization of organized centers of mass sociopolitical activity is another. Mass activity remains beyond the realm of realistic possibilities of people who are dependent in almost every respect on an omnipotent bureaucracy.

There is a growing awareness in Poland that sooner or later the economy must be based on principles that would eliminate clique interests, or at least significantly decrease their importance. Such principles could be the harsh laws of an open market. The autonomy of state enterprises, which has been fought for by the more enlightened Polish economists for so many years, signifies nothing other than the subordination of production and consumption to the laws of a market. The return of capitalism is not the issue, but the removal of the national economy from dependence on the subjective whims of people in power.

Every economic reform that aims at increasing efficiency and productivity hits at the interests of some portion of the blue-collar workers' class. Polish workplaces are full of people who would not be able to maintain their positions under harsh market laws—they would have to be retrained and would lose their privileges. Polish intellectuals, who may advocate reform, cannot count on the immediate support of the blue-collar workers. Enormously strong willpower and much foresight will be needed in order to minimize the losses and and the injustices inevitably caused by reform. What would be done with the great mass of people who would suddenly become superfluous? Only a great and fearless move toward industrialization can guarantee enough employment positions both for the younger generations and for people forced to leave their present positions as a result of economic reform.

POLAND IN THE SOVIET BLOC

As Jan Drewnowski (1972) points out, a knowledge of the developmental tendencies within Poland is a sine qua non for predicting the trends of social forces in the country. Neither the "cries of despair" of such disillusioned Communists as Wladyslaw Bienkowski nor the fragmentary and gradual reformist pressures proposed by Leszek Kolakowski (1971b), nor even the strengthening of social forces set into motion by the contradictions inherent in the nature of the Sovietism prevailing in Poland (Drewnowski 1972, p. 25) will be of much help if they are not appropriately situated in a historical context. Whether she likes it or not, Poland shares her fate with contemporary communism; and what is happening in the country cannot be separated from the fate of a considerably broader structure.

Many Polish emigrants in the West still dream of an arrangement excluding Russia from a future East European structure. For example, Bohdan Osadczuk (1972) would like to push Russia into Eurasia. Both in the satellite countries and among their émigrés there is still a strong conviction that Russians are similar to Asians and therefore somehow inferior. But the USSR is a world power. And what hope is there that the East European nations, after the exclusion of Russia, could manage to get together and agree? Would not a "liberated" Eastern Europe again become an area of bloody struggles envenomed by particular interests?

The contemporary history of Eastern Europe is shaped by the following factors:

1. Progress of industrialization and the growing pressure of necessities connected with it (the anachronism of authoritative management, the need to pass from a system of giving orders to a system of stimulating and coordinating, the growing role of experts and of educated people).

2. The rapid growth of aspirations of the masses to continually higher level of education and culture, having contact with a broader world, freeing themselves of traditional provincialism, requiring more and demanding participation in decisions.

3. A deepening ideological, moral, and political crisis of institutionalized Marxism based on might, banality, boredom and lying versus an increasing common demand for democratic socialism based on freedom, creative searching, elasticity, and truth.

4. A growing social loss of face by the ruling elite, which does not want to learn anything and which, after temporary concessions to the masses, stubbornly returns to the defunct system of privileges, repression, and arbitrariness.

5. A consciousness of the collective strength of the Soviet bloc and its enormous significance on a world scale (by contrast with the interwar period, when few people in the West worried much about or even noticed Eastern Europe).

It is worth seeing how contemporary transformations in Eastern Europe are viewed from a North American perspective. P. A. Toma et al. (1970) demonstrate the gradual desatellization of particular countries in connection with the development of local nationalism (that are, incidentally, the simple and direct consequence of Soviet chauvinism), with stronger Western contacts, and above all with the disintegration of the ideological unity of the bloc. The new Communist elites of the Warsaw Pact countries are national Communists fighting against Party intellectuals (revisionists) whose disillusionment with Soviet utopianism and disenchantment with the imperialist policy of the Soviet Union have led to a reexamination of Marxist theories in the light of humanism and democracy. Local patriotism, ably manipulated by the Soviet authorities, is today of greater importance than ideology.

It seems right to claim that the growing polycentrism of the Soviet bloc can by no means be identified with de-Stalinization. At present, much of what happens within the bloc can be explained in terms of the elites, created by Stalin and trying to maintain their power. For these elites are threatened above all by the transformation of the present face of communism toward fundamental democratic freedoms. This is the cause of continual waverings by bloc countries between increased economic and social effectiveness, which requires democratic reforms, and the oppression identified with spiritual stagnancy in practically every field of human endeavor (except for the military).

Johnson (1970) presents a number of very penetrating approaches to the matter under discussion. First of all, the cognitive usefulness of the totalitarian interpretation of communism is shown to be very doubtful. As collective management becomes more common and political significance is acquired by various pressure groups (blue-collar workers, experts, Party organizers), it becomes increasingly difficult to talk about full centralization of political power. Terror, under the conditions of peaceful coexistence of systems and of the ever sharper division of labor in Communist societies, is losing its significance. The revolutionary elite is giving way to a technocratic elite. Market socialism, taking into account the law of supply and demand, is inching its way into the uniform economic model based on orders from above. The organisms that compose the Soviet bloc are gaining more and more experience in how to acquire comparative independence while retaining the pretense of complete obedience (Hungary and Rumania, as well as Armenia, are good examples in this respect). The mobilization of all social forces within the framework of a model of blind subordination to the top level is beginning to result in greater social losses than advantages—not only from the point of view of the good of the population, but even considering the significance of the Soviet bloc in the world. The malady of the system, consisting in its insufficient elasticity and negligible conduciveness to peaceful transformations, is being more fully realized by the Party intelligentsia. One can discern a tendency of the ruling elites to search for new, more subtle methods of stimulating effort by the masses and of controlling this effort.

All this taken together has the result of strengthening a pragmatic orientation and of weakening the doctrinal and ideological approach. The number of different versions of communism is being multiplied, not only outside the Soviet bloc but within it as well. Faith and utopia are giving way to rational thinking that leads to concrete programs aimed at solving internal problems. All this evolves in a crossfire of sharp conflicts between various pressure groups: experts oppose Party organizers, nationalists throw off the yoke of internationalism, utilitarians oriented toward improvement of the population's standard of living obstruct the endeavors of dogmatists, and pacifists try to negate the activity of militarists and neo-Stalinists. These conflicts pave the way for innovations, but at the same time they introduce more elements of differentiation to the superficially homogeneous Soviet bloc.

What significance is there to the long fashionable Western theory that systems are becoming more and more similar? Both its pessimistic version, prophesying the spreading of totalitarianism, or at least omnipotent bureaucracy, to every part of the world, and its optimistic version, prophesying universal democratic socialism, are turning out to be utopian, for they do not sufficiently take into account the conflicting nature of social evolution.

To the question of petrification of the system or its growing pluralism, J. F. Hugh (1972) answers that the Soviet system, superficial appearances to the contrary, is undergoing a gradual, very careful transformation in the direction of pluralism. This pluralism is still, however, very far removed from Western democracy, and from democracy in general, for its foundation is the multiplicity of institutions whose representatives take part in making decisions. In any case, changes in the Soviet political system are not going, and probably will not go for a long time, toward formalized representative democracy and thus of free elections.

BETWEEN RUSSIA AND THE WEST

The location of Poland on the border between the Western world and the European East has for centuries shaped the fate of the nation, its culture, ideology, and politics. "Although on one hand closely bound to Western European civilization, and representing on the other hand a transition between West and East, Poland has frequently found herself in a sort of contradiction with the historical evolution of the countries of both Eastern and Western Europe" (Lednicki 1944, p. 4).

Until the 18th century, when Russia became strong, Poland expanded to the east. This expansion began in the middle of the 14th century through the efforts of the Cracow lords. It was welcomed by the patricians of Little Poland and by the Church, who were interested in the occupation of the southeastern border territories, which were coveted by Lithuania and Hungary. That land was a gate to the fertile fields of Podolia, and through it passed the trade routes to the Black Sea.

A fairly sizable part of those territories was united with Poland in the second half of the 14th century. "In this manner the Polish State expanded beyond its ethnic frontiers and entered upon a multinational stage in its development" (Gieysztor et al. 1968, p. 131).

This expansion into Eastern Europe continued for the next three centuries. According to prominent Polish historians, such as Jozef Szujski, it exceeded the capacity of the nation. "The best, most active and creative elements of the nation were lost, absorbed by the immense territories united to the Republic" (Lednicki 1944, p. 24). In accomplishing its civilizing mission in the East, Poland gradually lost or at least attenuated its occidental characteristics.

The fate of Poland depends to a very large extent on how she is able and willing to deal with great powers that for centuries have been invading Eastern Europe. "When both [Russia and Germany] were weak or divided, Poland could expand her boundaries. When one or the other was strong and united the tendency was for Poland to pull in her boundaries on this side and to expand on the other. Only when both have been strong and allied with one another has the security of Poland been really endangered. This conjunction has occurred twice in the long history of Poland: in the eighteenth century when it culminated in the partitions of Poland; and in the late 1930s, when an unholy alliance of Nazi Germany and Stalinist Russia again led to the partition and destruction of the state" (Benes and Pounds 1970, p. 22).

Oskar Halecki, the prominent historian who remained in exile after World War II, represents the pro-Western interpretation of Poland's destiny. According to him, the Polish nation has been "separated from Russia by a thousand of years of completely different development and at the same time intimately associated to the West" (Halecki, ed. 1957, p. ix). The future of Poland, from this perspective, is in "the integration of a free and independent Poland with a freely united Europe integrated in turn with the modern Atlantic Community for the defence of Western civilization and the heritage of Christendom" (Halecki, ed. 1957, p. 16). Many Poles in exile have spent much time and effort to convince the West that it should actively help Poland return to the West. "What is our fate today would be yours tomorrow. Our will for the deliverance from our present plight and all its misfortunes should meet and equal your will for self-defence against the menace of a similar lot in the near future" (Ostaszewski 1971, p. 142).

Writing on the Polish victory over the Soviet army in 1920, the prominent Polish general Kazimierz Sosnkowski suggests, "After the defeat of the Soviet armies, the Western countries together with a victorious Poland were in a position to institute in Russia the rule of justice; together they would have accomplished a task which had proved too difficult for the Western Powers to undertake without Poland and too difficult for Poland without them" (Pilsudski 1972, p. vi).

There are various Russias just as there are various Polands. Reading Roy A. Medvedev's book on Stalinism (1971) or Solzhenitsyn's The Gulag Archipelago (1974) is probably a traumatic experience, even though so much has already been written on this subject. Of importance in this respect is not only the atmosphere of those times, when even the formal head of the Soviet State, M. I. Kalinin, managed to extract his wife from a detention camp very shortly before his death, and when even Stalin's closest associates lived in perpetual fear for their lives. More important is the enormous influence of totalitarianism on the people's mentality (Hollander 1973).

Poles may be vitally interested in supporting a Russia that will gradually rid itself of dogmatism and provincialism, that will revise outdated premises, that will search for new truths. Nothing can be more of an obstacle for Poles to a dialogue with such a Russia than their own provincialism, unjustified feeling of superiority, and contempt for everything east of Poland's present eastern border. Russia was and is great even in its deterioration and provincialism. Under no circumstances can Poles turn their backs on Russia.

Does the West really have a vested interest in breaking up the present Soviet bloc by feeding the fires of local nationalism? There are good reasons for doubting this. The West never was, and probably never will be, interested in "liberating" Eastern Europe, despite earnest proclamations to the contrary. It must, however, be concerned with making sure that Eastern Europe does not become a seeding ground for world cataclysms. After all, both world wars grew out of conflicts within Eastern Europe. Left to themselves, local nationalisms must sooner or later lead to new conflicts. On the other hand, it is the nationalist feelings that to a considerable extent form the foundation of the present conservative status quo of the Soviet bloc. Local elites prey on nationalism for their own goals, whereas Russian chauvinism cements the entire bloc by force. The gradual democratization of the Soviet bloc will increasingly come up against obstacles raised by nationalisms. It is not by chance that Boleslaw Piasecki, the leader of Poland's prewar radically nationalistic group, played the role of a status quo supporter in People's Poland (Blit 1965).

A dialogue with the new Russia, which is gradually crystallizing its program of breaking through self-illusions, concealments, and various kinds of simplification, can develop to the advantage of Eastern Europe solely on the basis of thinking in universal categories. Russian fundamentalism has in this respect superiority over the thinking in terms of personnal relations, sympathies and antipathies, local traditions and rituals so common in non-Russian Eastern Europe. It is not by chance that strength of character is a characteristic mainly of the new Soviet opposition, which defends law and order, demands fundamental liberties, and, in short, knows what it wants.

Some of the European entries are incomplete because the sources are now unavailable to the author. In all entries, however, enough information is given for the source to be identified and used as a reference.

Adamski, Franciszek. 1965. "The Steel Worker's Occupation and Family." Polish Sociological Bulletin 1: 103-07.

_____. 1966. Hutnik i jego rodzina (The steelworker and his family). Katowice: Slaski Instytut Naukowy.

Adamski, Wladyslaw. 1972. "Tendances des changements dans les attitudes sociales des paysans polonais." Paper for the Third World Congress of Rural Sociology. Baton Rouge.

Altkorn, Jerzy. 1963. "Identifikacja pracownikow handlu z zawodem" (Identification of trade employees with their profession). Handel wewnetrzny 5.

Anuarul statistic al Republicii Socialiste Romania 1972. Bucarest: Directia Centrala de Statistica.

Arnold, Stanislaw, and Marian Zychowski. 1962. Outline History of Poland. Warsaw: Polonia Publishing House

Bartnicki, T., and T. Czajkowski. 1936. Struktura zatrudnienia i zarobki pracownikow umyslowych (Structure of employment and salaries of white-collar workers). Warsaw.

Barycz, Henryk. 1957. The Development of University Education in Poland. Warsaw: Polonia Publishing House.

Baucic, Ivo. 1972. The Effects of Emigration from Yugoslavia and the Problems of Returning Emigrant Workers. The Hague: Martinus Nijhof. Bauman, Zygmunt. 1962. "Social Structure of the Party Organization in Industrial Works." Polish Sociological Bulletin 3-4: 50-64.

_____. 1966. "Economic Growth, Social Structure, Elite Formation." In Class, Status, and Power, eds. R. Bendix and S. M. Lipset. New York: Free Press.

_____. 1971a. "Social Dissent in the East European Political System." Archives européenes de sociologie 12: 38-39.

_____. 1971b. "Uses of Information: When Social Information Becomes Desired." Annals of the American Academy of Political and Social Sciences 393.

_____. 1971c. "The Crisis of Soviet-Type Systems." Problems of Communism 20 (6): 45-53.

Benes, Vaclav L., and Norman G. J. Pounds. 1970. Poland. London: Benn.

Berger, Peter, ed. 1969. Marxism and Sociology. Views from Eastern Europe. New York: Appleton-Century-Crofts.

Berliner, J. S. 1957. Factory and Manager in the USSR. Cambridge, Mass.: Harvard University Press.

Bethell, Nicholas. 1969. Gomulka. His Poland, His Communism. New York: Holt, Rinehart, and Winston.

Bielicki, Waclaw, and Krzysztof Zagorski. 1966. Robotnicy wczoraj i dzis (Blue-collar workers yesterday and today). Warsaw: Wiedza Powszechna.

Bienkowski, Wladyslaw. 1966. Problemy teorii rozwoju spolecznego (Theoretical problems of social change). Warsaw: Ksiazka i Wiedza.

_____. 1970. Motory i hamulce socjalizmu (The driving and inhibiting forces of socialism). Paris: Instytut Literacki.

Blauner, Robert. 1964. Alienation and Freedom. Chicago: University of Chicago Press.

Blit, Lucjan. 1965, The Eastern Pretender. London.

_____. 1971. The Origins of Polish Socialism. The History of Ideas of the First Polish Socialist Party 1876-1886. Cambridge: Cambridge University Press.

Blumberg, Paul. 1968. Industrial Democracy. London: Constable.

Bochenski, Aleksander. 1972. Rzecz o psychice narodu polskiego (On the psychology of the Polish nation). Warsaw: Panstwowy Instytut Wydawniczy.

Borowski, S. 1967. "New Forms and Factors Affecting Rural-Urban Migration in Poland." In Proceedings of the World Population Conference, IV. New York: United Nations.

Borucki, Andrej. 1962. "Study of the Socio-Occupational Position of the Pre-War Intelligentsia in People's Poland." Polish Sociological Bulletin 1-2.

Boswell, A. Bruce. 1967. "Poland." In The European Nobility in the 18th Century, ed. Albert Goodwin, pp. 154-71. New York: Harper & Row.

Breed, W. 1955. "Social Control in the Newsroom. A Functional Analysis." Social Forces 33.

Brodzinski, Bohdan. 1971. "The Polish Economy in the Inter-war and Post-war Years." In Modern Poland Between East and West, ed. Jan Ostaszewski. London: Polish School of Political and Social Science.

Bromke, Adam. 1967. Poland's Politics. Idealism versus Realism. Cambridge, Mass.: Harvard University Press.

_____. 1971. "Beyond the Gomulka Era." Foreign Affairs 49 (4).

_____ and T. Rakowski-Harmstone, eds. 1972. The Communist States in Disarray 1965-1971. Minneapolis: University of Minnesota Press.

_____ and John W. Strong, eds. 1973. Gierek's Poland. New York: Praeger.

Brzeski, Andrej. 1967. "Finance and Inflation Under Central Planning." Osteuropa Wirtschaft 12 (3).

_____. 1968. "Forced-Draft Industrialization with Unlimited Supply of Money: Poland, 1945-1964." In Money and Plan, ed. Gregory Grossman. Berkeley: University of California Press.

_____. 1971a. "Intensification of Economic Growth in Eastern Europe." Jahrbuch der Wirtschaft Osteuropas 2.

227

_____. 1971b. "Poland as a Catalyst of Change in the Communist Economic System." Polish Review 16 (2).

Brzezinski, Zbigniew. 1970. Between Two Ages. America's Role in the Technetronic Era. New York: Viking Press.

Budzet czasu rodzin pracowniczych (Time budget of working families). 1970. Warsaw: Glowny Urzad Statystyczny.

Budzety czasu pracownikow zatrudnionych w gospodarce uspolecznionej poza rolnictwem i lesnictwem 1969 (Family Budgets of the non-agricultural employees of the nationalized economy in 1969). 1971. Warsaw: Glowny Urzad Statystyczny.

Bursche, Krystyna, and Grazyna Pomian. 1963. "The Role and Social Position of Foremen in Industrial Works." Polish Sociological Bulletin 1.

_____. 1965. "Doksztalcanie i szkolenie pracownikow" (Education of workers). In Problemy kadry przemyslowej, ed. Maria Hirszowicz. Warsaw: Wydawnictwo Zwiazkowe CRZZ.

_____. 1969. "Problemy jakosci pracy w swietle opinii robotnikow przemyslowych." (Problems of work quality in the opinion of industrial workers). Prakseologia 32.

Buszko, Henryk. 1967. Proba oceny aktualnej sytuacji architektury polskiej i zawodu architekta (Evaluation of the current situation of Polish architecture and of the architectural profession). Warsaw: SARP.

Byrne, Terence E. 1970. "Levels of Consumption in Eastern Europe." In Economic Development in Countries of Eastern Europe. A Compendium of papers submitted to the Subcommittee on Foreign Economic Policy of the Joint Economic Committee, Congress of the United States. Washington: U.S. Government Printing Office.

"Can Sociology Help?" 1971. Summary of papers presented at the annual meeting of the Polish Sociological Association in March 1971. Polish Perspectives 7-8.

Chalasinski, Jozef. 1946. Spoleczna genealogia inteligencji polskiej (Social origin of the Polish intelligentsia). Lodz: Czytelnik.

_____. 1958. Przeszlosc i przyszlosc inteligencji polskiej (Past and Future of the Polish intelligentsia). Lodz: Czytelnik.

_____. 1962. "Spenser's Sociology as Assimilated by the Intellectuals in Britain, Poland and America at the End of the 19th Century. A Comparative Study." Polish Sociological Bulletin 1-2.

_____. 1964. "The Young Generation of Rural Inhabitants in People's Poland as Seen from their Life-Records." Polish Sociological Bulletin 2.

Charkiewicz, Michal. 1961. Kadry wykwalifikowane w Polsce (Skilled personnel in Poland). Warsaw: PWE.

_____. 1966. "Employment of Trained Personnel." Polish Perspectives 2.

Chodak, Szymon. 1973. "How Was Political Sociology Possible in Poland?" International Journal of Contemporary Sociology 10 (1).

Cichomski, Bogdan. 1967. "Zdobywanie stopni naukowych w instytutach" (Work for academic degrees in the applied research institutes). In System spoleczny instytutu, ed. Alexander Matejko, pp. 133-51. Warsaw: PWN.

_____. 1969. "Rola doktoranta w katedrze" (Role of a doctoral candidate in departments). In System spoleczny katedry, ed. Alexander Matejko. Warsaw: PWN.

Cieplak, Tadeusz, ed. 1972. Poland Since 1956. New York: Twayne.
Concise Statistical Yearbook of Poland 1970. 1970. Warsaw: Central Statistical Office.

Concise Statistical Yearbook of Poland 1973. 1973. Warsaw: Central Statistical Office.

Conquest, Robert. 1967. Industrial Workers in the USSR. London: Bodley Head.

Culture in People's Poland. 1966. Warsaw: Panstwowe Wydawnictwo Ekonomiczne.

Czapow, Czeslaw. 1969. Ksztaltowanie postaw mlodziezy pracujacej (Shaping of the blue-collar youth's attitudes). Warsaw: Wydawnictwo Zwiazkowe CRZZ.

Czechoslovakia. Statistical Abstract. 1969. Prague: Orbis Czeczerda, Wanda. 1964. Warunki i zyczenia mieszkaniowe roznych grup ludnosci (Conditions and housing preferences of various population groups). Warsaw: Arkady.

Czerniewska, Maria. 1961. "Dochody gospodarstw chlopskich w 1959/60" (Incomes of peasant families in 1959/60). Zagadnienia ekonomiki rolnej supplement 6.

Czerwinski, Marcin. 1967. The Dissemination of Culture in Poland. Warsaw: Polonia Publishing House.

_____. 1969. Przemiany obyczaju (Transformation of mores). Warsaw: Panstwowy Instytut Wydawniczy.

Czyszkowska Janina, and Zdzislaw Grochowski. 1966. Efektywnosc gospodarowania rolniczych spoldzielni produkcyjnych w porownaniu z gospodarka indywidualna (Comparison of economic effectiveness between private and collective farming). Warsaw: Zaklad Wyd. Centrali Roln. Spoldz.

Daniluk, Wlodzimierz. 1968. "Organizacyjne i psychospoleczne aspekty pracy sprzedawcow" (Organizational and psychosocial aspects of salesclerks' work). Studia socjologiczne 3/4.

Davies, Ioan. 1970. Social Mobility and Political Change. London: Macmillan.

Davies, Norman. 1972. White Eagle, Red Star. The Polish-Soviet War 1919-20. New York: St. Martin's Press.

Deschner, Gunther. 1972. Warsaw Uprising. New York: Ballantine.

Dmoch, Teodozja. 1971. "Zarobki przed i po grudniu." (Incomes before and after December). Polityka-statystyka 11.

Dobrowolska, Danuta. 1965. Gornicy salinarni Wieliczki w latach 1880-1939 (The saltworks employees of Wieliczka in the period 1880-1939). Wroclaw: Ossolineum.

_____. 1972. "Social Changes in Suburban Villages." Paper for the Third World Congress of Rural Sociology. Baton Rouge.

Drewnowski, Jan. 1970. "Socjalizm w Polsce" (Socialism in Poland). Kultura (Paris) 9:25-39.

_____. 1972. "Jedyna droga" (The only way). Kultura (Paris) 3:3-26.

Drewnowski, Tadeusz, et al. 1964. Poland 1944-1964. Warsaw: Polonia Publishing House.

Dyoniziak, Ryszard. 1967. Spoleczne warunki wydajnosci pracy (Social conditions of effective work). Warsaw: Ksiazka i Wiedza.

Dzida, Jan. 1969. Rozpietosc i zasieg kierowania w teorii i praktyce (Span of control in theory and practice). Warsaw.

Dziecielska, Stefania. 1967. Sytuacja spoleczna dziennikarzy polskich (The social situation of Polish journalists). Wroclaw: Ossolineum.

Dzieciolowska, Stefania. 1973. "The People's Council in the Eyes of the Inhabitants." In People's Councils in Poland in the Light of Empirical Research, ed. Sylwester Zawadzki, pp. 187-230. Warsaw: Institute of Legal Sciences, Polish Academy of Sciences.

Dziecielska-Michnikowska, Stefania, and Joanna Kulpinska. 1967. "Women's Promotion." Polish Sociological Bulletin 1: 85-93.

Dziewicka, Maria. 1963. Chlopi-robotnicy (Peasant-workers). Warsaw.

_____. 1972. "Changes in the Families and Forms of Part-Time Farmers 1957-1967." Paper for the Third World Congress of Rural Sociology. Baton Rouge.

Dziewonski, K., and M. Jerczynski. 1970. "Urbanization of Poland." Studia demograficzne 22/23: 161-71.

Eberhardt, P., et al. 1971. "Polska 2000" (Poland in the year 2000). Polityka-statystyka 5.

Eisenstadt, Shmuel N. 1963. The Political Systems of Empires. London: Free Press.

Ellias, Andras. 1970. "Magnitude and Distribution of the Labour Force in Eastern Europe." In Economic Developments in Countries of Eastern Europe. Washington: U.S. Government Printing Office.

Fainsod, Merle. 1963. How Russia Is Ruled. Cambridge, Mass.: Harvard University Press.

Feiwel, George. 1965. The Economics of a Socialist Enterprise. A Case Study of the Polish Firm. New York: Praeger.

_____. 1971a. Poland's Industrialization Policy: A Current Analysis. New York: Praeger.

_____. 1971b. Problems in Polish Economic Planning: Continuity, Change and Prospects. New York: Praeger.

Feuer, Lewis S. 1964. "Marxism and the Hegemony of the Intellectual Class." In Transactions of the Fifth World Congress of Sociology, IV, pp. 83-96. International Sociological Association.

Fialkowski, W. 1971. "Czlowiek zwany kierownikiem—w drodze z piekla do nieba" (Man called manager—on the way from hell to heaven). Polityka 32.

Fiszman, Joseph R. 1970. "Poland: Continuity and Change." In The Changing Face of Communism in Eastern Europe, ed. P. A. Toma. Tucson: University of Arizona Press.

_____. 1972. Revolution and Tradition in People's Poland. Education and Socialization. Princeton University Press.

Flakierski, Henryk. 1973. "The Polish Economic Reform of 1970." Canadian Journal of Economics 6 (1).

Ford, James L. 1972 (?). The Role of Poland's "Recovered Western Territories" in Her Economy. Lawrence: University of Kansas Press.

Forster, G. M. 1965. "Peasant Society and the Image of a Limited Good." American Anthropologist 67.

Fox, Paul. 1971. The Reformation in Poland. Westport, Conn.: Greenwood Press.

Friedrich, Carl J., and Zbigniew Brzezinski. 1965. Totalitarian Dictatorship and Autocracy. New York: Praeger.

Galaj, Dyzma. 1965. "Attitudes of the Rural Population to the Part-Time Farmers." Polish Sociological Bulletin 1.

Galbraith, John K. 1962. The Affluent Society. Baltimore: Penguin Books.

Galdzicki, Zygmunt. 1967. Pracownicy przedsiebiorstwa elektronicz-nego (Employees of an electronic company). Wroclaw: Ossolineum.

Galeski, Boguslaw. 1963. "Farmers' Attitude Towards Their Occupation." Polish Sociological Bulletin 1: 57-68.

_____. 1964. "From Peasant into Farmer." Polish Sociological Bulletin 2.

_____. 1972. Basic Concepts of Rural Sociology. Manchester: Manchester University Press.

Galinowski, K. 1971. "Placa zasadnicza-podstawa" (Basic salary as a principle). Zycie gospodarcze 13.

Gella, Aleksander. 1970. "The Fate of Eastern Europe under 'Marxism'" Slavic Review 29: 187-200.

_____. 1971a. "Contemporary Sociology in Poland." International Journal of Contemporary Sociology 2-3.

_____. 1971b. "The Life and Death of the Old Polish Intelligentsia." Slavic Review 30: 1-27.

Gieysztor, Alexander, et al. 1961. Millenium. A Thousand Years of the Polish State. Warsaw: Polonia Publishing House.

_____. 1968. History of Poland. Warsaw: PWN.

Gniazdowski, A. 1969. "Zwartosc malych zespolow roboczych" (Cohesiveness of small work teams). Studia socjologiczne, 2: 225-48.

Golanski, Henryk. 1966. "Planning for the Future." Polish Perspectives 12.

Gömöri, George. 1973. "The Culutral Intelligentsia. The Writers." In Social Groups in Polish Society, eds. David Lane and George Kolankiewicz, pp. 152-79. New York: Columbia University Press.

Gontarski, Z. 1971. "Dojazdy do pracy" (Commutation to work). Polityka-statystyka, 2.

Gorecki, Jan. 1963. "Matrimonial Property in Poland." Modern Law Review (March): 156-73.

_____. 1970. Divorce in Poland. The Hague: Mouton.

_____. 1971. "Industrial Accident Compensation in Eastern Europe. An Empirical Study." Stanford Law Review 23 (2).

_____. 1972. "Communist Family Patterns. Law as an Implement of Change." University of Illinois Law Forum 1: 121-36.

Gospodarek, Tadeusz. 1971. "Z badan nad kultura polityczna w zakladach wielkoprzemyslowych" (Studies on political culture in big industrial works). Studia socjologiczne 2: 235-52.

Gouldner, Alwin W. 1970. The Coming Crisis of Western Sociology. New York: Basic Books.

Granick, David. 1950. The Red Executive. Garden City, N.Y.: Doubleday.

Gross, Felix. 1945. The Polish Worker. New York: Roy.

Groth, Alexander J. 1972. Peoples' Poland. Government and Politics. San Francisco: Chandler.

Grzelak, Anna. 1965. "Problemy adaptacji mlodych inzynierow" (Adaptation problems of young engineers). In Problemy kadry przemyslowej, ed. Maria Hirszowicz. Warsaw: Wydawnictwo Zwiazkowe CRZZ.

Gumkowski, Janusz, and Kazimierz Leszczynski. 1961. Poland Under Nazi Occupation. Warsaw: Polonia Publishing House.

Gwiszani, D. M. 1966. "Problemy upravlenija socyalisticzeskoj promyszlennostiu" (Problems of management in socialist industry). Voprosy filosofii 11.

Haire, Mason, et al. 1966. Managerial Thinking. An International Study. New York.

Halecki, Oskar. 1950. The Limits and Division of European History. London: Sheed and Ward.

_____. 1956. A History of Poland. London: Dent.

_____, ed. 1957. Poland. New York: Atlantic Books.

Harbison, Frederick H. and Charches A. Myers, eds. 1959. Management in the Industrial World. New York: McGraw-Hill.

Heilbroner, Robert L. 1970. Between Capitalism and Socialism. New York: Vintage Books.

Heller, Celia Stopnicka, ed. 1969. Structured Social Inequality. New York: Macmillan.

_____. 1969. "Anti-Zionism and the Political Struggle Within the Elite in Poland." Jewish Journal of Sociology 11 (2).

Herod, C. 1969. "Opinie mlodych robotnikow na temat ksztalcenia sie" (Opinions of young workers about learning). Studia socjologiczne 3: 237-52.

Hertz, Alexander. 1942. "The Social Background of the Pre-War Polish Political Structure." Journal of Central European Affairs (July): 145-60.

_____. 1951. "The Case of an Eastern European Intelligentsia." Journal of Central European Affairs 11 (1).

Hirszowicz, Maria. 1973a. "Marxism, Revionism and Academic Sociology in Poland." International Journal of Contemporary Sociology 10 (1): 40-52.

_____. 1973b. Komunistyczny lewiatan (The Communist leviathan). Paris: Instytut Literacki.

Hiscocks, Richard. 1963. Poland. Bridge for the Abyss? London: Oxford University Press.

Hollander, Paul. 1973. Soviet and American Society. London: Oxford University Press.

235

Holzer, Jerzy. 1968. Fifty Years of Polish Independence. Warsaw: Interpress.

Hozer, Jan. 1969. "Inzynierowie w przemysle" (Engineers in industry). In Przemysl i spoleczenstwo w Polsce Ludowej, ed. Jan Szczepanski, pp. 104-40. Wroclaw: Ossolineum.

_____. 1970. Zawod i praca inzyniera (Profession and work of an engineer). Wroclaw: Ossolineum.

Hugh, Jerry F. 1972. "The Soviet System. Petrification or Pluralism?" Problems of Communism 2.

Hunek, Tadeusz. 1965. Spoldzielczosc produkcjna w rolnictwie polskim (Collective farming in Polish agriculture). Warsaw: Panstn. Wyd. Roln. i Lesne.

Hunnius, Gerry, et al., eds. 1973. Workers' Control. New York: Vintage Books. International Encyclopaedia of the Social Sciences. 1968. New York: Free Press.

Iwanicka-Lyra, Elzbieta. 1972. "Changes in the Character of Migration Movements from Rural to Urban Areas in Poland." Geographia Polonica 24: 71-80.

Jablonski, Henryk. 1966. "O potrzebie usprawnienia pracy wyzszych uszelni" (On the need to improve the functioning of higher education institutions). Nowe drogi 11.

Jakubowicz, Szymon. 1971. "Organizacja to nie schematy" (A nonformalistic approach to organization). Zycie gospodarcze 20.

Janicki, Janusz. 1968. Urzednicy przemyslowi w strukturze spolecznej Polski Ludowej (Industrial clerks in the social structure of People's Poland). Warsaw: Ksiazka i Wiedza.

Jarosinska, Maria. 1964. Adaptacja mlodziezy wiejskiej do klasy robotniczej (Adaptation of peasant youth to the blue-collar class). Wroclaw: Ossolineum.

Jarosz, Maria. 1967. Samorzad robotniczy w przedsiebiorstwie przemyslowym (Workers' self-government in an industrial establishment). Warsaw: Panstwowe Wydawnictwo Ekonomiczne.

Jasienica, Pawel. 1965. Polska Jagiellonow (Jagiellonian Poland). Warsaw: PiW.

_____. 1966. Polska Piastow (Piast Poland). Warsaw: PiW.

_____. 1972. Rzeczpospolita obojga narodow. Dzieje agonii (The gentry commonwealth of two nations. The story of agony). Warsaw: PiW.

Jedrzycki, Wieslaw. 1971. Socjolog w zakladzie pracy (The Sociologist at the workplace). Wroclaw: Ossolineum.

Johnson, Charles. 1970. "Comparing Communist Nations." In Changes in Communist Systems, ed. Charles Johnson. Stanford: Stanford University Press.

Jozefowicz, Zofia. 1958. "Students. Their Views on Society and Aspirations." Polish Perspectives 7/8.

_____, et al. 1958. "Students. Myth and Reality." Polish Perspectives 3/4.

Kalecki, Michal. 1964. "Porowanie dochodu robotnikow i pracownikow umyslowych z okresem przedwojennym" (Comparison of workers' and white collars' incomes at the present time and before the war). Kultura i spoleczenstwo 1.

Karpinski, Andrzej. 1963. Problems of Socialist Industrialization in Poland. Warsaw: Panstwowe Wydawnictwo Ekonomiczne.

Kasinska, Barbara. 1970. "Student Activism in Poland. 1968." M. A., thesis, University of Calgary.

Keller, Suzanne Infeld. 1963. Beyond the Ruling Class. New York: Random House. Kiezun, Witold. 1968. Dyrektor (The executive). Warsaw: Ksiazka i Wiedza.

_____. 1968/69. "Niektore zagadnienia formalizacji w biurokracji" (Some problems of formalization in bureaucracy). Prakseologia 30.

_____. 1969. "Style kierownictwa na tle zadan organizacyjnych" (Styles of management and organizational tasks). In Socjologia kierownictwa, ed. Aleksander Matejko, pp. 117-54. Warsaw: Panstwowe Wydawnictwo Ekonomiczne.

Kilbach, D. 1971. "Kary, reklamacje i co z tego wynika" (Penalties, complaints and their consequences). Zycie gospodarcze 10.

Klimczyk, Marian. 1973. "Metodologiczne problemy migracji wahad-lowych" (Methodological problems of daily migrations). Wiadomosci statystyczne 4.

Kloskowska, Jolanta. 1964. "Mass Culture in Poland." Polish Sociological Bulletin 2.

Kolaja, Jiri T. 1960. A Polish Factory. Lexington: University of Kentucky Press.

Kolakowski, Leszek. 1968. Toward a Marxist Humanism. Crowe Press.

_____. 1969, Chrétiens sans église. Paris: Gallimard.

_____. 1971a. "A Pleading for Revolution. A Rejoinder to Z. Bauman." Archives Européenes de sociologie 12 (1).

_____. 1971b. "Tezy o nadziei i beznadziejnosci" (Theses on hope and hopelessmess). Kultura (Paris) 6.

Kolankiewicz, George. 1973. "The Technical Intelligentsia." In Social Groups in Polish Society, eds. David Lane and George Kolankiewicz. New York: Columbia University Press.

Kolko, Gabriel. 1962. Wealth and Power in America. New York: Praeger. Koncentracja przestrzenna ludnosci, tempo i skala zmian w latch 1950-1970. (Dynamics of the territorial concentration of the population in the period 1950-1970). 1973. Warsaw: Glowny Urzad Statystyczny.

Korbonski, Andrzej. 1965. Politics of Socialist Agriculture in Poland 1945-60. New York: Columbia University Press.

Korbonski, Stefan. 1966. Warsaw in Exile. New York: Praeger.

Kornilowicz, Maria, ed. 1962. Western and Northern Poland. Poznan: Zachodnia Agencja Prasowa.

Kosinski, Leszek. 1969. "Migration of Population in East Central Europe 1939-1955." Canadian Slavonic Papers 12 (3).

_____. 1970a. "The Internal Emigration of Population in Poland 1961-1965." Geographia Polonica.

_____. 1970b. The Population of Europe. London: Longman.

_____. 1971. "Population Trends in Poland after the Second World War." Paper presented to the Symposium of the Institute of British Geographers. Brighton.

Kotarbinski, Tadeusz. 1955. Traktat o dobrej robocie (Treatise on good work). Lodz.

Kowalewska, Salomea. 1962. Psychospoleczne warunki pracy w przedsiebiorstwie przemyslowym (The social psychological conditions of work in an industrial enterprise). Wroclaw: Ossolineum.

_____. 1971. Humanizacja pracy (Humanization of work). Warsaw: Wydawnictwo Zwiazkowe CRZZ.

Kowalewski, J. 1970. "Niektore konsekwencje demograficzne migracji ludnosci wiejskiej do miast w europejskich krajach socjalistycznych 1950-1965" (Some demographic consequences of the migration of rural population to urban areas in socialist countries of Europe 1950-1965). Studia demograficzne 21:81-97.

Kowalewski, Stanislaw. 1967. Przelozony-podwladny (Supervisor-subordinate). Panstwowe Wydawnictwo Ekonomiczne.

Kowalewski, Zdzislaw. 1962. Chemicy w Polskiej Rzeczypospolitej Ludowej (Chemists in People's Poland). Wroclaw: Ossolineum.

Kowalik, Tadeusz. 1971. "Oskar Lange. His Influence on Polish Economics." Polish Perspectives 6:9-17.

Kozakiewicz, Mikolaj. 1972. "Accessibility to Rural Youth of Different Levels of Schooling." Paper presented at the Third World Congress of Rural Sociology. Baton Rouge.

Kozlowski, Czeslaw, and Wieslaw Turos. 1973. "Ostateczne wyniki NSP w zakresie danych o ludnosci" (Final results of the 1970 census on population) Wiadomosci statystyczne 4.

Krall, Hanna. 1970. Pobiezny szkic do portretu klasy (Essay on the working class). Polityka-statystyka 5.

Kraus, Gabriel. 1968. Spoleczne aspekty wdrazania postepu technicznegozw gornictwie wegla kamiennego (Social aspects of technical progress in coal mining). Katowice: Slaski Instytut Naukowy.

Krawczewski, A. 1970. Zawod nauczyciela (Teacher's profession). Warsaw: Ksiazka i Wiedza.

Kridl, Manfred, et al., eds. 1944. The Democratic Heritage of Poland. London: Allen and Unwin.

Krol, Henryk. 1970. Postep techniczny d kwalifikacje (Technical progress and qualifications). Warsaw: Ksiazka i Wiedza

Kruszewski, Z. Anthony. 1972. The Oder Neisse Boundary and Poland's Modernization. New York: Praeger.

Kryczka, Piotr, et al. 1971. Socjologia wsi i miasta w Polsce (Sociology of villages and towns in Poland). Warsaw: Polish Academy of Sciences.

Krysiak, J. 1971. "Jak wykorzystujemy urlopy wypoczynkowe?" (How do we spend our leaves?). Polityka-statystyka 2.

Krzyzaniak, Marian. 1971. Transformation of Polish Agriculture from 1920 on. Houston: Rice University.

Kucharski, W. 1971. "Zwiazki zawodowe-ale jakie?" (Trade unions —but of what kind?). Polityka 10.

Kulczycka, Barbara. 1973. "Niektore problemy kobiet pracujacych zawodowo" (Some problems of working women). Wiadomosci statystyczne 4:44-45.

Kupis, Tadeusz. 1966. Zawod dziennikarza w Polsce Ludowej (The journalistic profession in People's Poland). Warsaw.

Kurczweski, Jacek, and Kazimierz Frieske. 1973. "Prawo jako narzedzie regulacji zycia gospodarczego w swietle badan empirycznych" (The law as a tool of regulation of economic life in the light of empirical research). Warsaw. Paper.

Kuron, Jacek, et al. 1968. Revolutionary Marxist Students in Poland Speak out 1964-1968. New York: Roy.

Kurowski, Stefan. 1971. "Granice usprawnienia systemu planowania i zarzadzania" (The limits of reforming the system of planning and management). Gospodarka planowa 4.

Kwasniewicz, Wladyslaw. 1964. Czytelnictwo prasy w Nowej Hucie —jego podloze i funkcje spoleczne (Newspaper reading in Nowa Huta—its background and socio-cultural functions). Cracow: Osrodek Badan Prasoznawczych.

Lachs, Manfred. 1964. The Polish-German Frontier. Warsaw: PWN.

Laevan, Harald. 1972. Polen nach dem Sturz Gomulkas. Stuttgart: Seewald.

Lane, David. 1971. The End of Inequality? Stratification Under State Socialism. Baltimore: Penguin Books.

_____. 1972. "Dissent and Consensus Under State Socialism." Archives Européenes de sociologie 13 (1).

_____. 1973a. "Structural and Social Change in Poland." In Social Groups in Polish Society, eds. David Lane and George Kolankiewicz, pp. 1-28. New York: Columbia University Press.

_____. 1973b. "The Role of Social Groups." In Social Groups in Polish Society, eds. D. Lane and G. Kolankiewicz, pp. 302-76. New York: Columbia University Press.

_____, and George Kolankiewicz, eds. 1973. Social Groups in Polish Society. New York: Columbia University Press.

Latuch, M. 1970. Migracje wewnetrzne w Polsce na tle industrial-izacji 1950-1960 (Internal migrations in Poland and industrialization 1950-1960). Warsaw: Panstwowe Wydawnictwo Ekonomiczne.

Lednicki, Waclaw. 1944. Life and Culture in Poland. New York: Roy.

_____. 1954. Russia, Poland, and the West. London: Hutchison.

Lenski, Gerhard, and Jean Lenski. 1974. Human Societies. New York: McGraw-Hill.

Lepa, Eugene, and Olga Lepa. 1966. Culture in People's Poland. Warsaw: Panstwowe Wydawnictwo Ekonomiczne.

Leslie, R. 1969. Reform and Insurrection in Russian Poland 1856-1865. Westport; Conn.: Greenwood Press.

Leszczycki, Stanislaw. 1964. "Patterns of Industrialization." Polish Persectives 8.

_____, and L. Kosinski, eds. 1967. Zarys geografii ekonomicznej Polski (Outline of the economic geography of Poland). Warsaw: PWN.

_____, and T. Lijewski, eds. 1972. Geografia przemyslv Polski (Geography of industry in Poland). Warsaw: Panstwowe Wydawnictwo Naukowe.

Lewis, Paul. 1973. "The Peasantry." In Social Groups in Polish Society, eds. D. Lane and G. Kolankiewicz. New York: Columbia University Press.

Lijewski, Teofil. 1967. Dojazdy do pracy w Polsce (Commutation to work in Poland). Warsaw: PWN.

Likert, Rensis. 1967. The Human Organization. New York: McGraw-Hill.

Lipinski, Edward. 1968. "The Theory of the Socialist Enterprise." In Economic Development for Eastern Europe, ed. M. C. Kaser. London: MacMillan.

_____. 1971a. "Czwarta sila wytworcza-zarzadzanie" (The fourth element in the forces of production-management). Zycie literackie 4.

_____. 1971b. Marks i zagadnienia wspolczesnosci (Marx and contemporary problems). Warsaw: PWN.

_____. 1972. "System wartosci spoleczenstwa socjalistycznego" (The value system of socialist society). Zycie gospodarcze 27 (28).

Lipset, Seymour M., and R. Bendix. 1967. Social Mobility in Industrial Society. Berkeley: University of California Press.

_____, and R. B. Dobson. 1973. "Social Stratification and Sociology in the Soviet Union." Survey 3:114-85.

242

Lipski, Witold. 1962. Agriculture in Poland. Warsaw: Polonia Publishing House.

_____. 1973. "Changes in Agriculture." Canadian Slavonic Papers 15 (1-2).

Ludz, Peter C. 1972. The Changing Party Elite in East Germany. Cambridge, Mass.: MIT Press.

Lukacs, George. 1971. History and Class Consciousness. London: Merlin Press.

Lutynska, Krystyna. 1964. "Office Workers' Views on Their Social Position." Polish Sociological Bulletin 1:79-83.

_____. 1967. Pozycja spoleczna urzednikow w Polsce Ludowej (Social position of office workers in People's Poland). Warsaw.

Lysiowa, Ewa. 1963. "Research on the Occupation of Farming." Polish Sociological Bulletin 3.

_____. 1969. Zawod rolnika w w swiadomosci spolecznej dwoch pokolen (The farming occupation in social consciousness of two generations). Warsaw.

Machonin, P. 1970. "Social Stratification in Contemporary Czechoslovakia." American Journal of Sociology 75 (5).

Madej, Zbigniew. 1963. O funkcjonowaniu gospodarki narodowej (Functioning of the national economy). Warsaw: Ksiazka i Wiedza.

Majchrzak, Irena. 1965. Pracownicze przestepstwo gospodarcze i jego sprawca (The White-collar crime and the people responsible for it). Warsaw: Wiedza Powszechna.

Maly Rocznik Statystyczny Warsaw: 1973. (Small statistical yearbook). Glowny Urzad Statystyczny.

Marczak, J. 1970. "Warunki rodzinne i socjalno-bytowe wlokniarek lodzkich" (Family and living conditions of working women in the textile industry in Lodz). Studia demograficzne 21:69-80.

Markiewicz, Wladyslaw. 1962. Spoleczne procesy uprzemyslowienia (Social processes of industrialization). Poznan: Wydawnictwo Poznanskie.

Markiewicz-Lagneau, Nina. 1969. Éducation, égalité et socialisme. Paris: Anthopos.

Matejko, Aleksander. 1956. "Struktura ludnosci Nowej Huty" (The population structure of Nowa Huta). Przeglad statystyczny 2.

_____. 1959. "Wartosc uzytkowa nowych mieszkan w swietle doswiadczen ich mieszkancow" (Utilization of apartments by their inhabitants). In Zaludnienie i uzytkowanie mieszkan w nowych osiedlach. Warsaw: Arkady.

_____. 1962. Kultura pracy zbiorowej (The culture of teamwork). Warsaw: Wydawnictwo Zwiazkowe CRZZ.

_____. 1964a. Hutnicy na tle ich srodowiska pracy (Steelworkers and their work environment). Katowice: Slaski Instytut Naukowy.

_____. 1964b. "Zespol redakcyjny w oczach socjologa" (The journalistic team from the sociological viewpoint). Zeszyty prasoznawcze 4.

_____. 1965. "Steelworkers' Attitude to Their Occupation." Polish Sociological Bulletin 1.

_____. 1966a. "Les conditions psycho-sociales du travail dans les groupes scientifiques." Sociologie du travail 1:51-66.

_____. 1966b. "Status Incongruence in the Polish Intelligentsia." Social Research 4:611-38.

_____. 1966c. System spoleczny zespolu naukowego (The Social system of basic research teams). Warsaw: PWN.

_____. 1967a. Nastin sociologie prace (Outline of the sociology of work). Prague: Nakladatelstvi Prace.

_____. 1967b. "The Organization and Stratification of Scientific Workers in Poland." Sociology of Education 40 (3):367-76.

_____. 1967c. "Workers' Aspirations." Polish Perspectives 10: 29-37.

_____. 1968. Socjologia pracy (Sociology of work). Warsaw: Panstwowe Wydawnictwo Ekonomiczne.

_____. 1969a. "Planning and Tradition in Polish Higher Education." Minerva 7 (4):621-48.

_____. 1969b. Socjologia zakladu pracy (Sociology of the workplace). Warsaw: Wiedza Powszechna.

_____. 1969c. "Some Sociological Problems of Socialist Factories." Social Research 3:448-80

_____. 1970a. "Newspaper Staff as a Social System." In Media Sociology, ed. J. Tunstall, pp. 168-80. London: Constable.

_____. 1970b. Uslovia tworczeskogo truda (Conditions of creative work). Moscow: Izdatelstvo Mir.

_____. 1970c. "Task versus Status." International Revue of Sociology 1-3:329-54.

_____. 1971a. "The Executive in Present Day Poland." Polish Review 16 (3).

_____. 1971b. "From Peasant into Worker in Poland." International Review of Sociology 7 (3):27-75.

_____. 1971c. "Swiadomosc inteligencka" (The consciousness of the intelligentsia). Kultura (Paris) 7-8.

_____. 1972a. "Sociologists In-between." Studies in Comparative Communism 5 (2-3).

_____. 1972b. "O wòdzu" (About a leader). Robotnik 3.

_____. 1972c. "The Theatre of J. Grotowski." International Review of Sociology 8 (2-3):57-73.

_____. 1973a. "Institutional Conditions of Scientific Inquiry." Small Group Behavior 4 (1).

_____. 1973b. "The Self-Management Theory of Jan Wolski." International Journal of Contemporary Sociology 10 (1):66-87.

_____. 1973c. "Industrial Democracy." Our Generation 9 (1): 24-41.

_____. 1974a. The Social Dimensions of Industrialism. Meerut: Sadhna Prakashan.

_____. 1974b. "The Sociotechnical Principles of Workers' Control" in Proceedings of the First International Conference on Participation and Self-Management Dubrovnik December 1972. Zagreb: Institute for Social Research.

_____, ed. 1967. System spoleczny instytutu (Social System of the applied research institutes). Warsaw: PWN.

_____. 1968. System spoleczny katedry (Social system of departments in the institutions of higher education). Warsaw: PWN.

_____. 1969. Socjologia kierownictwa (Sociology of management). Warsaw: Panstwowe Wydawnictwo Ekonomiczne.

Matejko, Joanna. 1966. "Profesorowie uczelni warszawskich" (Professors in the institutions of higher education in Warsaw). In Spoleczenstwo krolestwa polskiego, ed. Witold Kula, pp. 173—98 Warsaw: PWN.

Mazur, Marian. 1970a. Historia naturalna polskiego naukowca (The natural history of Polish scientists). Warsaw: Panstwowy Instytut Wydawniczy.

_____. 1970b. Jakosciowa teoria informacji (The qualitative information theory). Warsaw: Wydawnictwo Naukowo-Techniczne.

Medvedev, Roy A. 1971. Let History Judge. The Origins and Consequences of Stalinism. New York: Knopf.

Meissner, Hans Otto. 1966. A History of Modern Poland. London: Eyre and Spottiswoode.

Michajlow, W. 1966. "Research." Polish Perspectives 12.

Michon, Ferdynand. 1964. Psychospoleczne uwarunkowania wydajnosci pracy w zawodzie ksiegowego (Psychosociological conditions of effective work in the accounting profession). Warsaw.

Milosz, Czeslaw. 1953. The Captive Mind. New York: Vintage Books.

Minc, Bronislaw. 1967. "Ekonomiczna teoria przedsiebiorstwa socjalistycznego" (The economic theory of a socialist enterprise) In Przedsiebiorstwo w polskim systemie spoleczno-ekonomicznym. Warsaw.

Misztal, Stanislaw. 1972. "Industrializacja ziem polskich w okresie kapitalizmu" (Industrialization of the Polish territory in the period of capitalism). In Geografia przemyslu Polski, ed. S. Leszczycki and T. Lijewski. Warsaw: PWN.

Mlicka, Wanda. 1967. "Porownanie zespolow naukowych w naukach podstawowych z zespolami w naukach stosowanych" (Comparison of basic research teams with applied research teams). In System spoleczny instytutu, ed. A. Matejko, pp. 109-32. Warsaw: PWN.

Mond, Georges H. 1973. "The Role of the Intellectuals." Canadian Slavonic Papers 15 (1-2).

Montias, John Michael. 1962. Central Planning in Poland. New Haven: Yale University Press.

Morawski, Witold. 1969. "Funkcje samorzadu robotniczego w systemie zarzadzania przemyslem" (Functions of the workers' self-government in managing industry). In Prezemysl i spoleczenstwo w Polsce Ludowej, ed. Jan Szczepanski, pp. 249-52. Wroclaw: Ossolineum.

Morrison, James F. 1968. The Polish People's Republic. Baltimore: Johns Hopkins Press.

Mrozek, Wanda. 1965. "Social Transformations of Family Relations and Environment of Coal Miners in Upper Silesia." Polish Sociological Bulletin 1:108-12.

_____. 1966. Rodzina gornicza (The miner's family). Katowice: Slaski Instytut Naukowy.

Muller, Otto Wilhelm. 1971. Intelligenz. Untersuchungen zur Geschichte eines politischen Schlagwortes. Frankfurt am Main: Athenaeum Verlag.

Najduchowska, Halina. 1969a. "Drogi zawodowe kadry kierowniczej" (Professional careers of executives). Studia socjologiczne 3:253-69.

_____. 1969b. "Dyrektorzy przedsiebiorstw przemyslowych" (Industrial executives). In Przemysl i spoleczenstwo w Polsce Ludowej, ed. Jan Szczepanski, pp. 79-103. Wroclaw: Ossolineum.

Negandhi, Anant R., and S. Benjamin Prasad. 1971. Comparative Management. New York: Appleton-Century-Crofts.

Nicki, Henryk. 1969. "Niektore spoleczne problemy socjalistycznego wspolzawodnictwa pracy w swietle badan opinii pracownikow" (Some social problems of socialist work competition in the opinion of workers). Studia socjologiczne 2:203-24.

Nowak, Irena. 1966. "Some Differences in Social Contact Patterns Among Various Social Strata." Polish Sociological Bulletin 2.

Nowak, Stefan. 1960. "Egalitarian Attitudes of Warsaw Students." American Sociological Review 25:219-31.

_____. 1962. "Social Attitudes of Warsaw Students." Polish Sociological Bulletin 1-2:94-95.

_____. 1963. "In Memory of Stanislaw Ossowski." Polish Sociological Bulletin 2.

_____. 1964. "Changes of Social Structure in Social Consciousness." Polish Sociological Bulletin 2.

_____. 1969. "Changes of Social Structure in Social Consciousness." In Structured Social Inequality, ed. Celia S. Heller, pp. 235-47. London: MacMillan.

Nowakowska, Irena. 1964. "The Social View of Academic Workers." Polish Sociological Bulletin 1.

_____. 1970. "Struktura spoleczna mlodziezy szkolnej" (Social structure of the school youth). Kultura i spoleczenstwo 3.

Nowicki, Miroslaw. 1968. "Adaptacja mlodych robotnikow w zakladach przemyslowych" (Adaptation of young workers in industrial establishments). Studia socjologiczne 3-4:365-84.

Nowatorzy w zakladzie przemyslowym (Innovators in industrial establishments). 1968. Wroclaw: Ossolineum.

Oledzki, Michal.1967. Dojazdy do pracy (Commutation to work). Warsaw: Ksiazka i Wiedza.

Olszewska, Anna. 1969. Wies uprzemyslowiona (The industrial village). Wroclaw: Ossolineum.

Osadczuk, Bohdan. 1972. "Neodmowszczyzna Gierka" Gierek's Neodmowskism). Kultura (Paris) 3.

Osipov, Gennadii V., ed. 1966. Industry and Labour in the USSR. London: Tavistock Publications.

_____, and Jan Szczepanski, eds. 1970. Spoleczne problemy pracy i produkcji. Polsko-radzieckie badania porownawcze (Social problems of work and production. Polish-Soviet comparative studies). Warsaw: Ksiazka i Wiedza.

Ossowski, Stanislaw. 1957. Marksizm i tworczosc naukowa w spoleczenstwie socjalistycznym (Marxism and scientific creativity in the socialist society). Warsaw.

_____. 1963. Class Structure in the Social Consciousness. London: Routledge and Kegan Paul.

Ostaszewski, Jan, ed. 1971. Modern Poland Between East and West. London: Polish School of Political and Social Science.

Ostrowski, Krzysztof. 1968. "Funkcja mobilizacji w dzialalnosci zwiazkow zawodowych" (The function of social mobilization in the activity of trade unions). Studia socjologiczne 3-4:137-51.

_____. 1970. Rola zwiazkow zawodowych w polskim systemie politycznym (Role of trade unions in the Polish political system). Wroclaw: Ossolineum.

Pajestka, Jozef. 1971. "Streamlining the Economy." Polish Perspectives 2:7-22.

Paradysz, S. 1971. "Ile naprawde pracujemy?" (How effectively do we work?). Polityka-statystyka 8.

249

Parkin, Frank. 1969. "Class Stratification in Socialist Societies." British Journal of Sociology 20 (4):355-74.

_____. 1971. Class Inequality and Political Order. London: Paladin.

_____, 1972, "System Contradiction and Political Transformation." Archives Européenes de Sociologie 13 (1).

Parsons, Talcott. 1951. The Social System. New York: Free Press.

_____. 1970. "The Intellectual." In On Intellectuals, ed. P. Rieff. Garden City, N.Y.: Doubleday.

Pasieczny, Leszek. 1963. Kierownik a bodzce materialnego zainteresowania (Manager and material stimulants). Warsaw: PWE.

_____. 1968. Inzynier w przemysle (The engineer in industry). Warsaw: PWE.

Pateman, Carole. 1970. Participation and Democratic Theory. Cambridge: Cambridge University Press.

Pawelczynska, Anna, and Stefan Nowak. 1962. "Social Opinions of Students in the Period of Stabilization." Polish Perspectives 2:38-50.

Pietraszek, Edward. 1966. Wiejscy robotnicy koplan i hut (The rural workers in mines and foundries). Wroclaw: Ossolineum.

_____. 1968. "Zroznicowanie a typologia wsi robotniczych" (The differentiation and typology of workers' villages). Studia socjologiczne 2:111-39.

Pilsudski, Jozef. 1972. Year 1920. London and New York: Pilsudski Institute.

Piotrowski, W. 1966. "Life and Work of Rural Migrants in Urban Communities." Polish Sociological Bulletin 2:149-58.

Pipes, Richard, ed. 1961. The Russian Intelligentsia. New York.

Pirages, Dennis Clark. 1972. Modernization and Political Tension Management: A Socialist Society in Perspective. Case Study of Poland. New York: Praeger.

250

Pirog, Stanislawa. 1966. Bodzce materialnego zainteresowania w opiniach pracownikow biur projektow (Material incentives as viewed by the design bureau employees). Warsaw.

Podgorecki, Adam. 1962. Charakterystyka nauk praktycznych (Nature of applied sciences). Warsaw.

_____. 1964. Zjawiska prawne w opinii publiciznej (Legal phenomena in public opinion). Warsaw: Wydawnictwo Prawnicze.

_____. 1966a. Prestiz prawa (The prestige of law). Warsaw: Ksiazka i Wiedza.

_____. 1966b. Zasady socjotechniki (Principles of sociotechnique). Warsaw: Wiedza Powszechna.

_____. 1971a. Poglady spoleczenstwa polskiego na moralnosc i prawo (Views of Poles on morality and law). Warsaw: Ksiazka i Wiedza.

_____. 1971b. "Swiadomsc prawna Polakow" (Law consciousness of Poles). Polityka 13.

_____, ed. 1972. Socjotechnika. Style dzialania (Sociotechnique. Styles of Action). Warsaw: Ksiazka i Wiedza.

_____, and Andrzej Kojder. 1972. Ewolucja swiadomosci prawnej i postaw moralnych spoleczenstwa polskiego (Evolution of legal consciousness and moral attitudes in the Polish society). Warsaw: Wydawnictwa Radia i Telewizji.

_____, and Rolf Schulze. 1969. "Sociotechnique." Social Science Information 7 (4).

Pohoski, M. 1964a. "Interrelation Between Social Mobility of Individuals and Groups in the Process of Economic Growth in Poland." Polish Sociological Bulletin 2.

_____. 1964b. Migracje ze wsi do miast (Migrations from villages to towns). Warsaw: PWN.

Polonsky, Anthony. 1972. Politics in Independent Poland 1921-1939. Oxford: Clarendon Press.

Pomian, Grazyna. 1969. "Robotnik jako pracownik i jako kolega-wzory zachowan w spolecznosci robotniczej" (The Worker as an employee and as a colleague. Patterns of behavior in the blue-collar community). In Z zagadnien kultury pracy robotnikow przemyslowych. Warsaw: Wydawnictwo Zwiazkowe CRZZ.

Pracownicy handlu (Trade employees). 1967. Warsaw: Wydawnictwo Zwiazkowe CRZZ.

Preiss, Anna. 1967. "Robotnicy i pracownicy inzynieryjno-techniczni" (Workers, technicians, and engineers). Socjologiczne problemy przemyslu i klasy robotniczej 2:19-42.

Problemy wyznan i laicyzacji (Problems of denominations and secularization). 1973. Warsaw: Central Committee of the Polish United Workers' Party.

Przeclawska, A., and J. K. Sawa. 1971. "Studenckie idealy" (Students' ideals). Polityka 20.

Przedsiebiorstwo w polskim systemie spoleczno-ekonomicznym (Enterprise in the Polish socioeconomic system). 1967. Warsaw: Panstwowe Wydawnictwo Ekonomiczne.

Radzko, Andrzej, and Barbara Majewska. 1968. "Pracownicy nauki na tle mikrosrodowiska katedry (Academic staff in the framework of a department). In System spoleczny katedry, ed. A. Matejko, pp. 23-134. Warsaw: PWN.

Rajkiewicz, Antoni. 1965. Zatrudnienie w Polsce Ludowej w latach 1950-1970 (Employment in People's Poland in 1950-1970). Warsaw: Ksiazka i Wiedza.

Rawin, Solomon J. 1965. "The Manager in the Polish Enterprise. A Study of Accommodation Under Conditions of Role Conflict." British Journal of Industrial Relations (March):1-16.

_____. 1968. "The Polish Intelligentsia and the Socialist Order. Elements of Ideological Compatibility." Political Science Quarterly 83(3).

_____. 1970. "Social Values and Managerial Structure: The Case of Yugoslavia and Poland." Journal of Comparative Administration 2(2).

Reddaway, William F. et al. n.d. The Cambridge History of Poland. Cambridge: Cambridge University Press.

Rees, John. 1971. Equality. London: MacMillan.

Reiss, Albert J. 1961. Occupations and Social Status. Glencoe: Free Press.

Richman, Barry M. 1965. Soviet Management. New York: Prentice-Hall.

Robotnicy na tle przemian struktury spolecznej w Polsce (Blue-collar workers and dynamics of social structure in Poland). 1970. Warsaw: Glowny Urzad Statystyczny.

Rocznik demograficzny 1972 (Demographic yearbook). 1972. Warsaw: Glowny Urzad Statystyczny.

Rocznik statystyczny (Statistical yearbook). 1970, 1971, 1972. Warsaw: Glowny Urzad Statystyczny.

Rocznik statystyczny pracy 1948-1968 (Statistical yearbook of work 1948-1968) 1970. Warsaw: Glowny Urzad Statystyczny.

Rocznik statystyczny szkolnictwa 1944/45-1966/67. 1968 (Statistical yearbook of education). Warsaw: Glowny Urzad Statystyczny.

Rogger, Hans, and Eugen Webber, eds. 1965. The European Right. Berkeley: University of California Press.

Rosner, Jan. 1957. "Management by the Workers in Poland." International Labour Review 76 (3).

Rostow, Walt W. 1971. Politics and the Stages of Growth. Cambridge: Cambridge University Press.

Rozwoj gospodarczy krajow RWPG 1950-1968. 1969. (The economic development of Comecon countries). Warsaw: Glowny Urzad Statystyczny.

Rupinski, Gabriel, and Stanislaw Taubwurcel. 1961. Elementy organizacji zarzadzania przedsiebiorstwem (Elements of management organization in enterprises). Lodz.

253

Rychlinski, Stanislaw. 1938. "Ujecie wiezi spolecznej w socjologii Ludwika Krzywickiego" (The concept of social bond in sociology of Ludwik Krzywicki). In Ludwik Krzywicki. Warsaw: Instytut Gospodarstwa Spolecznego

Sadownik, H. 1971. "Miejsce Zjednoczenia" (Role of industrial corporations). Zycie Gospodarcze 17.

Sarapata, Adam. 1963. "Iustum Pretium." Polish Sociological Bulletin 1:41-56.

_____. 1965. Studia nad uwarstwieniem i ruchliwoscia spoleczna w Polsce (Studies on stratification and social mobility in Poland). Warsaw: Ksiazka i Wiedza.

_____. 1966a. "Social Mobility." Polish Perspectives 1.

_____. 1966b. "Stratification and Social Mobility." In Empirical Sociology in Poland, ed. Jan Szczepanski. Warsaw: PWN.

_____. 1967. Plynnosc i stabilnosc zalog (Mobility and Stability of personnel). Warsaw: Wydawnictwo Zwiazkowe CRZZ.

_____. 1970. "Motywacje i satysfakcje dyrektorow-studium porownawcze" (Motivation and satisfaction of executives. A Comparative study). Studia socjologiczne 3:61-89.

_____, ed. 1965a. Socjologia zawodow (Sociology of occupations). Warsaw: Ksiazka i Wiedza.

_____. 1965b. Socjologiczne problemy przedsiebiorstwa przemyslowego (Sociological problems of industrial enterprises). Warsaw: Panstwowe Wydawnictwo Ekonomiczne.

_____. 1968. Plynnosc zalog (Labor turnover in industrial crews). Warsaw: Panstwowe Wydawnictwo Ekonomiczne.

_____. 1971. Etyka zawodowa (Professional ethics). Warsaw: Ksiazka i Wiedza.

_____, and Wlodzimierz Wesolowski. 1961. "The Evaluation of Occupations by Warsaw Inhabitants." American Journal of Sociology 66 (6).

_____, and Kazimierz Doktor. 1963. Elementy socjologii przemy-
slu (Elements of industrial sociology). Warsaw: Ksiazka i
Wiedza.

Searing, Marjory E. 1970. "Estimates of Educational Attainment in
Poland 1950-1969. Mimeographed. Washington: U.S. Bureau
of the Census.

Selucky, Radoslav. 1970. "Economic Reforms in the Countries of the
Soviet Bloc." Paper presented at the University of Alberta.

Seton-Watson, Hugh. 1972. "Is There an East Central Europe?" In
Eastern Europe in the 1970s, eds. Sylvia Sinanian et al., pp.
3-12. New York: Praeger.

Sicinski. Andrzej. 1964. "Expert-Innovator-Adviser." Polish Sociological Bulletin 1:54-66.

_____. 1966. "Television and Radio in the Structure of Material
and Cultural Needs in the Polish Society." Polish Sociological
Bulletin 2.

Slomka, Jan. 1941. From Serfdom to Self-Government: Memoirs of
a Polish Village Mayor 1842-1927. London: Minerva.

Skorzynski, Zygmunt. 1962. "Mass Entertainment Among Urban
Population in Poland." Polish Sociological Bulletin 3-4.

_____. 1965. Miedzy praca i wypoczynkiem (Between work and
leisure). Warsaw.

Smolinski, Leon. 1971. "Socialism and Technocracy. A Problem
of Polish Planning." Paper for the Second Congress of Polish-
American Scholars and Scientists. New York.

Snell, Edwin M. 1970. "Economic Efficiency in Eastern Europe."
In Economic Developments in Countries of Eastern Europe.
Washington: U.S. Government Printing Office.

Sokolowska, Magdalena. 1969. "Funkcjonowanie przemyslu a zdrowie"
(Health and functioning of industry). In Przemysl i spoleczenstwo w Polsce Ludowej, ed. Jan Szczepanski, pp. 277-98. Wroclaw: Ossolineum.

_____, and K. Wrochno. 1965. "Pozycja spoleczna kobiet w swietle statystyki" (Social position of women in the light of statistics). Studia socjologiczne 1.

Staar, Richard F. 1971. The Communist Regimes in Eastern Europe, 2nd ed. Stanford: Hoover Institution.

Statistical Abstract of the United States. 1972. Washington: U.S. Bureau of the Census.

Statistical Yearbook 1970. 1972. Budapest: Hungarian Central Statistical Office.

Statistical Yearbook 1971. 1973. Budapest: Hungarian Central Statistical Office.

Statisticka rocenka Ceskoslovenske Socialisticke Republiky 1971. 1971. Prague: SNTL.

Statisticka rocenka Ceskoslovenske Socialisticke Republiky 1972. 1972. Prague: SNTL.

Statistisches Jahrbuch der Deutschen Demokratischen Republik. 1972. Berlin: Staatsverlag.

Statistisches Jahrbuch der Deutschen Demokratischen Republik. 1973. Berlin: Staatsverlag.

Stehle, Hans Jakob. 1965. The Independent Satellite. Society and Politics in Poland since 1945. New York: Praeger.

Stipczynski, T., and Z. Szeliga. 1971. "Polskie 'wedrowki ludow'" (social mobility in Poland). Polityka-statystyka 8.

Strefy wplywow duzych miast w swietle dojazdow do pracy (The scope of big cities' influence in the light of commutation). 1973. Warsaw: Glowny Urzad Statystyczny.

Strong, John, W., ed. 1971. The Soviet Union Under Brezhnev and Kosygin. New York: Van Nostrand-Reinhold.

Struktura i dynamika spoleczenstwa polskiego (The structure and dynamics of Polish Society). 1970. Warsaw: PWN.

Strzeminska, H. 1970. Praca zawodowa kobiet a ich budzet czasu (Women's employment and their time budget). Warsaw: Panstwowe Wydawnictwo Ekonomiczne.

Sufin, Zbigniew, and W. Wesolowski. 1964. "Work in the Hierarchy of Values." Polish Sociological Bulletin 1.

Surmaczynski, Marian. 1965. "Informacja w zakladzie przemyslowym" (Information in an industrial establishment). Studia socjologiczno-polityczne 19.

Swaniewicz, Stanislaw. 1968. "World Economic Growth and the Soviet Challenge." Review of Politics 4:455-75.

_____. 1969. "The Impact of Ideology on Soviet Economic Policy." Canadian Slavonic Papers 1:66-81.

Szarfenberg, Janina. 1966. Materialy do charakterystyki zawodu i pozycji architekta (Data on the profession and the position of architects). Warsaw.

Szarras, Henryk. 1969. "Warunka pracy mlodej kadry pracownikow naukowych" (Working conditions of the junior academic staff). In System spoleczny katedry ed. Alexander Matejko. Warsaw: PWN.

Szczepanski, Jan. 1957. "Proba Diagnozy" (A diagnosis). Przeglad kulturalny 36.

_____. 1960a. "Z badan nad inteligencja polska XIX wieku." (Studies on the 19th century Polish intelligentsia). Kultura i spoleczenstwo 4, (3).

_____. 1960b. "Struktura inteligencji w Polsce" (Structure of the Polish intelligentsia). Kultura i spoleczenstwo 4, (1-2).

_____. 1961. "Problems of Sociological Research on the Polish Intelligentsia." Polish Sociological Bulletin 1.

_____. 1962. "The Polish Intelligentsia. Past and Present." World Politics 14 (3).

_____. 1963. Socjologiczne zagadnienia wyzszego wyksztalcenia (Sociological problems of higher education). Warsaw: PWN.

_____. 1964a. "Sociological Problems of Higher Education in Poland." In Social and Political Transformations in Poland, ed. Stanislaw Ehrlich. Warsaw: PWN.

_____. 1964b. "Some Characteristics of Contemporary Polish Society." Polish Sociological Bulletin 2.

_____. 1966. "Sociologist's View." Polish Perspectives 9 (2).

_____. 1969. "Pracownicy administracyjno-biurowi" (The clerical staff). In Przemysl i spoleczenstwo w Polsce Ludowej, ed. Jan Szczepanski. Wroclaw: Ossolineum.

_____. 1970. Polish Society. New York: Random House.

_____. 1971a. Odmiany czasu terazniejszego (Diversity of Present Reality). Warsaw: Ksiazka i Wiedza.

_____. 1971b. Rozwazania o Rzeczypospolitej (Comments on Commonwealth). Warsaw: PIW.

_____, 1959-60. Wyksztalcenie a pozycja spoleczna inteligencji (Education and the social status of intelligentsia). Warsaw.

_____. 1961. Studia nad rozwojem klasy robotniczej (Studies on the development of the blue-collar class). Lodz: PWN.

_____. 1965. Socjologiczne problemy industrializacji w Polsce Ludowej (Sociological problems of industrialization in People's Poland). Warsaw: PWN.

_____. 1969. Przemysl i spoleczenstwo w Polsce Ludowej (Industry and Society in People's Poland). Wroclaw: Ossolineum.

Szlapczynski, J. K. 1968. Zarzad szkola wyzsza w Polsce Ludowej (Management of institutions of higher education in Poland). Warsaw: PWN.

Szostkiewicz, Stefan. 1962. "Two Researches in Industrial Sociology." Polish Sociological Bulletin 1-2.

Taras, Ray. 1973. "The Local Political Elites." In Social Groups in Polish Society, eds. D. Lane and G. Kolankiewicz. New York: Columbia University Press.

"Targets for Tomorrow." 1971. Interview with Antoni Rajkiewicz. Polish Perspectives 7-8:7-12.

Taylor, Jack. 1952. The Economic Development of Poland 1919-1950. Ithaca, N.Y.: Cornell University Press.

Theodorson, George A., and Achilles Theodorson. 1969. Modern Dictionary of Sociology. New York: Thomas Y. Crowell.

Thomas William and Florian Znaniecki. 1918. The Polish Peasant in Europe and America. Boston.

Toma, Peter A., ed. 1970. The Changing Face of Communism in Eastern Europe. Tucson: University of Arizona Press.

Trzeciakowski, Witold. 1973. "Foreign Trade. A Retrospective View." Canadian Slavonic Papers 15 (1-2).

Tulski, Jozef. 1971. Mlodzi robotnicy w zakladzie przemyslowym (Young workers in the industrial establishment). Warsaw: Ksiazka i Wiedza.

Turowski, Jan. 1964. Przemiany wsi pod wplywem zakladu przemyslowego (Changes of villages under the impact of an industrial establishment). Warsaw: PWN.

Turski, Ryszard. 1961. Dynamika przemian spolecznych w Polsce (Dynamics of social changes in Poland). Warsaw.

_____. 1965. Miedzy miastem i wsia. Struktura spoleczno-zawodowa chlopow robotnikow w Polsce (Between town and village. The socio-occupational structure of peasant-workers in Poland). Warsaw: PWN.

_____. 1970. Les transformations de la campagne polonaise. Wroclaw: Ossolineum.

Tuszko, Aleksander, and Stefan Chaskielewicz. 1968. Bandania naukowe. Organizacja i kierownictwo (Scientific research. Organization and management). Warsaw: PWN.

Twenty Years of the People's Polish Republic. 1964. Warsaw: Panstwowe Wydawnictwo Ekonomiczne.

Tymowski, Andrzej. 1971. "W sprawie minimum socjalnego" (The issue of basic income). Zycie gospodarcze 8

Tymowski, Janusz. 1963. "Educating Specialists." Polish Perspectives 8-9.

Tyrmand, Leopold, ed. 1970a. Explorations in Freedom. Prose, Narrative, and Poetry from Kultura. New York: Free Press.

_____. 1970b. Kultura Essays. New York: Free Press.

Tyszka, A. 1971. Uczestnictwo w kulturze. O roznorodnosci stylow zycia (Participation in culture. On the variety of life styles). Warsaw: PWN.

Urban, Jerzy. 1971. "Zwiazki zawodowe" (Trade unions). Polityka 5.

Waclawek, Juliusz. 1970. Socjalistyczne stosunki w zakladzie pracy (Socialist relations in workplaces). Warsaw: Ksiazka i Wiedza.

Wacowska, Ewa. 1972. "Polska klasa robotnicza" (The Polish working class). Kultura (Paris) 7-8.

Walicki, Jerzy. 1970. Religious Life in Poland. Warsaw: Interpress.

Wallis, Aleksander. 1964. Artysci plastycy (Plastic Artists). Warsaw.

Wawrzecka, B. 1971. "Poszukuje pracy . . . (Searching for a job). Polityka 37.

Webber, Ross A., ed. 1969. The Culture of Management. Homewood, Ill.: Irwin.

Wellisz, Leopold. 1938. Foreign Capital in Poland. London: Allen and Unwin.

Wesolowski, Wlodzimierz. 1962. "Robotnicy o swojej pracy i o zakladach" (Workers speaking about their jobs and workplaces). Studia socjologiczno-polityczne 12.

_____. 1969a. "The Notions of Strata and Class in Socialist Society." In Social Inequality, ed. André Beteille. Baltimore: Penguin Books.

_____. 1969b. "Strata and Strata Interest in Socialist Society." In Structured Social Inequality, ed. Celia Stopnicka-Heller. London: MacMillan.

_____, ed. 1970. Zroznicowanie spoleczne (Social differentiation). Wroclaw: Ossolineum.

Whyte, William H. 1966. The Organization Man. Garden City, N.Y.: Doubleday.

Wiatr, Jerzy J. 1962. "Stratification and Egalitarianism." Polish Perspectives 12.

_____. 1964. "The Intelligentsia." In Twenty Years of the People's Polish Republic. Warsaw: Panstwowe Wydawnictwo Ekonomiczne.

_____. 1965. "Inteligencja w Polsce Ludowej' (The Polish intelligentsia). In Przemiany spoleczne w Polsce Ludowej. Warsaw.

_____, ed. 1971. The State of Sociology in Eastern Europe Today. Carbondale: Southern Illinois University Press.

Widerszpil, Stanislaw. 1965. Sklad polskiej klasy robotniczej (Structure of the Polish blue-collar class). Warsaw: PWN

_____, and A. Owieczko. 1971. "Management and Workers' Control." Polish Perspectives 1:7-16.

Wierzbicki, Zbigniew T. 1972. "Some Theoretical Issues in Collective Farming." Paper for the Third World Congress of Rural Sociology. Baton Rouge.

Wilder, E. 1964. "Impact of Poland's Stabilization on Its Youth." Public Opinion Quarterly 3.

Wiles, P. J. D., and Stefan Markowski. 1971. "Income Distribution Under Communism. Some Facts about Poland, the UK, the USA, and the USSR." Soviet Studies 22 (1 and 3).

Wisniewski, W. 1963. "Tolerance and Egalitarianism." Polish Sociological Bulletin 2.

Wolf, Eric R. 1966. Peasants. Englewood Cliffs, N.J.: Prentice-Hall.

Woods, William Howard. 1968. Poland. Eagle in the East. New York: Hill and Wang.

Worach-Kordas, H. 1970. "Problem feminizacji zawodu nauczyciels-kiego" (Feminization of the teacher's profession). Studia demograficzne 21:119-27.

Woskowski, Jan. 1964. "Primary School Teachers and Their Social Position in People's Poland." Polish Sociological Bulletin 1.

Wyderko, Adam. 1972. "Demographic Transformation in Poland's Rural Areas." Paper for the Third World Congress of Rural Sociology. Baton Rouge.

Zabkowicz, L. 1969. "The Role of Amalgamated Corporations in Management of Polish Industry." Polish Foreign Trade 6.

Zagorski, K. 1971. "Robotnicy w strukturze spolecznej Polski" (Blue-collar workers in the social structure of Poland). Polityka-statystyka 7.

Zajaczkowski, Andrzej. 1961. Glowne elementy kultury szlacheckiej w Polsce (Basic characteristics of the gentry culture in Poland). Wroclaw: Ossolineum.

_____. 1962. Z dziejow inteligencji polskiej (On the history of the Polish intelligentsia). Wroclaw: Ossolineum.

Zakrzewski, Pawel. 1969. Zjawisko wykolejenia spolecznego mlod-ziezy na terenach uprzemyslawianych (Social deviance in industrializing areas). Warsaw: Wydawnictwo Prawnicze.

Zakrzewski, Witold. 1973. "The System of People's Councils in the Polish People's Republic." In People's Councils in Poland in the Light of Empirical Research, ed. Sylwester Zawadzki, pp. 4-40. Warsaw: Polish Academy of Sciences. Institute of Legal Sciences.

Zaleski, Bogdan. 1963. Chlopi i zawod rolnika (Peasants and Farmers). Warsaw.

Zaluski, Zbigniew. 1960. Siedem polskich grzechow glownych (Seven main Polish sins). Warsaw: Iskry.

Zarnowski, Janusz. 1964. Struktura spoleczna inteligencji w Polsce miedzywojennej (Social structure of the intelligentsia in interwar Poland). Warsaw.

_____. 1973. Spoleczenstwo Drugiej Rzeczypospolitej 1918-1939 (Society of the Second Commonwealth 1918-1939). Warsaw: Panstwowe Wydawnictwo Naukowe.

Zawadzki, Sylwester, ed. 1973. People's Councils in Poland in the Light Empirical Research. Warsaw: Polish Academy of Sciences, Institute of Legal Sciences.

Zegzdryn, R. 1971. Studenci studiow dziennych. Rok szkolny 1969/70. Rozmieszczenie terytorialne (Students of regular courses. Academic year 1969/70. Territorial distribution). Warsaw: Glowny Urzad Statystyczny.

Zemankowa, Z. 1963. "Science and Higher Education." Polish Perspectives 3.

Zieleniewski, Jan. 1967. Organizacja zespolow ludzkich (Organization of teams). Warsaw: PWN.

_____. 1968/69, "Organizational Research on Bureaucracy." Prakseologia 30

_____. 1970. O problemach organizacji (Problems of organization). Warsaw: Wiedza Powszechna.

Zielinski, Janusz G. 1964. Big Business. Warsaw. PWN.

_____. 1971a. "On the Effectiveness of the Polish Economic Reforms." Soviet Studies 22.

_____. 1971b. "Planners' Growth Priorities and System Remodelling." Co-existence.

Ziolkowski, Janusz. 1966. "Sociological Implications of Urban Planning." In City and Regional Planning in Poland, ed. Jack C. Fisher. Ithaca, N.Y.: Cornell University Press.

Ziomek, Maksymilian J. 1964. Abencja w pracy (Absenteeism at work). Warsaw: PWE.

Znaniecki, Florian. 1935. <u>Ludzie terazniejsi a cywilizacja przysz-</u>
<u>losci</u> (People of the present and civilization of the future). War-
saw.

_____. 1940. <u>The Social Role of the Man of Knowledge</u>. New York:
Columbia University Press.

Zweig, Ferdynand. 1944. <u>Poland Between Two Wars</u>. London:
Secker and Warburg.

Halecki, Oskar, 223
Hapsburgs, 54
Harbison, F., 127
Heller, Celia Stopnicka, 2, 31
Hertz, Alexander, 59, 61, 62, 140
Hollander, Paul, 27, 223
Hozer, Jan, 164, 165, 166
Hugh, Jerry F., 222
Humboldt von, Alexander, 183
Hunek, Tadeusz, 79

Iwanicka-Lyra, Elzbieta, 70

Jagiello-Lysiowa, Ewa, 71, 72, 79
Jakubowicz, Szymon, 137
Jarosinska, Maria, 105, 106, 107
Jasienica, Pawel, 208-209
Johnson, Charles, 134, 221
Jozefowicz, Zofia, 167

Kalecki, Michal, 87, 145
Kalinin, Mikhail I., 223
Karpinski, Andrzej, 31
Kasinska, Barbara, 167
Keller, Suzanna Infeld, 154, 183
Kiezun, Witold, 129, 132
Kilbach, D., 136
Klimczyk, Marian, 73
Kloskowska, Jolanta, 147
Kojder, Andrzej, 168
Kolaja, Jiri T., 123
Kolakowski, Leszek, 218, 219
Kolankiewicz, George, 118, 165
Kolko, Gabriel, 15
Korbonski, Stefan, 67
Kosinski, Leszek, 13, 14
Kotarbinski, Tadeusz, 179
Kowalewski, Stanislaw, 131
Kowalewski, Zdzislaw, 163, 164
Kowalik, Tadeusz, 137
Kozakiewicz, Mikolaj, 73
Kozlowski, Czeslaw, 6, 76
Krall, Hanna, 165
Kraus, Gabriel, 136
Kruszewski, Z. Anthony, 64, 65

Kryczka, Piotr, 79
Krzywicki, Ludwik, 207
Krzyzaniak, Marian, 69
Kucharski, W., 127
Kulczycka, Barbara, 36
Kupis, Tadeusz, 173
Kurczewski, Jacek, 124
Kurowski, Stefan, 137

Lachs, Manfred, 64
Lane, David, 1, 2, 3, 7, 8, 10
Lange, Oskar, 137
Lednicki, Waclaw, 222
Lenski, Gerhard, 1
Lenski, Jean, 1
Leszczycki, Stanislaw, 13, 68, 84
Lewis, Paul, 76, 77
Lijewski, Teofil, 84
Lipinski, Edward, 30, 116, 126,
    134, 136, 137
Lipset, Seymour M., 5, 117
Lipski, Witold, 68, 78
Lutynska, Krystyna, 156, 157, 158

Machonin, P., 1
Madej, Zbigniew, 136
Majchrzak, Irena, 213
Majewska, Barbara, 197, 198
Malewski, Andrzej, 150
Markowski, Stefan, 11, 12
Matejko, Aleksander, 96, 97, 101,
    112, 115, 118, 152, 170, 174,
    189, 213-215
Matejko, Joanna, 194
Medvedev, Roy A., 223
Michajlow, W., 188
Michon, Ferdynand, 158
Milosz, Czeslaw, 112
Minc, Bronislaw, 134
Misztal, Stanislaw, 82
Mlicka, Wanda, 198, 199
Moczar, Mieczyslaw, 56
Mond, Georges H., 148
Montias, John M., 31
Morawski, Witold, 130

Mrozek, Wanda, 95
Myers, Charles A., 127

Najduchowska, Halina, 116-117
Negandhi, Anant R., 123, 127
Nicki, Henryk, 127
Nowak, Irena, 98
Nowak, Stefan, 20, 86, 108, 149, 150, 151, 167
Nowakowska, Irena, 90, 196

Osadczuk, Bohdan, 219
Ossowski, Stanislaw, 1, 149
Ostaszewski, Jan, 223

Pajestka, Jozef, 137, 138
Parkin, Frank, 3, 4, 117
Parsons, Talcott, 208
Pasieczny, Leszek, 118, 165
Pawelczynska, Anna, 167
Piasecki, Boleslaw, 56, 224
Piast dynasty, 58
Pilsudski, Jozef, 223
Pipes, Richard, 141
Pirages, Dennis C., 85
Pirog, Stanislawa, 169, 171, 172
Podgorecki, Adam, 137, 168
Pohoski, Michal, 70, 72, 73
Polonsky, Anthony, 59, 62, 120
Pomian, Grazyna, 92
Pounds, Norman G. J., 223
Prasad, Benjamin S., 123, 127
Preiss, Anna, 167
Przeclawska, Anna, 168

Radzko, Andrzej, 197, 198
Rawin, Solomon J., 123, 143, 145
Rees, John, 2
Reiss, Albert J., 196
Richman, Barry M., 123, 124
Rosner, Jan, 123
Rostow, Walt W., 27
Rupinski, Gabriel, 132
Rychlinski, Stanislaw, 207

Sarapata, Adam, 1, 7, 22, 85, 86,
87, 90, 93, 108, 132, 134, 146, 151, 157, 180
Sawa, J. K., 168
Searing, Marjory E., 38
Selucky, Radoslav, 139
Sicinski, Andrzej, 98
Skorzynski, Zygmunt, 98, 99, 100
Slomka, Jan, 69
Smolinski, Leon, 118
Snell, Edwin M., 28
Solzhenitsyn, Alexander, 223
Sosnkowski, Kazimierz, 223
Staar, Richard F., 54
Stalin, Joseph V., 220, 223
Stopnicka-Heller, Celia (see Heller, Celia Stopnicka)
Stys, Wincenty, 69
Swaniewicz, Stanislaw, 129, 135
Szarfenberg, Janina, 171, 172
Szarras, Henryk, 200
Szczepanski, Jan, 5, 93, 119, 134 136, 137, 141, 143, 144, 147, 154, 155, 156, 158, 188, 205, 207, 212
Szlapczynski, J. K., 189
Szujski, Jozef, 222

Taras, Ray, 23, 24
Taubwurcel, Stanislaw, 132
Taylor, Jack, 7
Theodorson, George A., 140
Theodorson, Achilles, 140
Thomas, William I., 69
Toma, Peter A., 220
Trzeciakowski, Witold, 78
Turos, Wieslaw, 6, 76
Turski, Ryszard, 149
Tymowski, Janusz, 146

Urban, Jerzy, 211

Wacowska, Ewa, 111, 113
Wallis, Aleksander, 182
Webber, Ross A., 127
Wesolowski, Wlodzimierz, 7, 22, 87, 130, 133, 146, 151, 157, 180
Wiatr, Jerzy J., 140, 145, 149, 151

Widerszpil, Stanislaw, 74, 91
Wierzbicki, Zbigniew, 79
Wilder, E., 167
Wiles, P. J. D., 11, 12
Wolf, Eric R., 67
Woskowski, Jan, 160
Wyderko, Adam, 74, 76

Zabkowicz, L., 138

Zajaczkowski, Andrzej, 142, 143
Zakrzewski, Witold, 24
Zarnowski, Janusz, 7, 61, 70, 83, 144, 156
Zieleniewski, Jan, 136
Zielinski, Janusz, 3
Znaniecki, Florian, 69, 154
Zweig, Ferdynand, 7

decision making, 132, 133, 138
democratic management, 132, 133
demoralization, 215
dialogue of Poles with Russia,
    223-224
differentiation of system, 25
dissemination of culture, 30

earnings: in Czechoslovakia, 12;
    in the interwar period, 60; occu-
    pational disparities, 17, 20; in
    Poland, 11; in Rumania, 12; in the
    USSR, 12; of steel workers, 101,
    workers' demands, 108, 109
economic reform, 3
education, 21, 37-41; enrollment,
    37-38; equality of educational
    perspectives, 17, 18; hopes and
    disillusions, 41; training level
    of working people, 38, 41
efficiency versus bureaucracy,
    25-26
egalitarianism, 7, 20-21; aspira-
    tions, 20-21; ideal and reality,
    21; in Poland, 7
elites and elitism, 21, 23
engineers, 163-169; as managers,
    118-119; friendship ties, 164;
    growth, 163; managerial aspira-
    tions, 164; motivation, 163-164;
    Party commitment, 165, 167,
    168; pragmatism of engineers,
    167-169; preferences, 164;
    satisfaction, 164-165
enterprise as a social system,
    121-123
executive style of work, 131-133
executives and intellectuals, 216
exposure to contrary pressures,
    119-121

family structure, 34, 36
fate of executives, 215-216
favoritism, 214
feeding of population, 31, 32
foreign capital, 60

fringe benefits, 15, 17
functioning of bureaucracy, 124,
    125

gentry tradition, 57-59
governance of souls, 143-144,
    152-153
growth of white-collar workers,
    156

higher education, 183-189
historical background, 54-57
household budget, 17, 20
housing, 51

idealism versus realism, 142
idlers, 217
incomes differentiation, 100
industrial democracy, 115
industry in the economy, 31, 32
ineffectiveness of the system, 22
inequalities, 2, 4
informal structure/grapevine, 114,
    131, 207-211
intelligentsia, 8, 9, 140-154; am-
    biguity, 153, 154; aspirations,
    143; attractiveness, 144; con-
    sciousness, 149-151; definition,
    140; discontent, 150; education,
    144; growth, 144-145; honor,
    142; ideals, 142, 144; influence
    on apparatchiks, 120; influence
    on society, 147, 148; opposition,
    148; origin, 141-144; relation
    to other strata, 146-148, 155,
    172; snobbishness, 142, success,
    150, 151; status, 144, 145, 146-
    149, 153
interwar period, 59-62, 67-70,
    141-144; destruction, 59; differ-
    ential perspectives, 60; earnings,
    60-61; elite, 61; intelligentsia,
    61, 62, 142-144; minorities, 60;
    peasants, 60, 68-70; social
    structure, 59-61; state, 60

institutions of higher education,
201-206
investments versus consumption,
28, 30

Jews, 60
journalists, 173-181; ambitions,
175-176; earnings, 177; formal
organization, 177-178; links
with other strata, 176; informal
organization, 177-179; management, 174; political pressures,
177; publicists, 174; role ambiguity, 173-174; satisfaction,
179-181; standards, 177; work
atmosphere, 173-174

Latin tradition, 58
limited goods orientation, 139

managers, 116-139; bargaining
with superiors, 130; inferiority
feeling, 120; intellectual level,
120-121; manipulation of people,
130; origin, 117; Party affiliation, 122-123; personal model,
121; professionalism versus
politics, 120; promotion, 116-
117; role ambiguity, 120, 121,
129-131; self-actualization, 135;
status, 118, 133, 135; strategy
of success, 123
massive social upgrading, 2
minorities, 60
motivation for work, 126-127

nationalism versus universalism,
54-56

opposition, 137

participatory democracy, 10
partitions of Poland, 59
Party membership, 31, 122
peasants and farmers, 9, 10, 60-

61, 67-81; acculturation in towns,
73, 79-80; aging, 76; agrarian
policy, 78; allocation, 71; emigration to towns, 70-74; Gomulka
policy, 76; in the interwar period,
69, 70; in Western territories,
64-66; landless peasants, 69;
modernization of farming, 78-81;
peasant-workers, 67, 68, 74, 75;
relation to the state, 76-78;
social and economic structure,
76-77; traditional conditions, 67;
transformation into farmers, 73;
transformation into workers,
70-76; youth, 71-73
parasitism, 216
personalities and a formal structure, 209, 211
perspectives of democratization,
218, 219
petrification versus pluralism, 222
planning of specialists' training,
184
planning in practice, 124, 125, 136
Poland and Soviet communism,
219-222
Poland between West and East,
222-224
Poland's Western territories,
64-66
Polish mentality, 208, 209
political loyalty versus professionalism, 128
population, 34
pragmatic orientation, 168, 169,
221
pressure groups, 222
pro-Western Poles, 222, 223
professional oligarchy, 205
purchasing preferences, 48, 49

reference groups, 52
reform and reformists, 24, 25,
134-135, 138, 218-219
religion, 208, 209

271

risk-taking by managers, 134
Roman Catholic Church, 31

Sarmatism, 57
secrecy, 122
shift work, 125
"small stabilization," 113
social and territorial mobility, 13-14
social stratification: in the eighteenth century, 57; in the interwar period, 59-62; in Czechoslovakia, 7; in East Germany, 7; in Hungary, 8; in Poland, 4-7; in Rumania, 8; socialist, 1
social structure, 1
socialist work competition, 127
span of control, 132
standard of living, 41-53; in Czechoslovakia, 42, 45, 46, 47; in East Germany, 42-45; in Hungary, 43, 49; in Poland, 47, 48; international comparisons, 54-57; political aspect, 41
state intervention, 60
state versus citizen, 53
status ambiguity, 215, 216
status of clerks, 132
structural disproportion, 30

structure of employment, 32, 34
student body, 183-189; admittance, 186-187; origin, 185; scholarships, 187; selection, 185, 187, 188; structure, 184, 185; territorial allocation, 187-188
superfluous people, 217

teachers, 159-163; church affiliation, 161, 162; growth, 159, 160; origin, 160, 162; Party affiliation, 160, 161; role ambiguity, 161-163; status, 162, 163; training, 160
technical progress, 136
time budget of executives, 131-133
trade unions, 126, 127
"transfer culture," 134

universities, 185
urbanization, 13, 32

white-collar workers, differentiation, 155, 156
women, discrimination against, 37; employment of, 36, 37
workers' councils, 130

xenophobia, 57-59

ALEXANDER J. MATEJKO is Professor of Sociology at the University of Alberta in Edmonton. He settled in Canada in 1970 after having spent two years as a visiting professor at the University of Zambia. Until 1968 Dr. Matejko taught at the University of Warsaw. He was also active in the field of management training in Poland.

Dr. Matejko has published widely in the area of industrial sociology, management participation, teamwork, and Polish society. His articles and reviews have appeared in Minerva, Social Research, International Review of Sociology, and Studies in Comparative Communism. He has published several books on Eastern Europe in Polish, Russian, and Czech.

Dr. Matejko holds an M.A. from Jagiellonian University and a Ph.D. from the University of Warsaw.

GIEREK'S POLAND

edited by Adam Bromke
and John W. Strong

THE USES OF SOCIAL SCIENCE IN EASTERN
EUROPE

Bogdan D. Denitch and
Vladimir Gligorov

THE POLITICS OF MODERNIZATION IN
EASTERN EUROPE: Testing the Soviet Model

edited by Charles Gati

CRISIS IN SOCIALIST PLANNING: Eastern
Europe and the USSR

Jan Marczewski

CONSUMPTION IN EASTERN EUROPE: Social and
Economic Dimensions in Poland, Czechoslovakia, Hungary, and East Germany

Bogdan Mieczkowski

POLITICAL SOCIALIZATION IN EASTERN
EUROPE

edited by Ivan Volgyes

TECHNOLOGY IN COMECON: Acceleration of
Technological Progress through Economic
Planning and the Market

J. Wilczynski